THE BEDFORD SERIES IN HISTORY AND CULTURE

Southern Horrors and Other Writings

The Anti-Lynching Campaign of Ida B. Wells, 1892–1900

THE BEDFORD SERIES IN HISTORY AND CULTURE

Southern Horrors and Other Writings

The Anti-Lynching Campaign of Ida B. Wells, 1892–1900

SECOND EDITION

Edited with an Introduction by

Jacqueline Jones Royster

Georgia Institute of Technology

bedford/st.martin's
Macmillan Learning

Boston | New York

For Bedford/St. Martin's

Vice President, Editorial, Macmillan Learning Humanities: Edwin Hill
Publisher for History: Michael Rosenberg
Senior Executive Editor for History: William J. Lombardo
Director of Development for History: Jane Knetzger
Developmental Editor: Mary Posman
Executive Marketing Manager: Sandra McGuire
Production Editor: Lidia MacDonald-Carr
Production Coordinator: Carolyn Quimby
Director of Rights and Permissions: Hilary Newman
Permissions Assistant: Michael McCarty
Permissions Manager: Kalina Ingham
Cover Design: William Boardman
Cover Photo: Portrait of Ida B. Wells Barnett, ca. 1893 (sepia photo), American School
    (19th century) / Private Collection / Prismatic Pictures / Bridgeman Images
Project Management: Books By Design, Inc.
Composition: Achorn International, Inc.
Printing and Binding: RR Donnelley and Sons

Manufactured in the United States of America.

1   0   9   8   7
f   e   d   c   b

For information, write: Bedford/St. Martin's, 75 Arlington Street, Boston, MA 02116
    (617-399-4000)

ISBN 978-1-319-04904-1

At the time of publication all Internet URLs published in this text were found to accurately link to their intended Web site. If you do find a broken link, please forward the information to history@macmillan.com so that it can be corrected for the next printing.

Foreword

The Bedford Series in History and Culture is designed so that readers can study the past as historians do.

The historian's first task is finding the evidence. Documents, letters, memoirs, interviews, pictures, movies, novels, or poems can provide facts and clues. Then the historian questions and compares the sources. There is more to do than in a courtroom, for hearsay evidence is welcome, and the historian is usually looking for answers beyond act and motive. Different views of an event may be as important as a single verdict. How a story is told may yield as much information as what it says.

Along the way the historian seeks help from other historians and perhaps from specialists in other disciplines. Finally, it is time to write, to decide on an interpretation and how to arrange the evidence for readers.

Each book in this series contains an important historical document or group of documents, each document a witness from the past and open to interpretation in different ways. The documents are combined with some element of historical narrative — an introduction or a biographical essay, for example — that provides students with an analysis of the primary source material and important background information about the world in which it was produced.

Each book in the series focuses on a specific topic within a specific historical period. Each provides a basis for lively thought and discussion about several aspects of the topic and the historian's role. Each is short enough (and inexpensive enough) to be a reasonable one-week assignment in a college course. Whether as classroom or personal reading, each book in the series provides firsthand experience of the challenge — and fun — of discovering, recreating, and interpreting the past.

Lynn Hunt
David W. Blight
Bonnie G. Smith

Preface

Since the 1997 publication of *Southern Horrors and Other Writings*, research and scholarship related to African American life and culture, and specifically social activism and leadership, have gained considerable momentum. This trend has cast a far more intense light on the importance of looking beyond just the facts of activism as a set of events to the larger historical frameworks in which those events occurred and by which they can be more fully understood. Within this scholarly context, Ida B. Wells, as a high-performing social activist, is a persistent subject of choice. Born into slavery, Wells overcame many barriers to garner respect as a nationally and internationally prominent journalist, social activist, public speaker, and leader in various social movements. Part One of this edition adds more insight into the historical dynamics, exploring, for example, the yellow fever epidemic, that greatly steered Wells's life trajectory toward activism, and the importance of her legacy for today's students. Wells became one among a relatively small number of "public" women in an era when public arenas were not considered the place for women, and she earned a reputation as an outspoken and steadfast crusader for justice. The three selections in this volume — *Southern Horrors: Lynch Law in All Its Phases*, *A Red Record*, and an excerpt from her autobiography, *Crusade for Justice* — testify to her achievements and the importance of understanding her legacy of activism.

Wells's documents continue to play a key role in understanding complex race relations and in understanding peace and justice as global concepts. I have retained *Southern Horrors: Lynch Law in All Its Phases* and *A Red Record* from the first edition. As complements to each other, these titles clearly state Wells's position on lynching, revealing the insight and perception with which she was able to launch the most successful of the early anti-lynching campaigns. Wells disassembled and targeted separately the many contradictions and hypocrisies built into the broad myths that white apologists had used to justify lynching, making a case for justice at a particular moment in time. Through the pamphlets we can recognize lynchings as more than isolated incidents arbitrarily happening to African Americans and occasionally to Americans of other ethnic groups. We see instead lynching's complex relationships to systems of power and domination, to public discourse, and to social activism, including the activism of African American women. Wells's courageous analysis helps us understand the told and untold stories of this sinister thread in the fabric of American life.

With the current deepening of scholarly concerns, there is an additional opportunity in this second edition to further illuminate Wells as a distinctive exemplar of leadership and action. I have therefore shifted priorities away from *Mob Rule in New Orleans*, a case study of lynching and its consequences in a specific site, to include instead a set of chapters from Wells's autobiography. The section that I chose to include focuses on a crucial moment in her campaign, her first British tour, when Wells gained leverage in pushing lynching to a higher level of attention nationally and internationally. In *Crusade for Justice*, Wells tells her own story, not so much as an intimate self-reported account of her life, but more as a personal narrative of her growth and performance as a professional, or what might be considered the telling of an "inside story" of her lifelong campaign for social justice. By interrogating the dynamic convergences of action, context, and actor, we broaden and deepen knowledge, not just of the worthiness of historical acts as stand-alone deeds, but also the making of them.

With the combination of *Southern Horrors*, *A Red Record*, and an excerpt from *Crusade for Justice*, we can explore with a more holistic point of view, not just Wells's anti-lynching campaign, but also her operational processes as an activist. This edition draws more attention to her pathway toward activism and leadership, her view of what it meant for her to stay the course, as well as the actions, contexts, and societal consequences of her activism. The effort is to make more evident the importance of ethos, agency, and voice in fomenting social action, as well as the complex interface of civil rights with human rights in the United States and internationally. This approach underscores the idea that, for Wells, her campaign was not just professional work—a thing to do. It was an act of passion.

Fundamentally, *Southern Horrors and Other Writings: The Anti-Lynching Campaign of Ida B. Wells, 1892–1900* remains an occasion to look at the anti-lynching movement at the turn of the twentieth century and at lynching and other violent acts over time as a disquieting antithetical phenomenon in a nation that takes such pride in being a place for justice and equality for all. For contemporary audiences, Wells's achievements remain an excellent springboard from which to bring visibility to the dynamic interconnections among social justice movements—from abolition to the modern civil and human rights movements to the Black Lives Matter and Black Girls Matter campaigns. When we connect these dots, we highlight the importance of supporting exactly what Wells was advocating for: fairness and equity under the rule of law and keeping public sentiment attuned to the urgency of engendering peace and social justice for all.

Several editorial features have been designed to help students understand the historical context of the documents and the questions they raise about Ida B. Wells and her activism. These features include a chronology, questions for consideration, a bibliography, and an index.

A NOTE ON THE DOCUMENTS

In the interest of preserving historical accuracy, we have reprinted the documents in this collection as they originally appeared. Rather than correct obvious mistakes or impose contemporary writing conventions, we have preserved the spelling and punctuation of the original documents. When an error makes the meaning unclear, I have explained it in my annotations, noting for example when words and phrases are out of order.

ACKNOWLEDGMENTS

As has been the case throughout my career, I am grateful to my spouse, Patrick Royster, for his unconditional support of my work. I also remain grateful to the editorial group at Bedford/St. Martin's, particularly Publisher Michael Rosenberg, Director of Development Jane Knetzger, Executive Marketing Manager Sandra McGuire, Production Editor Lidia MacDonald-Carr, Cover Designer William Boardman, and Production Coordinator Nancy Benjamin of Books By Design for the attention and care that they have given to this project. I am especially grateful to Senior Executive Editor William Lombardo, and Developmental Editor Mary Posman, whose encouragement of my ideas for change provided significant leverage to move ahead—and in a timely way.

Jacqueline Jones Royster

Contents

Illustrations

PART ONE

Introduction:
Equity and Justice for All

A LYNCHING AT THE CURVE

Eight Negroes lynched since last issue of the *Free Speech* one at Little Rock, Ark., last Saturday morning where the citizens broke (?) into the penitentiary and got their man; three near Anniston, Ala., one near New Orleans; and three at Clarksville, Ga., the last three for killing a white man, and five on the same old racket—the new alarm about raping white women. The same programme of hanging, then shooting bullets into the lifeless bodies was carried out to the letter. Nobody in this section believes the old threadbare lie that Negro men assault white women. If Southern white men are not careful, they will over-reach themselves and public sentiment will have a reaction; a conclusion will then be reached which will be very damaging to the moral reputation of their women.[1]

Ida B. Wells wrote this editorial on May 21, 1892. An African American woman who was co-owner, editor, reporter, and publisher of the *Free Speech*, a weekly newspaper in Memphis, Tennessee, Wells was what we might today call an investigative journalist. Typically, she would identify a problem or issue, collect data that served to instruct and enlighten, and report the findings to her readers. She was known for stating her case simply and directly, without mincing words. This editorial, however, which describes eight incidents of lynching, was incredibly bold, even for an outspoken journalist, because of what it suggested about the "truth" of lynching.

Inspired by the data that she had been collecting for more than two months, Wells raised several very uncomfortable specters between the lines of this editorial. The unstated question was, "If assaulting white women is a threadbare lie, then what might the truth be?" In suggesting such a question, Wells permitted all sorts of codes of etiquette to be broken by alluding to relationships between black men and white women that in 1892 would have been unspeakable, and certainly not spoken about in the newspaper by an African American woman. She hinted that the truth might be more obvious than the crafters of the threadbare lie were willing to acknowledge — more obvious, that is, if readers actually paid attention to the facts. The editorial invited the readers to do just that — to pay attention to the facts.

In *Southern Horrors: Lynch Law in All Its Phases* and in *A Red Record*, Wells chronicled a change in her understanding of lynching that began with the lynching of three friends (*SH*, pp. 61–63; *RR*, pp. 127–128). On the morning of March 9, 1892, the bodies of Thomas Moss, Calvin McDowell, and Wil Stewart[2] were found shot to pieces in a field a mile north of Memphis, Tennessee, "by hands unknown." The men had owned and operated the People's Grocery Store, a store in competition with a grocery owned and operated by a white man. The stores were located across the street from each other in an area known in Memphis as the Curve, an area that was beyond the Memphis city limits and beyond police protection. A few days before, an altercation instigated by the white store owner had resulted in a late-night shoot-out at the People's Grocery and the wounding of three white men. In the wake of the shoot-out, numbers of African American men were randomly arrested, guns were confiscated throughout the African American community, and the three business partners were jailed and charged with wounding white men, despite their doing so in what was arguably the defense of their property. By law, the wounding of a white person, as compared with the killing of a white person, was not punishable by death. Nonetheless, on March 9, lynch law prevailed, and between two and three o'clock in the morning the three men, who were not yet convicted by law, were removed from their jail cells, put in a railroad car, carried north of the city, and shot to death.

Word came to Wells about the lynching while she was in Natchez, Mississippi, on one of her many trips as co-owner, editor, and reporter for the *Free Speech*.[3] Thomas Moss and his family were Wells's closest friends. She was devastated by the news but also incensed that such a thing could happen. Before this incident, Wells reports that she had abhorred lynching but had accepted the idea that it was the horror of rape and other crimes that incited such violence. With this lynching, however—the lynching of men whom she knew to be leading citizens of Memphis—her eyes were opened to the truth. Lynching was not simply a spontaneous punishment for crimes but an act of terror perpetrated against a race of people in order to maintain power and control. She began to see that these ritualized murders were acts of violence and intimidation designed to retard the progress of African Americans in their efforts to participate more fully in social, political, and economic life. As she explained in her autobiography, *Crusade for Justice*,

> Thomas Moss, Calvin McDowell, and Lee Stewart had been lynched in Memphis, one of the leading cities of the South, in which no lynching had taken place before, with just as much brutality as other victims of the mob; and they had committed no crime against white women.This is what opened my eyes to what lynching really was. An excuse to get rid of Negroes who were acquiring wealth and property and thus keep the race terrorized and "keep the nigger down."[4]

Wells's immediate response to the lynchings was to write editorials that encouraged African Americans in Memphis to leave a city that offered no protection of their rights of citizenship and to go west to Kansas and Oklahoma. Her editorials were successful, affecting in a significant way the migration of thousands of African Americans to the West.[5] Wells also began collecting data on other lynchings, and on May 21, 1892, she wrote the editorial quoted at the start of this introduction.

Wells's actions were extraordinary for her time. To appreciate fully just how bold and courageous she was, we need to examine shifts in mob violence against African Americans after the Civil War; a range of factors that affected how Wells came of age during the post–Civil War era and that informed her life choices; her impressive record of leadership and rhetorical prowess; and her distinctive display of courage and action in the face of danger.

A Short Overview of Lynching

A look at the history of lynching in the United States offers evidence of a shady and questionable past. Uses of lynching against African Americans in the nineteenth century (and throughout the decades since that era), however, offer provocative evidence that these practices were particularly malevolent and barbarous. According to *The Oxford English Dictionary* (*OED*), the origins of the word *lynching* are rather obscure. Its earliest discovered use in any form in literature was in 1817. The historian W. Fitzhugh Brundage,[6] on the other hand, posits two even earlier origins—one in seventeenth-century Ireland and a second in eighteenth-century United States. Whatever the case, lynching was an established custom in the United States by the end of the colonial period, as evidenced by the sources in the *OED* for the term *lynch law*.

The *OED* attributes *lynch law* to Judge Charles Lynch, a justice of the peace in Virginia who in 1780 illegally fined and imprisoned British loyalists. The entry states that Judge Lynch's name (or perhaps that of another perpetrator of illegal punishment named Lynch) came to be associated with any acts of punishment not sanctioned by law, including whipping, tarring and feathering, and other acts of humiliation and degradation. As time passed, though, *lynch law* came to refer mainly to unlawful sentences of death.

A second explanation in the *OED* for *lynch law* indicates that it might also be attributed to a place, Lynche's Creek in South Carolina. By 1768, this place was known as a meeting site for the Regulators, a group of men who committed many acts of violence throughout the Carolinas against people who were suspected of being loyalists and thus enemies of local efforts to establish and maintain power structures. The Regulators circumvented the law by attacking people who could be perceived as vying with them for economic and political power and control.

A conception of lynching that has helped to make its lawlessness more palatable has been its relation to the notion of "frontier justice,"[7] whereby punishments outside the law are deemed a necessary, even an appropriate, response to two situations. The first situation is when law and order does not exist, as in the early western frontier. In such cases, people are compelled to take justice into their own hands in paving the way for the establishment of legal systems. When legal systems are in place, "frontier justice" is expected to end. The second situation is when law and order does not satisfy the needs of justice and can therefore be "rightly" ignored or circumvented. Such was the position taken by late-nineteenth-century lynchers of African Americans. This group justified lynching with the basic argument that "law" was out of order and civilization needed to be preserved. By the post-Reconstruction era, southerners coded all that they considered to be wrong in the South by asserting the urgent need to defend their women and stop "black brutes." They believed that virtuous white women should see their evil attackers punished quickly and with finality. Nonetheless, such justifications were inadequate to account for actual lynching practices.

The formal public record of lynchings in the United States reveals that during the post–Civil War era, lynching and other acts of mob violence against African Americans (for instance, the destruction of farms, businesses, and other property owned or operated by African Americans) steadily increased, with the first peak occurring in 1892. In the antebellum period, lynching was not typically used against blacks but against whites who deviated in some way from the local norm—for example, as batterers of wives and children or as people who held unorthodox beliefs or unpopular political positions (as in the case of British loyalists in the eighteenth century). The lynching of slaves was rare, first and foremost because it would result in a loss of "property" and profit. Obviously, it was more profitable to sell slaves than to kill them. Second, there was more advantage to planters when slaves were executed within the law, as planters were compensated for their lost "property." Third, the lynching of slaves served to undermine the power base of the South's wealthy, white, landowning aristocracy. In effect, mob violence against slaves would have transferred the power of life and death from the hands of planters to the hands of the mob, whose numbers were quite likely to include non-elite whites as well. Such a transfer of power would have loosened the systems of control, the general stronghold of the landed aristocracy over both economic and political life. The lynching of African Americans before the Civil War, therefore, was exceptional indeed.

After the Civil War, however, a distinctive shift occurred. While the victims of lynching across the country still included whites, Native Americans, Chicanos, and Asians, by 1892, as reported by Wells in *A Red Record* (1900), the majority of the victims were African American and the majority of the lynchings were in the South. Wells reported that during a single year, 1892, 241 men, women, and children across twenty-six states were lynched. Of that number, 160 were identified as African Americans, which represented an increase of 200 percent over the ten-year period since 1882, when the number of African Americans lynched was fifty-two. This change cemented a connection between lynching and both race and region that continued to gain strength until 1953, the first year with no recorded lynchings. Between 1882 and 1968, 4,743 lynchings were recorded, including fifty African American women between 1889 and 1918. These data indicate the dramatic increase of African Americans in the total number of lynchings from 46 percent in 1882 to an average of 89 percent between 1900 and 1910, with seven of the eleven years showing rates above 90 percent.[8]

The increased lynchings of the post–Civil War era targeted not only African Americans but African American sympathizers as well. This group included, among others, anyone who worked for the Freedmen's

Bureau.[9] The response to the Bureau's activities by southerners ranged from tolerance with resentment to open and bitter opposition. Some southerners rebelled through the violent and intimidating practices of their secret organizations and other acts of resistance directed against African Americans and their white allies. These actions offered evidence of the passionate desire of southern leadership to regain control of their governments and to secure white supremacy. Despite acts of violence and intimidation, however, the Bureau functioned successfully until about 1870 and with limited activity until about 1874, much to the benefit of millions of African Americans across the South.

The Response of the African American Community

Reconstruction as a positive force in the lives of freed men and women is marked roughly from the end of the Civil War in 1865 until President Rutherford B. Hayes issued orders in 1877 removing the last of the federal troops from the South. By 1876, most of the Reconstruction coalitions had already lost control of local legislatures. In Virginia, North Carolina, Tennessee, and Georgia, Confederates had been quickly reenfranchised. The process took much longer in Mississippi, Louisiana, and South Carolina, where shifts in political power were sometimes violently wrought through coercion, intimidation, and other acts of force. By removing federal oversight in 1877, President Hayes returned home rule to the South and full power to ex-Confederates and Southern Democrats. By the 1878 national elections, Democrats, rather than Republicans, controlled the U.S. Senate and the House of Representatives. The erosion of gains for African American people was well on its way.

Chief among the reasons for the failure of Reconstruction was that without the redistribution of land in the South, African Americans were unable to develop an economic base for their newly acquired political rights. In addition, after years of turmoil the attention of northerners was focusing more on reconciliation and economic opportunities in the South and less on the terrorist methods by which power and control were being reestablished and maintained. Further, with the return of home rule, southerners were free to construct white supremacy as they chose. Unmistakably, by the 1880s the era of post-Reconstruction had begun. While African Americans continued to struggle for voting rights and civil liberties, hindering their progress was yet another reenactment of many of the provisions of the Black Codes in the newly established Jim Crow laws. These laws firmly re-inscribed boundaries between whites and African Americans; controlled their social, political, and economic lives; and became the way of southern life until such overt practices were finally ended with the passage of the Civil Rights Act of 1964.[10]

During this time of increased mob activity, African American leaders recognized the precarious position of their people and spoke out passionately against the rising tide of violence. They saw that it was open season on them—for intimidation, wanton destruction of their crops and property, and open "punishment" outside of the law without fear of retaliation or formal prosecution. African Americans found themselves disenfranchised, economically at risk, and powerless to protect themselves, and they recognized that these patterns of domination needed to be vehemently resisted. Leaders called for various forms of community action. Conservative positions envisioned change as slow and incremental: This stance would later be epitomized by Booker T. Washington, president of Tuskegee Institute and national spokesperson for African American concerns. More radical positions (such as those assumed by T. Thomas Fortune, editor of the *New York Age*, and Monroe Trotter, editor of the Boston *Guardian*) saw change emerging from a more direct confrontation with the issues.

One early form of community action was mass meetings to raise support funds and to develop responses to specific outrages in a given community. National and statewide political conventions constituted another strategy. Community leaders such as Frederick Douglass (noted abolitionist, writer, orator, diplomat), Blanche K. Bruce (senator from Mississippi), John Mercer Langston (U.S. representative from Virginia), Bishop James Alexander Shorter of the African Methodist Episcopal Church, and others called meetings to draw the attention of the African American community to an array of concerns.

The national convention called by Frederick Douglass was typical. On September 24, 1883, three hundred delegates from twenty-seven states met in Louisville, Kentucky. At this meeting, Douglass denounced lynching, setting a pattern for future conventions in placing lynching prominently on the agenda. The need for solidarity and for cooperation with white allies was also discussed. These meetings demonstrated the active commitment of African Americans to causes of justice, equality, and empowerment, but despite their dedication to reform, the political conventions were largely unsuccessful in stemming the tide of mob violence.[11]

In addition to political conventions, other organizational efforts signaled that African Americans were far from passive in response to mob violence. While leaders like Douglass sought to forge alliances with white activists, more radical leaders such as T. Thomas Fortune had come to prefer independent action that did not seek alliances with whites.[12] In May 1887, Fortune established the Afro-American League, envisioned as an all-black self-help organization. At the beginning, the league established lynching as a central issue, but after the first convention, attention shifted to antidiscrimation activities, agitating for social equality as well as political and economic opportunity. Fortune was endorsed in this effort by African American newspaper editors across the country, including Ida B. Wells, and he was successful in organizing local branches of the organization and in holding two national conventions.

By 1893, however, the national organization no longer functioned. A central problem was that Fortune and the other leaders were unable to garner a base of support among the masses of African Americans in critical sectors of community activity—for example, within the black church and among black Republicans. The majority of these leaders were southern and were not inclined to defy southern attitudes about social behavior or to forego white patronage in agitating for social equality. In essence, the league did not develop effective lines of communication with the majority of African Americans, and their attention to antidiscrimation action and social equality rather than to protection from lynching as the common problem across socioeconomic strata set them apart as elitist.

A second organization established to address the problem of lynching was the Equal Rights Council. Bishop Henry McNeal Turner of the African Methodist Episcopal Church issued a call for a convention to be held in Cincinnati, Ohio, from November 28 through December 1, 1893. George L. Knox, editor of the Indianapolis *Freeman*, was instrumental in publishing the ideas of prominent leaders about the convention and in establishing a national organization. After a short while the council merged with the Afro-American League, but in neither configuration did these organizations garner strength as an anti-lynching movement.

A PATHWAY TO ACTIVISM

Ida B. Wells was born a slave in Holly Springs, Mississippi, on July 16, 1862, the eldest daughter of James Wells, a carpenter, and Elizabeth Warrenton Wells, a cook. After the Civil War, Wells's parents were politically active in Holly Springs. Her father became locally known as a "race" man, a term assigned to African American men, and women, who were intimately involved in the leadership of African American communities, the securing of civil rights, and the betterment of political, economic, and social conditions. James Wells was a local entrepreneurial leader; he was active in the Masons and the Loyal League, a Republican political organization; and he was a member of the Board of Trustees of Shaw University (founded in 1866 and supported by the Freedmen's Bureau), which later became Rust College.

Both of Wells's parents provided her with strong role models. They worked hard and held places of respect in the community as forward-looking people. They educated their children in Freedmen's Bureau schools and were committed to helping forge a brighter world around them. Despite the considerable odds against African Americans in making the transition from slavery to freedom, the Wells family shared with others a sense of great expectation for a future in freedom. Released from the legal restrictions of slavery, James and Elizabeth Wells and their children expected justice under the law for all.

In *Crusade for Justice*, Wells discusses the spirit of activism and achievement that enriched her family's lives during the early years:

> My earliest recollections are of reading the newspaper to my father and an admiring group of his friends. He was interested in politics and I heard the words Ku Klux Klan long before I knew what they meant. I knew dimly that it meant something fearful, by the anxious way my mother walked the floor at night when my father was out to a political meeting. . . . Our job was to go to school and learn all we could. . . . My mother went along to school with us until she learned to read the Bible. After that she visited the school regularly to see how we were getting along. . . . She was not forty when she died, but she had borne eight children and brought us up with a strict discipline that many mothers who have had educational advantages have not exceeded.[13]

By such attitudes and actions, James and Elizabeth Wells instilled in their daughter a keen sense of duty to God, family, and community, lessons that would stand her well throughout her life but would come into play far sooner than anyone had expected. James and Elizabeth Wells, their youngest child, and James's half-brother all died in the 1878 yellow fever epidemic that swept the Mississippi Valley. With these deaths, the trajectory of Wells's life took a dramatic turn toward an independence and self-sufficiency that she might not otherwise have known in quite the same way.

The 1878 Yellow Fever Epidemic

As Margaret Humphreys reports in *Yellow Fever and the South* (1999), after the Civil War, African Americans in both urban and rural areas not only struggled to survive in an environment that had been devastated by war but were also plagued by sickness and disease: cholera, smallpox, yellow fever, malaria, influenza, and so forth. Many thousands of displaced people also struggled against the lingering conditions of exposure and starvation. As explained by Deanne Stephens Nuwer, in 1878 the Mississippi Valley experienced a mild winter, a long spring, and a hot summer, climatic conditions that led to an extended breeding season for mosquitoes. The cause of the 1878 yellow fever epidemic was a particularly virulent mosquito, *Aedes aegypti*. The disease, however, was not at all new to the Americas or the Mississippi Valley. The first recorded case in the Americas, according to Khalid J. Bloom, was in the Yucatán in 1648. By the 1800s, there had been several outbreaks in the United States along the East Coast, but the disease had become entrenched in New Orleans, a port that had frequent contact with Havana and other Caribbean ports where the disease had become a recurring problem.[14] The most recent epidemic of this horrific disease in the Mississippi Valley before 1878 occurred in 1873 and was quite fresh in the memories of many residents of the area.

According to Bloom, the 1878 epidemic was one of the worst disasters in American urban history, ultimately killing over twenty thousand people: Four thousand died in New Orleans, where the first case was documented as entering by means of the *Emily B. Souder*, a steamship from Cuba; one thousand died in Vicksburg; over five thousand in Memphis; and another five thousand in two hundred towns and villages in nine states, including 309 in Holly Springs, Mississippi. The disaster included economic losses of well over $200 million, caused by the flight of many people to surrounding states and places as far away as New York, Illinois, and Alabama, as well as by the disruptions to trade as a result of the quarantines from city to city of people who were suspected of being exposed to this fearsome disease.

In this situation, the vulnerability of African Americans was magnified. First, many African Americans had no way to remove themselves from disease hotspots and ultimately stayed in place, suffering through the epidemic and helping family and friends who had no other resources for care. Second, according to Gretchen Long, the residents of urban African American communities experienced inadequate housing, overcrowding, poor ventilation, a lack of safe water, no sewage system, unemployment, and poverty. Combined, these factors constituted ideal conditions for devastating diseases to take hold.[15] Ironically, an asset for the African American community might well have been their historic roots in tropical climates. Their forebears, who had lived over centuries in tropical areas, where diseases like yellow fever were more common, likely had prior exposure. The presumption is that, while African Americans were not immune to yellow fever, existing records suggest a possible resistance to it. Certainly, they did indeed suffer from a full range of tropical diseases. However, scholars speculate that their cases were frequently the milder forms that, with proper treatment and adequate environmental conditions, should not always have resulted in death.

Unfortunately, by 1878, access to adequate environmental resources and to proper health care was a precious privilege not easily gained given the erosion after the Civil War of even the inferior health-care infrastructure that had been in place for African Americans during slavery, the loss of the explicit support of the Freedmen's Bureau, and the long-standing overt and covert problems of race and class in the health system generally.[16] Many who might have recovered from yellow fever likely did not; the existing vital statistics for African American experiences are unclear. In Holly Springs, for example, according to Nuwer, among the 1,239 cases of yellow fever, there were 309 deaths, a statistic that must be contextualized within another statistic that Nuwer reports.[17] Out of the thirty-five hundred residents of Holly Springs, all but fifteen hundred became refugees, leaving three hundred whites and twelve hundred African Americans. One can easily conclude, then, that of the 309 deaths, many African Americans fell victim. The Wells family story was part of this larger scenario.[18]

According to *Crusade for Justice*, when news came of the yellow fever outbreak in Memphis (fifty miles from Holly Springs), Wells was visiting her grandmother, her father's mother, who lived on a farm outside the town, and they assumed that the rest of the family would leave Holly Springs to stay with Aunt Belle, her mother's sister, who also lived in a more rural area. Through correspondence, however, Wells discovered that their assumptions were not true. The family had stayed in Holly Springs. She received word that both her parents had succumbed to the disease and that the children were being taken care of by others. Her father died first on September 26; her mother on September 27.

According to her autobiography, Wells was urged to stay on the farm until the epidemic was over. She didn't. She took the train home to take care of her remaining siblings:[19] Eugenia, James, George, Annie, and Lily. When she arrived home, Wells found that all of the children except

Eugenia had been stricken by the disease; two remained in bed, and her baby brother, Stanley, died on October 3. In *Crusade for Justice*, Wells states,

> I had a chill the day after getting home. I will always believe it was one of the usual malarial kind I had been having, but the old nurse in the house who had taken care of the children would take no chances. She put me to bed and sweated me four days and nights on hot lemonade.[20]

Wells recovered from her symptoms, whether malaria or a milder form of yellow fever, but she awoke to the knowledge that she had become head of her household, the next person in the immediate family to shoulder the responsibilities of her five younger siblings.

A Turn toward Sociopolitical Action

In 1878, Wells was sixteen. History often records the beginning of her social resistance in the public space a few years later with her professional work as a teacher and even more dramatically starting a few years even later as a journalist. However, the intrusion of yellow fever in her life clearly signaled a shift in her horizon. First, she refused to leave her siblings in jeopardy while she remained safe with her grandmother, away from the threat of death. She returned home on a train, but a freight train rather than a passenger train, on which two conductors had died of the disease. Second, she defied the adults in her community, men who were her father's friends and members of his Masonic order. The Masons had taken it upon themselves to find homes for the younger children and to make sure that the family was well cared for. Wells adamantly refused this strategy and asked that, instead, they help her find work so that she could take care of the children herself. They did, and Wells's life trajectory was forever changed.

In keeping with the deeply felt sense of obligation inherited from her parents, Wells assumed responsibility for her family. Her childhood ended abruptly, and she embarked on a life of independence and service to others. She left school, made herself look older, passed the teaching examination in her county, and obtained a teaching position six miles outside town. During the week, Wells fulfilled her teaching responsibilities while first her grandmother, who was not strong herself, and then an old friend of her mother's took care of the children. On the weekends, Wells came home to become head of the family and take on the full burden of household chores before returning to her country school on Sunday evening.

After a year of this grueling schedule, Wells's Aunt Fanny (her father's sister-in-law), who had lost her husband to the epidemic and who had three children of her own, invited Wells to move to Memphis, Tennessee, to better her circumstances. Recognizing opportunity, Wells agreed to relocate. She arranged for her two brothers, James and George, to be apprenticed with local tradesmen; she asked relatives in Holly Springs to take care of Eugenia, who was physically handicapped; and she took her two youngest sisters, Annie and Lily, with her to Memphis. Wells also carried with her habits and preferences that would constitute a foundation for her new life. She had acquired a strong sense of self, and she was confident in her ability to work hard and to provide for her own needs and for those of her family. In having assumed adult responsibilities so successfully, she had an uncommon sense of independence as a young professional woman. In addition, given her parents' activist background, Wells had internalized a sense of social responsibility and social justice, as well as a desire to participate actively in community development.

After Wells reached Memphis, she secured a position in the Shelby County school system and began studying for an examination that would make her eligible for employment in the Memphis city schools. As in Holly Springs, the African American community of Memphis took pride in being forward-looking and culturally and intellectually vibrant. They worked aggressively to take advantage of opportunities and to operate as productive and responsible citizens. Wells's years in this highly engaged African American community were excellent training for the public life that she seemed destined to lead.[21]

Wells continued to be active in her own church, the African Methodist Episcopal (AME) Church, as well as in others. She came into contact with AME bishops, such as Henry McNeal Turner, who were learned men, excellent orators, and politically active. By 1891, she had met and heard nationally renowned, politically astute figures, including Frederick Douglass, Blanche K. Bruce, and Frances Ellen Watkins Harper (one of the most highly respected creative writers, public speakers, and community activists of her day). Wells also came to know and respect local African American leaders, such as Robert Church,[22] one of the first African Americans in the Memphis area to acquire wealth and property.

Wells joined a lyceum, composed primarily of public school teachers, whose members enjoyed music, read together, gave recitations, wrote and presented essays, and debated issues of the day. Associated with the lyceum was a periodical, the *Evening Star*. By 1886, Wells had been asked to assume its editorship. With her success as editor and because of a lawsuit that she filed against the Chesapeake, Ohio, and Southwestern Railroad Company (discussed below), she was also asked to write a regular column, in the form of letters to the readers, for the *Living Way*, a weekly religious paper. She signed the letters "Iola"[23] and wrote about conditions and problems that were of critical concern to her people. As she stated in *Crusade for Justice*,

> I had an instinctive feeling that the people who had little or no school training should have something coming into their homes weekly which dealt with their problems in a simple, helpful way. So in weekly letters to the *Living Way*, I wrote in a plain, common-sense way on the things which concerned our people. Knowing that their education was limited, I never used a word of two syllables where one would serve the purpose.[24]

Success with her "Iola" column led to Wells's syndication across the country in the African American periodical press.

During this period, Wells became a leading community activist through a sequence of pivotal events. First, in 1884 on a trip from Memphis back to her Shelby County school, Wells was forcibly removed from a train for taking a seat in the ladies' coach rather than the smoking car, a privilege to which, the conductor asserted verbally and physically, she had no right, given the entrenchments of Jim Crow laws after Reconstruction. Wells was not inclined to accept this treatment, believing it to be an infringement of her rights and an insult to her person. She sued the Chesapeake, Ohio, and Southwestern Railroad Company and won. The railroad company appealed to the Tennessee Supreme Court, and the decision was overturned. This ruling was one among many incidents during this period that confirmed the regaining of political and social control by the white southern power elite and the mending of the North/South rift in the interest of participating in a global economy. The Wells case became a minor pawn within a display of resurgent power.[25]

The retrenchments of the post-Reconstruction era were a blow for Wells. She was incensed when Jim Crow laws were instituted (they dictated, for example, that African Americans could not ride in the first-class car on the train even with the purchase of a first-class ticket). When she witnessed the inequities in the educational system with the removal of the advocacy of the Freedmen's Bureau (controlled by northerners) and the establishment of public schools (controlled by white southerners), she was appalled. And she was infuriated when she saw that African American citizens had little or no protection against violence. Wells recognized that such encroachments on the rights of American citizens were unlawful. She was inspired to speak out, and speak out she did.

After the disappointment with her lawsuit, Wells was asked to write her first article for the *Living Way* about her ordeal. With the success of this first editorial in 1884, she was invited to write the "Iola" column for the *Living Way*, and by 1889 she had become co-owner of a newspaper, the *Free Speech and Headlight*, with Reverend F. Nightingale and J. L. Fleming. During 1889, Wells represented the paper at the convention of the National Press Association, where she was elected secretary of that organization. By 1891, she and Fleming had bought out Nightingale's interest in the paper and shortened its name to the *Free Speech*, and she had also secured an income competitive with her teaching salary, which was an important achievement since her editorials against the school board were one of the factors that led to her being fired from her teaching post.

Wells had firmly established herself as a bold woman who spoke the truth and as a respected journalist of considerable renown. Within the decade following her parents' death, she had become a businesswoman, an active journalist in her own community, a syndicated columnist in African American periodicals throughout the country, and an office-holder in her professional organization during a time when very few women, and even fewer African American women, could make any such claims.

By March 9, 1892, when her three friends were murdered, Wells had a reputation as a sharp-tongued political observer. With these lynchings, however, she was touched much more deeply than she had ever expected to be by such events, for these had occurred in Memphis, a "civilized" city, and the victims were people whom she knew very well. She began asking herself basic questions—"How can this be? What's really going on here?"—and collecting data on lynchings more systematically. Her findings were eye-opening, and she was energized to launch an anti-lynching campaign in order to counter misconceptions and to encourage the application of justice.

When Wells published her May 21 editorial, she did so hurriedly. She was on her way to Philadelphia for the annual meeting of the African Methodist Episcopal Church. After the conference, Wells was to visit New York as the guest of T. Thomas Fortune, editor of the *New York Age*, a paper in which her "Iola" column was syndicated. When Wells reached New York, she learned from Fortune that the offices of her paper had been ransacked and the equipment destroyed; that her partner, J. L. Fleming, had barely escaped Memphis with his life; and that some white men in Memphis had promised to torture and kill her on sight if she ever set foot in Tennessee again. In effect, Wells was forced into exile. She would not go south again for another thirty years. Wells became a reporter for the *New York Age*, where she told her story of exile in a feature article on June 25, 1892. As she stated in her autobiography, "Having lost my paper, had a price put on my life, and been made an exile from home for hinting at the truth, I felt that I owed it to myself and to my race to tell the whole truth now that I was where I could do so freely."[26] Wells's anti-lynching campaign gained momentum.

Having become a victim of terrorism herself, Wells was transformed from a regional figure with readers in several cities to a national figure and ultimately to an international one. Her public status, however, was atypical of women's experience during this era. In the 1890s, women who discussed social and political issues (rather than concerns of the home) in public arenas were pioneers in territory that was fundamentally gender-restricted—that is, for males only. Wells, operating as an African American woman in such gender-defined space and writing about issues that were both race- and gender-sensitive, was remarkable indeed.

Woman's Sphere

At the same time that lines of power and authority were being drawn around issues of race, gender restrictions were being seriously questioned. Beginning as early as 1848 with the Seneca Falls Convention on Women's Rights, the organized struggle for female equality and autonomy was gaining momentum. Nineteenth-century white women activists had learned two important lessons from the abolitionist movement. On the one hand, they discovered striking similarities between chattel slavery and women's oppression. On the other, they accrued valuable strategies for organization, political activity, and especially public speaking. After the Civil War, these women established a matrix of organizations in the interest of women's causes (the Equal Rights Association in 1866, the Woman's Christian Temperance Union in 1874, and the National American Woman Suffrage Association in 1890, to name a few).

At the dawn of the nineteenth century, women's lives were significantly shaped by male-held economic and legal authority. By custom and by their invisibility in the law, women had no authority. For example, their property, whether inherited or acquired, was controlled legally by fathers, husbands, or even brothers. If a woman worked outside the home or had a business of some sort, any earnings legally belonged to the head of her household: her father or her husband. Further, a married woman was defined in law essentially as her husband's property. Only husbands could sue for divorce, and in the event of a separation, all family property, including the guardianship of the children, went to the husband. With very few exceptions, women could not vote or engage in political activity of any kind. Women also were not sanctioned—except, for example, in Quaker communities—even to speak in public. Their fathers and husbands spoke for them, and, of course, the doors to institutions of higher education and to the professions were generally closed to white women—and doubly so for African American women. The lives of women were thoroughly dominated by the power and privilege of men.

This context defined womanhood and specified the home as the "appropriate" sphere for women's activity, regardless of the extent to which particular women's lives did not fit the model. Two examples of a bad fit stand out. One was poor immigrant women and other working-class women who needed to work outside the home, often in mill town factories and urban sweatshops, to help provide for their families. Another was women of African descent. For more than half of the century, enslaved women had absolutely no control over their lives, and for the remaining part of the century they were compelled to work more often than not as field-workers or as caretakers of other women's homes, not their own. Despite such discontinuities, however, and the fact that this standard assumed middle- and upper-class privilege, it remained the ideal toward which all women, regardless of race or social class, were to aspire.

True womanhood was defined within the sphere of "domestic" or private rather than "public" interests. Women were supposed to be the moral, stabilizing, civilizing influence in the home. They were "responsible" for the heart and the spirit. "Good" women were supposed to be pure, pious, modest, above the weaknesses of the physical body (that is, uninterested in sexual pleasure), and focused on the care of children, husband, and household. Their space was not the street, not the workplace, not the podium, not the written page—nothing that would draw attention to them in a "public" way. "Public" women were not "good" women.

While the cult of true womanhood operated well into the twentieth century, particular forces and events from the early 1800s onward served to undermine this model of domesticity. Technological innovation in transportation, encouraged by the rise of industrialism in the

United States, permitted women to travel in unsupervised ways much more frequently and without automatically being labeled "public" women. The increase in stagecoach lines, train travel, and steamboat and canal boat travel made it possible for women to go from place to place and appear in public spaces, with their safety in those spaces significantly tied to their deportment as "good" women, as "ladies," rather than as bad women who invited the attention of men. Changes also resulted from the era's remarkable number of inventions, such as the vaccuum cleaner and washing machine, which redefined work in the home and provided women who were able to own them the privilege of more leisure time. Inventions also reshaped "office" work, as in the case of the typewriter. To accommodate the view that women were well suited for typing because of their finger dexterity, the position of "secretary" was redefined. In 1870, there were 9,982 women employed as secretaries; in 1900, there were 238,982.[27] The job of secretary was no longer an apprenticeship to management but instead had become basically a dead-end, low-paying job for women. Nevertheless, the entry of women into the world of office work was part of a general increase of women in the public workforce.

The struggle of women for higher education also expanded woman's sphere. Oberlin College was the first institution of higher education to open its doors to women and to people of color. The first women were admitted in 1837. Educational opportunities generally remained scarce, however, until after the Civil War, when the emergence of women's colleges and public universities offered many more choices. Vassar, one of the earliest women's colleges, was founded in 1865. Smith and Wellesley began in 1875. The Atlanta Baptist Female Seminary (later Spelman College), one of the first institutions for women of African descent, began in 1881. By 1870, 30 percent of colleges and universities were open to women, and by 1900, 70 percent were open.[28] By the post-Reconstruction era, women were college-educated and entering the professions for the first time in significant numbers. Most became teachers (with the rise in the 1870s of public education), but women were also entering the workforce as physicians, nurses, and other health-care providers; as lawyers, businesswomen, and social services agents; and as writers, public speakers, and political activists.

During this era, African American women could be counted in steadily increasing numbers among these professional groups. In 1864, Rebecca Lee was the first African American woman to become a physician. In 1872, Charlotte E. Ray was awarded a law degree and became the first

African American woman to practice law in the United States and among the first women of any race to be admitted to the bar in Washington, DC. In 1921, Sadie T. M. Alexander was the first African American woman to be awarded a PhD from an American university (in economics from the University of Pennsylvania). These African Americans constituted the first wave of college-educated women. They were women who not only had the general desire and the determination to participate actively in "public" arenas but also had the wherewithal to do so in both formal and informal training.

These changes in women's aspirations and activities were inspired and facilitated by the movement among women for social equality and legal reform. Even though the nineteenth-century women's movement has been perceived as essentially the domain of white middle-class women, working-class white women, African American women, and other women of color were actively involved in women's reform activities. They cooperated with elite white women (sometimes smoothly, sometimes not) in mutually beneficial activities, and they were also active in various groups of their own. Typically, though, the more publicized record of political activity for women is defined by the interests of middle- and upper-class white women. While this elite group learned and sometimes benefited from various alliances with other women, its members were more interested in furthering their own causes—women's suffrage, temperance, and educational opportunity, for example—than in addressing issues like workers' rights or anti-lynching reform.

The nineteenth century was indeed an era of tremendous change in the lives of women, even though the role of African American women in bringing about this change has been acknowledged only in recent decades. By the post-Reconstruction era, new possibilities for women's autonomy were very much in evidence. It was a "woman's era," as the women of that time described it. Women across all classes and races had opportunities to belong to clubs and other organized groups working collectively toward social change. These remarkable women questioned distinctions between women's sphere and men's sphere, and by their very existence they reshaped these domains and created new options for women's lives.

During this period, Ida B. Wells emerged as one of the most well known of these "new" women among African American women. Like other professional women, she was challenged to adhere to nineteenth-century standards of "ladyhood," modesty, decorum, and propriety, even as she ventured ever more boldly as an African American woman into male-dominated "public" space. For African American women, the need to maintain feminine decorum was especially troublesome. The lash of slavery cut deeply. A primary task was to define oneself not just as a "true woman" but as "human," as capable and deserving of human regard. Privileged African American women (the group to which Wells belonged because of her access to education, her status as a professional woman, and the elite circles in which she was able to travel) felt obligated to defend both their race and their gender in order to carve out a space for participation and achievement. The story of African American women in public arenas, then, is a story of passion — a passion for the acquisition of literacy and for the opportunity to develop one's talents and abilities fully, to demonstrate one's potential, and to commit oneself to the betterment both of self and of the race. Personal potential was inextricably tied to collective possibility in the ways race, gender, and class privilege were determined in the society and access to opportunity was allowed or denied.

The Black Clubwomen's Movement

On June 25, 1892, as an exile in New York, Wells published a feature story in the *New York Age* about her ordeal. One result is that two African American women, Victoria Earle Matthews of New York and Maritcha Lyons of Brooklyn, decided to host a testimonial dinner for her. Matthews, a fellow journalist for the *New York Age* and several other newspapers around the country, is perhaps best known as the founding director of the White Rose Mission, a shelter for African American women and girls who had recently migrated from the South. It also functioned as a community center for women and children, teaching self-improvement and Christian living. Maritcha Lyons, an educator and writer, was one of the first African American women to be named assistant principal in a Brooklyn public school. Both women were active in social reform and experienced in ministering to the needs of their communities. Two months after the testimonial dinner, they founded a club, (the Women's Loyal Union of New York and Brooklyn) with Matthews serving as the first president.[29]

In hosting the dinner for Wells, Matthews and Lyons wanted to pay tribute to Wells's admirable and courageous work and to raise funds to help her continue that work. On October 5, 1892, at Lyric Hall in New York, they brought together 250 African American women from New York, Philadelphia, and Boston, including some of the most recognized and notable women of the day. In attendance was Josephine St. Pierre

Ruffin, known for working across racial lines as a leader in the charitable work of women's clubs in Boston and throughout Massachusetts. She was also a journalist and a member of the New England Women's Press Association, composed largely of white women. Gertrude Bustill Mossell, a member of one of Philadelphia's most politically active African American families, was a nationally prominent journalist and creative writer. Susan McKinney Smith Steward and Sarah Smith Garnet were sisters who lived in New York. Both broke new ground for African American women, Steward as the first to practice medicine in New York State, and Garnet as the first to be named a principal of an integrated public school in Manhattan. Most, if not all, of the others in attendance were community leaders active in charities and social reform. After hearing Wells's story, the women awarded her five hundred dollars and a gold, pen-shaped brooch.

In drawing together groups from three states, the Wells testimonial dinner made clear that the seeds of organized reform at the national level were firmly rooted. Josephine St. Pierre Ruffin and her daughter Florida Ruffin Ridley played central roles in establishing the Boston Woman's Era Club a few months later. They also founded the first monthly magazine to be published by African American women for African American women, *Woman's Era*, which drew correspondents from clubs across the nation and whose department heads included Victoria Earle Matthews (New York), Fannie Barrier Williams (Chicago), Josephine Silone-Yates (Kansas City, Missouri), Mary Church Terrell (Washington, DC), Elizabeth Ensley (Denver), and Alice Ruth Moore (New Orleans). Read primarily by elite African American women, *Woman's Era* became a primary vehicle for messages of political and social reform. The magazine was a vital source of information about family life and fashion as well as a place to discuss critical issues such as health care, educational opportunities, the participation of women in community development, and, of course, lynching. Just as influential as the Woman's Era Club was the Colored Woman's League of Washington, DC, led by Helen A. Cook, Mary Church Terrell, Anna Julia Cooper, Charlotte Forten Grimké, Josephine B. Bruce, Mary Jane Patterson, and others.[30]

African American women had long valued volunteerism, cooperative endeavor, and community service. The first women's clubs were established as early as the 1790s as auxiliaries to churches—for example, the Daughters of Allen of the African Methodist Episcopal Church. These groups primarily sought to care for the weak and infirm, feed the hungry, clothe and shelter the needy, and provide education and cultural enrichment. By the 1830s, the organizational efforts in the North shifted away from the church and focused more directly on educational, political, and cultural activities, as would later be the case with the lyceum to which Wells belonged during her years in Memphis. The northern groups included the Afric-American Female Intelligence Society (formed in Boston in 1832), before which spoke Maria Stewart, long considered to be the first African American woman to have publicly addressed an audience of both men and women.

By the post-Reconstruction era, African American women had a long history of community activism and operated several different networks of literary, benevolent, and other community organizations. Before and during the Civil War, they had participated in both black and white abolitionist societies, and after the Civil War they joined in the women's suffrage movement and the temperance movement, which also concerned itself with issues related to home, family, and community development. On July 21, 1896, two national organizations—the Washington, DC–based National Colored Women's League and the Boston-based National Federation of Afro-American Women—joined to form the National Association of Colored Women (NACW).

In August 1896, the NACW's newly elected president, Mary Church Terrell, announced in *Woman's Era*:

> We, the Colored Women of America, stand before the country today a united sisterhood, pledged to promote the welfare of our race, along all the lines that tend to its development and advancement. . . . We hope to run the whole gamut of human progress and reform. . . . In myself I am nothing, but with the loyal support of conscientious, capable women, all things are possible to us. . . . The magnitude of the work to which we seem divinely called and are solemnly pledged, far from affrighting and depressing us, inspires to greater effort.[31]

With the motto "Lifting as We Climb," the NACW called for the careful and conscientious study of questions that deeply and directly affected African American people in general and African American women in particular. They sought to improve housing, education, health care, and other conditions, to better the lives of children, to improve conditions for working women, and to maintain a healthy public opinion about the race and its women. The agenda also included attention to issues such as Jim Crow laws, prison reform, and lynching.

African American clubwomen played a vital role in the anti-lynching movement from its beginning. Anti-lynching committees were formed at the NACW's local and national levels, and these groups made a special point of publicizing the lynching of African American women. Supported by this nationwide network of committees, NACW leaders were active on many anti-lynching fronts, including the National Association for the Advancement of Colored People (NAACP): Mary Church Terrell and Ida B. Wells participated in its formation and in establishing protection against mob violence as one of its priorities. NACW leaders spoke often in public against lynching and addressed the issue in various periodicals. In 1922, Mary Burnett Talbert, NACW president from 1916 to 1920, formed the Anti-Lynching Crusaders, a group whose membership went from sixteen women to more than nine hundred in just three months. The group included women who worked with settlement houses, black women's clubs, the Young Women's Christian Association, the women's committee of the Council of National Defense, and the NAACP. Like Wells, the Crusaders advocated for federal anti-lynching legislation and actively sought the support of white women, particularly southern white women.

The Crusaders and the other lobbyists were not successful in pushing forth federal legislation, but they were able to increase the awareness of lynching as a national problem. They managed to gain the support of some white women leaders on the Women's Committee of the Commission on Interracial Cooperation (CIC) and the National Council of Women, though not at the level they desired. In fact, among white women, substantial support for the anti-lynching cause did not occur until the 1930s with the formation of the Association of Southern Women for the Prevention of Lynching (ASWPL). Although the success of the Crusaders and others was modest, one point stands clear: The diverse national network of African American women leaders, Wells included, was significant in placing lynching on the national agenda.

THE CASE ACCORDING TO WELLS

Ida B. Wells wanted lynching to stop, and she understood that increasing public awareness and being persistent in calling for action were necessary to attain this goal. In *A Red Record*, she states that the first step was to tell the world the facts: "When the Christian world knows the alarming growth and extent of outlawry in our land, some means will be found to stop it" (*RR*, p. 151). She sought to recast lynching in the public eye so that it was no longer perceived as an understandable though unpleasant response to heinous acts but as itself a crime against American values.

The Power of Her Pen

Wells's pamphlets define "lynching" by example, painting a vivid picture of incredibly brutal acts at the hands of a lawless mob. She begins *Southern Horrors* with a recounting of her May 21 editorial about eight men lynched, pointing out that the first victim was removed unlawfully from the penitentiary (implying that it surely must have been purposely unguarded); that he, like all of the eight, was killed without being convicted of his alleged crime in a court of law; and that in all eight cases the killings followed a "programme," a ritual—a hanging and then the shooting of bullets into a lifeless body (*SH*, p. 49). She continues this account by referring to an editorial published on the same day as her own in the Memphis *Evening Scimitar*, a white newspaper. This editorial stated the consequences for "whoever" wrote the *Free Speech* editorial:

> If the negroes themselves do not apply the remedy without delay it will be the duty of those whom he has attacked to tie the wretch who utters these calumnies to a stake [typically for burning] at the intersection of Main and Madison Sts., brand him in the forehead with a hot iron and perform upon him a surgical operation [i.e., the removal of the male genitals] with a pair of tailor's shears. (*SH*, p. 49)

For condemning the lynchings, the *Free Speech* editorial writer was to be brutalized several times over by an unlawful, unnamed group of southern white men whose patience "he" had tried.

Wells presented lynching as an unlawful act of mob violence throughout her career,[32] chronicling and cataloging in her pamphlets specific examples of the horror in its many varieties and places. In her second pamphlet, *A Red Record* (1895, pp. 78–83), she cites four hundred cases that had been recorded in 1892 and 1893, not just through her own research as an African American woman journalist whose credibility might be questioned, but also by the *Chicago Tribune*, a well-respected white newspaper. She points out racial and regional patterns in the numbers, highlighting, for example, that 160 of the 241 lynchings reported in 1892 were of African Americans and that 180 of the 241 occurred in southern states.[33] She also shows discontinuities between the public perception of lynching—as being in defense of white women's virtue—and the details of actual lynchings. She notes that the alleged crimes ranged from murder to barn burning to no offense; that the victims included five African American women; and that one group of victims included a fourteen-year-old girl and her sixteen-year-old brother, who were hanged alongside their father, the alleged criminal.

In presenting a narrative of lynching that was anchored so securely in data, Wells was emphasizing that the data speak for themselves. In bringing forward these accounts, as told through the white press, and in listing the statistics with minimum modification, Wells made a compelling point. She underscored the fact that lynching, as practiced against African American people, was an act of terrorism waged against not just African American men but also women and children. She demonstrated that the public assumptions about the reasons for lynching were not the truth. She crafted a persuasive case against the rationale of lynching as a necessary act to stop black male brutes, showing instead that it was designed to conceal a racist agenda and to keep power in the hands of southern white men. Wells emphasized also that the law had been violated and that the United States, as a land of freedom and opportunity, needed to take immediate action.

While Wells benefited from several overlapping circles of reformist allies in the United States and in Great Britain,[34] her campaign was essentially a one-woman enterprise, with the primary weapons being her pen and voice. She unraveled the social and political complexities of lynching and identified four basic inconsistencies between the rationale for lynching and its actual execution. First, African Americans were being lynched in parts of the country where legal systems were in place and very much operational. Wells notes in *A Red Record* (p. 83) that a great majority of the lynchings recorded for 1892 took place in the South, an area under lawful jurisdiction; in the Far West, where one might expect to find greater lawlessness, there were comparatively few lynchings. Second, the charges being leveled against African American lynching victims were not limited to rape, indicating again that there was no urgent, unmet need for punishment outside the law. Third, Wells's investigations often revealed that the "crimes" were actually "achievements": Sometimes the victim was a successful merchant whose business (like the People's Grocery) would be ransacked during the lynching, or a prosperous farmer whose house and crops would be burned; sometimes the victim was simply exercising the right to vote, speaking out publicly for the rights and freedoms of African Americans, or not being "appropriately" deferential to whites. Fourth, the alleged rapists were often in consensual liaisons with white women.

Wells crafted her argument by examining these inconsistencies, concluding that the rape of white women was not the "cause" of lynching at all, often not even the charge. Blacks were being lynched for allegations of murder, burglary, arson, poisoning water and livestock, insulting whites, being insolent, and other perceived "offenses," and sometimes they were lynched on no charges at all. Wells also documented that several lynching victims were not men, the assumed perpetrators of rape, but women and children. With this evidence, she reasoned that if most lynchings could be shown not to be caused by the horror of rape, then the barbarity with which lynching was applied to African Americans was even more unjust, especially since all the offenses—including rape—were only alleged. The alleged crimes could and should have been handled in a court of law and not before an unlawful mob.

Wells also argued that even when rape was the charge, the charge was not always the truth. Wells cited evidence that some of the liaisons between African American men and white women were long-term, not incidental. She found also that many of the relationships, incidental and otherwise, were with the consent and quite often at the instigation and encouragement of white women. Wells suggested that white women were not being violated at all but were instead very willing partners, belying the fallacy that white women were uninterested in sexual pleasure and uninterested in African American men. She reasoned that because we know from centuries of historical fact that white men desire African American women, why wouldn't white women be comparably interested in African American men? Wells quotes J. C. Duke, editor of the Montgomery, Alabama *Herald*, who suggested that there was a "growing appreciation of white Juliets for colored Romeos" (*SH*, p. 50).

In raising such a question, Wells conceded that culpability in sexual liaisons between white women and African American men might indeed be placed on the men for succumbing to the ill-considered advances of white women, but she also reasoned that such culpability did not make them guilty as a group of being uncontrollably lustful. Her proof was that there were no such concerns before and during the Civil War and no evidence to suggest that African American men had at any time demonstrated character flaws that would support the opinion that women were unsafe in their presence.

Wells further asserted that African American women could not be held responsible for these "crimes" either. She pointed out that although black women were themselves long-standing victims of rape, they were also accused in these lynching scenarios of being amoral and "naturally licentious" and thereby incapable of providing a stabilizing and moral influence for their men. Wells stressed that African American women should not be blamed for their own victimization.

Wells's case suggested that lynching encoded several race and gender stereotypes regarding pleasure and desire: (1) White women were pure, virginal, and uninterested in sexual pleasure. They needed and deserved protection. (2) African American women were wanton, licentious, and promiscuous. White men (who had obviously engaged in sexual acts with African American women over the decades, given the range of skin colors among African Americans) could not be accused of raping "bad" women. "Bad," amoral women did not need or deserve protection. African American women, as amoral women, were not capable of providing a moral influence on African American men or anyone else. (3) African American men were lustful beasts who could not be trusted in the company of "good" women, white women. (4) White men were champions of justice in defense of their women and in the preservation of "civilization." Wells understood that white womanhood was portrayed as "respectable," chaste, and vulnerable; that African American womanhood was constructed as wanton, unredeemable, and irrelevant; and that African American men were made out to be ignorant, evil brutes. It was also clear to Wells that white manhood was positioned outside of this schema as rightfully in control.[35]

Wells's argument declared all this to be false: cover stories designed to perpetuate an evil mythology. As a writer, Wells faced a multilayered challenge. To defend African American people from mob violence, she had to dismantle stereotypes that were based on both gender and race. She was required to identify each of the players, their roles, and their culpability—white women, African American men, African American women, and white men. In her May 21 editorial, therefore, she was not simply casting aspersions on white womanhood, as the *Evening Scimitar* editorial would have its readers believe; she was debunking myths, trying to preserve the lives of her people as well as law and order and justice.

Wells's third argument drew from knowledge deeply imbedded in her second argument: She stated that the term *rapist* more logically applied to white men than to black men. Race mixing between white men and black women was indisputable, and Wells, like other opponents of lynching, reasoned that "mulattoes" existed in large part because white men were free, before the Civil War and after, to assault African American women without fear of accountability or retaliation. After Reconstruction, even if African American women or their families were courageous enough to bring charges of rape against white men and, by some remarkable twist, the men were actually found guilty by the courts, the obvious inequity between African American and white rapists was that the white rapists were never in danger of being lynched. If white men were held accountable at all, it was to the rule of law, not to the unlawful practices of mob violence.

Wells brought to light the reality that violations of African American womanhood by white men—much more frequent than that of white womanhood by African American men—went unacknowledged and unavenged. She states,

> A leading journal in South Carolina openly said some months ago that "it is not the same thing for a white man to assault a colored woman as for a colored man to assault a white woman, because the colored woman had no finer feelings nor virtue to be outraged!" Yet colored women have always had far more reason to complain of white men in this respect than ever white women have had of Negroes. (*RR*, p. 122)

Wells goes on to make a poignant case for the fact that rape as a justification for lynching only applied to some women, not all, and most certainly not African American women. Wells presents evidence to demonstrate that the African American community did not have the license to lynch and thus intensified her argument that lynching and mob violence were unjust on several counts.

In *Southern Horrors*, Wells says that

> to palliate this record (which grows worse as the Afro-American becomes intelligent) and excuse some of the most heinous crimes that ever stained the history of a country, the South is shielding itself behind the plausible screen of defending the honor of its women. (p. 58)

Wells seemed to intuit here what we have gone on to think about much more deeply since her day.[36] She recognized that white men did many things behind a screen, a code of "honor" and "manners." The rape of white women became a symbol for all that southerners believed was out of order in the post–Civil War world, and they attributed many of their feelings of disorder to the newly freed slaves and the "liberties" that African Americans were granted during Radical Reconstruction. Jacquelyn Dowd Hall observes that rape was not viewed so much as an act of violence against women as it was an assault on male honor:

> The "false chivalry" of lynching cast [white] women as Christ-like symbols of racial purity and regional identity and translated every sign of black self-assertion into a metaphor for rape—black over white, a world turned upside down.[37]

After the Civil War, African Americans were acquiring political and economic power and had the potential to achieve social equality. Their manners were no longer controlled by the total domination of their lives and bodies by white landowners. Neither African American men nor white women were compelled by law, as they had been in the past, to be deferential in the presence of whiteness in the case of African Americans and white maleness in the case of white women. They were constrained at this point mainly by social conditioning and, where there was mob violence, by intimidation. In both gender and race control, however, southern white men in the post-Reconstruction era reclaimed power, honor, pride, and their version of southern manners with the rope, the gun, and a cultural ideology that allowed them to define lynching and mob violence not as terrorism and race and gender control but as "right" action to avenge their honor, their manhood, their women.

Wells's fourth and most comprehensive argument was that the charge of the rape of white women was used to justify lynching and other mob violence in order to terrorize, oppress, and control African Americans. Crediting the arguments of Frederick Douglass, Wells pointed out that such rationales had evolved over the years until the post-Reconstruction era, when the rape narrative had finally placed African Americans "beyond the pale of human sympathy" (*RR*, p. 73). Using Douglass's analysis, she explained that immediately after the Civil War, lynching was said to be needed to repress alleged race riots. During Reconstruction, lynching was supposed to prevent an "unlawful" domination of whites by African Americans. After African Americans were disenfranchised in the post-Reconstruction era, the excuse that won the day was the rape of white women. Stripping away these mythological trappings, Wells called this problem by what she felt was its "true name."[38] She demonstrated how a well-entrenched patriarchal system was able to control the behavior of African American men and women as well as white women. In stories of lynching, white women were the instruments by which the signal was sounded for life or death, for rending apart African American families, and for controlling their social, economic, and political lives. In accepting "protection," the central place of "honor" in this tale of white male chivalry, white women, in general, did not systematically question (until the rise of the Association of Southern Women for the Prevention of Lynching[39]) the extent to which their own lives were controlled through myths and stereotypes.

Wells's analysis raised provocative questions about the "truths" imbedded and unacknowledged in mob violence. Over the course of her anti-lynching campaign, the shaping of her arguments remained constant—starting with her first editorial on May 21, 1892. Her pamphlets openly proclaimed that lynching was not punishment for the heinous crime of rape but a heinous act of terrorism and oppression. She based her case on reason, logic, and ethics and established that knowing the truth of injustice requires acting against it, not just in the interest of African Americans but in the interest of the nation. She established a line of thought that struck deeply into the core values and beliefs in both the South and the United States as a whole—values and beliefs that in complicated ways embodied a history of race and gender oppression and political and economic domination. As a strident and discordant voice in exile from the South, Wells became a champion of truth and justice and a highly visible international leader against mob violence, disorder, and lawlessness.

The Wells Campaign as a National Cause

At the time Ida B. Wells was writing, the United States was seeking economic expansion beyond its national boundaries in an age of global imperialism. Earlier in the nineteenth century, expansion had been confined to the continent, extending territorial boundaries westward in keeping with the notion of manifest destiny, the idea that the United States was destined to conquer the continent (prime examples are incursions into Indian Territory, the war with Mexico to acquire Texas, and the purchase of Alaska). Accompanying these imperialistic tendencies was the idea that Christian values made the United States duty-bound to create an "empire of liberty," to be exemplars of democracy. Moreover, manifest destiny was tied to the social Darwinist belief in the survival of the fittest. Those who made and influenced national policy believed that the United States needed to seize all the world resources it could to ensure its economic survival. The interests of business, industry, and finance thus became the interests of governments, and the competition among nations for new territory and new markets was intense.

By the post-Reconstruction era, national leaders began to see the United States as part of a larger Atlantic community wherein the respect of other industrial nations was essential to secure economic power. These leaders sought foreign markets for manufacturing and investment. They did not want the nation's reputation tarnished by accounts of lynching and other barbaric forms of violence.

In the interest of the United States as a world power, silence on such issues as lynching and mob violence became golden. The sociopolitical environment in the South and the nation as a whole supported two "master narratives" of what lynching was all about: One said that lynching and mob violence were isolated incidents of passion and not evidence of a systemic "race" problem; the other maintained that the United States championed truth, justice, and equality in the world and protected all of its citizens at home.

Wells's messages about lynching did not fit well with these narratives. She linked imperialism abroad to racism at home, connecting her campaign more explicitly to "human" rights discourses and not just "civil" rights discourses, just as African American activists had done from the very beginning of their activism for freedom, equity, and justice in the United States. In keeping with a persistent pattern in these discourses, Wells questioned racial and social hierarchies and most certainly the equation between whiteness and civilization. In making these discontinuities public, Wells was able to turn imperialist attitudes on their heads and position whites in the United States as "savages" in a "civilized" world. In *A Red Record*, she states,

> Surely the humanitarian spirit of this country which reaches out to denounce the treatment of the Russian Jews, the Armenian Christians, the laboring poor of Europe, the Siberian exiles and the native women of India—will not longer refuse to lift its voice on this subject. If it were known that the cannibals or the savage Indians had burned three human beings alive in the past two years, the whole of Christendom would be roused, to devise ways and means to put a stop to it. Can you remain silent and inactive when such things are done in our own community and country? (p. 148)

To Wells, the problem was straightforward: While the United States presented itself as a securer of freedom and democracy abroad, it had a very serious race problem at home. From the government's perspective, there was great incentive to pursue policies that would maintain delicate economic and political balances within and preserve face without, and its position was one of neglect and inaction. Calls from the African American community for an end to mob violence were ignored.[40]

Despite inattention by white power elites in the United States, Wells continued to attack the problem on a number of fronts. The 1892 testimonial dinner for her at Lyric Hall in New York was a new beginning. First of all, instead of reestablishing the *Free Speech*, she used the five hundred dollars generated by the dinner to publish her first pamphlet, *Southern Horrors: Lynch Law in All Its Phases*, thus expanding her instruments for action. More dramatically perhaps, her speech opened the way for a new set of skills as a public speaker with both national and international visibility.

Two British Tours

After the dinner, Wells received invitations to speak from cities and towns across the Northeast, including Boston and New Bedford in Massachusetts, Providence and Newport in Rhode Island, Wilmington in Delaware, and Chester and Philadelphia in Pennsylvania. Frederick Douglass invited her twice to Washington, DC. Fortuitously, her talk in Philadelphia was attended by Catherine Impey, who was the writer, publisher, and editor of the journal *Anti-Caste* (published from 1888 to 1895). In 1893, Impey was visiting family and friends in Philadelphia and gathering information about conditions in the United States. After Wells's talk, Impey arranged a meeting with Wells at the home of William Still (abolitionist leader and political activist), where Wells was staying. By the time Wells reached Washington, DC, as the guest of Frederick Douglass, she had received an invitation from Impey's reformist colleague, Isabelle Fyvie Mayo, a Scottish writer who was also very active in reform movements in Great Britain, to lecture in Great Britain. Mayo and Impey were appalled by an account of a human burning in Texas.[41] After requesting initially that Douglass come to Great Britain to speak about lynching practices, they followed Douglass's recommendation and asked Wells to come instead.

This invitation gave Wells the opportunity to bring British influence to bear against lynching and in support of human rights for African Americans within the larger scope of anti-imperialism and the rights of others globally. She welcomed the opportunity to link her cause to an international commitment to social reform, as Douglass and other abolitionists had done earlier by using British money and influence to internationalize the antislavery cause. The internationalized abolitionist movement sought to end the illegal slave trade by ending the need for slaves—that is, by ending slavery in the United States. Both the United States and Great Britain had already made the trading in human beings illegal, and Great Britain, whose trade partnership and whose good opinion the United States greatly desired, was well positioned to press for abolition. The importance of British influence had not changed by the time of the Wells campaign. In the case of the lynching problem as well, political and economic leaders of the United States wanted the country to be perceived as respectable, as a major player on the world scene, not as a barbaric "cousin" across the sea who demonstrated all the evils of imperialism. Having the high regard of British elites in her anti-lynching campaign was indeed leverage for Wells at home.

As indicated in this volume in the excerpt from *Crusade for Justice*, Wells left for Great Britain on April 5, 1893, on the first of two British tours. She was invited to speak in Scotland—in Aberdeen, Huntly, Glasgow, and Edinburgh. In England, she was invited to Newcastle, Birmingham, Manchester, and London. In her account of the trip in her autobiography, Wells includes responses to her speeches that appeared in local newspapers and referenced the large audiences that she was drawing. Ultimately, the potential of the tour was cut short because of a controversy that developed between Impey and Mayo, but even in two months Wells had gotten a taste of the difference that an international platform could make, and Great Britain had become more explicitly aware of lynching as an American horror.

Back in the United States, Wells's British campaign had received only very modest attention in the white community. However, there was a more targeted effect in keeping with its basic purpose. As a strategy designed to embarrass the United States and its "civilized" people, Wells and others sent back to Memphis British newspaper clippings about her activities. Memphis was one of the largest exporters of cotton, and leaders in the white community did not want to be looked upon unfavorably in the international marketplace. The Memphis Chamber of Commerce, which included owners of the local newspapers, felt compelled to print what Wells was saying and to respond. For the first time, the Memphis newspapers spoke out against lynching and apparently affected both public opinion and action in a positive way. After Wells's British campaign, no lynchings occurred in Memphis for more than twenty years.

In contrast to the U.S. response, the impact of Wells in the reform community in England was substantial. Before their split, Impey and Mayo had been leaders in organizing the Society for the Recognition of the Universal Brotherhood of Man, and in London the Anti-Lynching Committee was established, with a long, very distinguished membership list. Speaking engagements brought in funds to support Wells's stateside campaign and also connections, especially from the clergy, who used their influence to secure prestigious speaking engagements to which Wells would not otherwise have had access.

Another international forum for Wells's campaign came upon her return from her first tour. The year 1892 marked the four hundredth anniversary of Columbus's landing in North America, and the United States was planning the Columbian Exposition in Chicago, the city that would become Wells's home, to celebrate and showcase four centuries of progress, achievement, and civilization. Unfortunately, African Americans were systematically excluded from exhibiting or participating in the exposition, and leaders of the African American community were waging battles from several quarters to remedy the situation.

One effort was spearheaded by Frederick Douglass, who was allowed to participate not as a U.S. citizen but as the U.S. Minister to Haiti. Douglass co-produced an eighty-one-page booklet, *The Reason Why the Colored American Is Not in the World's Columbian Exposition*, in collaboration with Wells; her future husband, Ferdinand L. Barnett (a Chicago lawyer and the editor of that city's first African American newspaper, *The Conservator*); I. Garland Penn (secretary of the Freedmen's Aid Society of the Methodist Episcopal Church and a highly respected journalist); and Albion W. Tourgée (lawyer, author, judge, and social reformer). The production of the booklet was supposed to have been under way while Wells was on her first British tour. When she returned to Chicago, however, she found that the fund-raising plans for publication were failing. She and Douglass combined forces to raise the funds to proceed, with Wells bringing the issue to the particular attention of Chicago's African American clubwomen. The clubwomen assisted in raising five hundred dollars to help in the printing of several thousand copies of the booklet in English, with prefaces in French and German. Included in the booklet was an account by Wells of lynching. With Douglass drawing a steady stream of visitors at the Exposition, Wells distributed all of the copies, free of charge, from the Haitian Pavilion and subsequently received responses from several countries, including Germany, France, Russia, and India.

In February 1894, Wells was invited for a second British tour by the Society for the Recognition of the Universal Brotherhood of Man, one of the two organizations that had been founded during her first tour. She left for the second tour in March. After a rough logistical start, this tour was ultimately more successful than the first. Wells was welcomed in London by the second organization that was founded during her first tour, the British Anti-Lynching Committee. The leadership of this organization was composed of prominent clergy, members of Parliament, and top journalists, with Peter William Clayden, editor of the *London Daily News*, serving as her London host and Charles Aked (renowned Baptist minister) offering her first invitation to speak in Liverpool at Pembroke Chapel, where 1,500 people were reported to be in attendance. With such persistent success, Wells ultimately spent six months on the tour instead of the three that had been anticipated. She delivered more than one hundred speeches to various types of gatherings (at churches, clubs, civic meetings, boardrooms, etc.), and she was very well received by audiences and the press.

In the United States, the impact of the second tour was also more significant than that of the first. Before Wells left Chicago, she had been hired by the Chicago *Inter Ocean* (a white newspaper edited by William Penn Nixon) to send back dispatches about her experiences for publication under the byline "Ida B. Wells Abroad." As a white publication, the *Inter Ocean* provided Wells a vehicle for reaching a much larger audience. Garnering more attention, however, meant receiving both positive and negative responses.

While Wells and her campaign did indeed receive national attention in the United States through her column in the *Inter Ocean*, she also suffered retaliatory blows. In her British speaking engagements, she told stories about the horrors of lynching, presented statistics and other evidence, and stated the need for action. When word of what she was saying came back to the southern white community, counterattacks were made. The most pernicious was attempted by John W. Jacks, president of the Missouri Press Association, who wrote an incendiary letter to Florence Balgarnie, secretary of the British Anti-Lynching Society, in which he attacked Wells's character and blatantly stated that African American women in general were without morals. Jacks sought to damage Wells's credibility, to remove her British support, and to stop the tour, but Balgarnie, who was indeed outraged by the letter, actually sent it to a colleague in reform in the United States, Josephine St. Pierre Ruffin, the founder of the Woman's Era Club in Boston.

Ruffin's daughter, Florida Ruffin Ridley, served as corresponding secretary for the club and was authorized by the leadership to send an open letter to London in defense of the truth of what Wells was reporting about lynching and to counter Jacks's view of African American women's morality. The Wells tour was not stopped. In addition to the open letter, however, Ruffin led another strategy. Instead of focusing in the United States on the Jacks attack, she very astutely used the unsavory message of the letter as a call to arms for African American women to organize the First National Conference of Colored Women of America, which was held in Boston from July 29 to July 31, 1895. Jacks's letter was set aside and not discussed at all at the conference, and the women proceeded with their efforts to establish a national organization of clubwomen, which ultimately led to the formation of the National Association of Colored Women (NACW) in 1896. This organization has the distinction of being the first national secular organization to be established in the United States by African Americans—before the NAACP (February 12, 1909) and before the National Urban League (September 29, 1910). Today, it has the distinction, as an organization that is still actively engaged in fulfilling its mission, of being the oldest African American secular organization.

Another negative incident during Wells's second tour arose from her responses to some of the questions that she received during her first tour. Near the end of her first series of speaking engagements, Wells was asked about Frances Willard, who was the national president of the Woman's Christian Temperance Union (WCTU) from 1879 until her death in 1898. Willard was internationally recognized as an abolitionist, a highly respected social reformer, and a leader of great vision. The questioner began by asking Wells to explain what actions churches and reform organizations such as the WCTU had taken against lynching. This was a critical rhetorical moment for Wells. She chose to respond truthfully and say that these voices were silent and that they ignored the problem. When the questioner asked more directly about Frances Willard, Wells explained that Willard accepted the southern position that lynchings were caused by the rape of white women by menacing black men and that she condoned lynching as the response. Wells concluded that Willard apparently was "no better or worse than the great bulk of white Americans on the Negro questions" (*RR*, p. 138), and she offered Willard's own words as evidence of this assertion.

When Wells returned to England on her second tour, the questions about Willard were increasingly problematic, as Willard was actually in England at the time on an extended visit. Willard responded in an interview to reports of what Wells was saying. She denounced Wells as being wrong about white women and overly zealous. In effect, Willard defended white women. She did not condemn lynching, although she did join the British Anti-Lynching Committee. The controversy caused a rift between Willard and Wells and added to Wells's reputation for being too radical and outspoken. In *A Red Record*, Wells devotes Chapter VII, "Miss Willard's Attitude," to an explanation of the turmoil that her response created, defending her character and the accuracy of her comments about Willard. She begins the chapter with her usual boldness:

> No class of American citizens stands in greater need of the humane and thoughtful consideration of all sections of our country than do the colored people, nor does any class exceed us in the measure of grateful regard for acts of kindly interest in our behalf. It is, therefore, to us a matter of keen regret that a Christian organization so large and influential as the Woman's Christian Temperance Union, should refuse to give its sympathy and support to our oppressed people who ask no further

favor than the promotion of public sentiment which shall guarantee to every person accused of crime the safeguard of a fair and impartial trial, and protection from butchery by brutal mobs. (p. 132)

With *Southern Horrors*, two British tours, and the Columbian Exposition behind her, Wells redirected her campaign to speaking out against lynching at engagements throughout the United States. *A Red Record*, published in 1895, presented her most comprehensive argument. In it, she acknowledges that *A Red Record* was influenced by a pamphlet prepared by Douglass, *Why Is the Negro Lynched?* She elaborates on his analysis to reconstruct the basic argument in *Southern Horrors* and to synthesize the data on lynching that she had been collecting over the years. Wells ends the document with a five-point plan of action and a call for readers to support the Blair Bill,[42] which was offered as a resolution in the House of Representatives in August 1894. The resolution began,

Resolved, By the House of Representatives and Senate in congress assembled, That the committee on labor be instructed to investigate and report the number, location, and date of all alleged assaults by males upon females throughout the country during the ten years last preceding the passing of this joint resolution. (*RR*, p. 149)

The resolution did not pass.

Neither Victory nor Defeat

In 1895, much about the anti-lynching movement was changing: Frederick Douglass died on February 20, 1895, and on the rise were the black clubwomen's movement, a cadre of African American male intellectual and political leaders, and an ideology of accommodation (that is, the view of change as a slow and incremental process and an agreement not to push for social equality) espoused by Booker T. Washington. Amid this environment of change, on June 27, 1895, Wells married Ferdinand L. Barnett and proceeded immediately to raise a family.

While her activism never ended, Wells limited its scope and entered what she called a "semi-retirement." She became more actively engaged as a community leader in Chicago and throughout Illinois but periodically still assumed a national role against lynching. When the Afro-American Council was revived, Wells was named chairperson of its Anti-Lynching Bureau. In 1909, she was one of the founders of the National Association for the Advancement of Colored People,[43] a racially integrated organization that assumed a lead position against lynching and continued to do so relentlessly through the civil rights movement of the 1950s and 1960s. Most notably, Wells continued to investigate incidents of lynching, to write newspaper articles and editorials, and to speak occasionally about mob violence. In 1899, she published *Lynch Law in Georgia* and, in 1900, *Mob Rule in New Orleans*. After the rise in lynching activity at the end of World War I, she published two more pamphlets: *The East St. Louis Massacre* (1917) and *The Arkansas Race Riot* (1920).

Wells died of uremic poisoning on March 25, 1931, at sixty-eight years of age, in Chicago. At her death, W. E. B. Du Bois[44] wrote,

> Ida Wells-Barnett was the pioneer of the anti-lynching crusade in the United States. As a young woman in Memphis, she began her work and carried it over the United States and even to England. She roused the white South to vigorous and bitter defense and she began the awakening of the conscience of the nation.[45]

Over a lifetime of activism and leadership, Wells never reduced her passion for justice or wavered in her commitment to people who were disenfranchised politically or economically, demonstrating her passionate desire to make the world a better place. Worthy of note, Wells found it difficult sometimes to remain attached to groups or allied with individuals, but these challenges show evidence of complex conditions and causes, including the following:

- Her ideological positions were often more radical than the positions of those around her.
- She defied "woman's place" in an era when respectability and tolerance were typically linked to a conservative sense of women's possibilities for participation and leadership.
- She had a passionate and intense personality.
- She was relentless in her commitment to what she considered to be reasonable action.
- She had a tendency to be direct and sharp-tongued in her engagements.

Despite complications, however, Wells was a very successful investigative journalist who waged campaigns that had public consequence. She was an insightful political observer whose analysis of events and circumstances was clear, useful, and well documented. She was a creative community organizer who was able to put together a network of services in support of specific needs. She was an intellectual with a provocative vision of possibility for the African American community. Perhaps most clearly of all, she was a leader who helped usher in a new century by identifying innovative strategies for social and political action that continue to constitute a framework for positive change.

Making a Difference

In accounting for Wells's specific impact on lynching, one noteworthy point stands out. From the beginning of her campaign, she saw her most central task to be placing the facts before the American people and ultimately before the world. Her primary effort was not really to change the law, though she certainly felt that the protection of all citizens within the rule of law was a central priority. Her personal imperative was instead to intervene boldly in public discourse and to change public opinion so that the ideal of justice for all could prevail. She believed that the public influence of good and righteous citizens should be brought to bear on the unspeakable horror of mob violence. She believed that white citizens had the power, authority, and resources for change and, thereby, the obligation to bring it about. She believed that African Americans also had obligations, central among which was the responsibility to be well informed about atrocities and not to remain silent in the face of injustice.

Wells herself was never silent. Her campaign established a pathway to change: documenting, agitating, shifting public sentiment, changing the law, upholding the law. Sadly, although the number of lynchings was significantly reduced from 1892 to 1900, they did not end. They continued to spike regularly over the subsequent decades and into the current day. Most disappointing of all, the legal history of anti-lynching action in terms of specific protections under the law also shows little success. Congress was unable to pass the Blair Bill, the Dyer Bill,[46] and any other legislation that would stem the tide of violence.

Still, Wells's basic strategies have prevailed. While violence against African Americans has continued to the present day, resistance (both individual and collective) has also continued. Activists have kept the national debate focused on critical issues and the need for change in public sentiment. For example, in the twentieth century, the anti-lynching campaign continued to be a priority for black clubwomen. By the 1920s and 1930s, white southern liberal organizations emerged (such as the Commission on Interracial Cooperation and the Association of Southern Women for the Prevention of Lynching). Although this agitation did not change laws, it did begin to change the cultural ethos that permitted mob violence without retribution. By the late twentieth century, perpetrators of mob violence were brought before the courts through the persistent activism of organizations such as the NAACP and the Southern Poverty Law Center (founded in 1971), with often hard-fought success in several cases, including high-profile ones. Consider, for example, the case of Byron De La Beckwith, a member of the White Citizens Council, who was accused of murdering Medgar Evers, a civil rights activist in Jackson, Mississippi, in 1963. After three trials and thirty years of delay, Beckwith was found guilty in 1994.

What has changed dramatically in the twenty-first century is the availability of technological resources. Wells had a printing press and the postal service, and she traveled by train and boat. Now, social activists have multimodal opportunities to put a human face on each victim, to connect the face with a personal history, and to put forward relevant information from databases of various kinds. Through photography, videos, audio recordings, and other documents that can be uploaded and examined directly, we can preserve an actual record of an incident in process, not just create a narrative account as a witness or retell a story in reflection. Perhaps most noticeably, various uses of social media platforms have become more normalized not just by creators, but also by audiences, who now share the privilege of public voice and vision and are free to engage in direct response. Contemporary audiences talk back. They assume their own agency and authority, and they participate more actively than any generation before them in sharing their viewpoints and conveying information. In addition, I dare say, unlike the postal service, train travel, or travel by sea, these conveying processes occur at mind-boggling speed, including the capacity to traverse the globe without moving an inch. With Skype and other communication technologies, we can travel, virtually, around the world in seconds.

What has also changed is the global landscape for sociopolitical activism. Various peoples around the world have made visible their own desires for and commitments to freedom, justice, equality under the rule of law, self-determination, and empowerment. In fact, the post–World War II period marks a critical crossroads, nationally and internationally, for seeing, interrogating, and understanding the complex historic and contemporary conditions and relationships that have given rise to various calls for reform in geopolitical context. One symbol of this crossroads was the formation of the United Nations on October 24, 1945, and the ways in which over subsequent decades this international agency has been called on, not simply to provide a forum for multinational discussions and to negotiate treaties and protocols for sustaining world peace, but also to offer workable operational frameworks (declarations) that support the rule of law, justice, equitable change, security, and peace for all people, regardless of national boundaries. Among the UN declarations are these: Universal Declaration of Human Rights (1949), Declaration of the Rights of the Child (1959), Millennium Declaration (2000), and Declaration of the Rights of Indigenous Peoples (2007).

Lingering issues, whether they emerge at home or abroad, often become more transparent in this larger framework as we go beyond concerns for autonomous power, privilege, and entitlement within the scope of a nation-state to articulate and address issues that touch the fullness of humanity: the need to conquer poverty and devastating disease; the need for healthy food, clean air, and water; the need to take seriously climate change and natural disasters; and the urgent need to seek innovative sustainable solutions for peace, prosperity, safety, and security. While violence and its resident ills still thrive, the rule of law has come to be a specific leverage point to push against patterns of domination, discrimination, oppression, and injustice, and a leverage point also for centralizing the notion of human dignity. In contemporary terms, the focus is not so much on the particulars of lynching and mob violence in their specific effects, although these concerns are still there, but often on the need for fairness and equity; self-determination, meaningful work, and fair compensation; food, clothing, shelter, education, and health care; and safety and security, with particular regard for the importance of freedom from terrorism, intimidation, and war.

In other words, the imperatives that created the occasion for Ida B. Wells to become a passionate crusader for justice continue. The question going forward may necessarily be whether we, like Wells, have the will to persist, whether we can learn from past successes to face ever more vigilantly and innovatively these basic challenges, and whether we can forge the empathy and compassion to hold ourselves responsible for the welfare of not simply our own nation or group within a nation, but the future of all human beings and the earth itself. The quest for civil and human rights for all continues, with the Wells campaign serving as an instructive example.

NOTES

[1]See, in this volume, *A Red Record*, pp. 74–75. All further references to the Wells pamphlets will be included parenthetically in the text using the abbreviations *SH* (*Southern Horrors: Lynch Law in All Its Phases*) and *RR* (*A Red Record*). Wells's autobiography, *Crusade for Justice*, will be abbreviated *Crusade* in text citations.

[2]Stewart is listed variously by Wells and others as Wil, William, Henry, and Lee.

[3]Details about Wells's life and work are based on information presented in Alfreda M. Duster, ed., *Crusade for Justice: The Autobiography of Ida B. Wells* (Chicago: University of Chicago Press, 1970), and Mildred I. Thompson, *Ida B. Wells-Barnett: An Exploratory Study of an American Black Woman, 1893–1930* (New York: Carlson, 1990).

[4]Duster, *Crusade for Justice*, 64.

[5]More information about her campaign to get African Americans to migrate west is available in the following sources: William Greaves, producer, *Ida B. Wells: A Passion for Justice*, installment of the PBS series *The American Experience* (New York: Video Dub, 1990); Mary M. B. Hutton, "The Rhetoric of Ida B. Wells: The Genesis of the Anti-Lynch Movement," PhD diss., University of Indiana, 1990; and David M. Tucker, "Miss Ida B. Wells and Memphis Lynching," *Black Women in American History: From Colonial Times through the Nineteenth Century,* ed. Darlene Clark Hine (New York: Carlson, 1990), 1085–95.

[6]W. Fitzhugh Brundage, *Lynching in the New South: Georgia and Virginia, 1880–1930* (Urbana: University of Illinois Press, 1993).

[7]See Donald L. Grant, *The Anti-Lynching Movement: 1883–1932* (San Francisco: R & E Research Associates, 1975).

[8]The sources of these data include Thompson, *Ida B. Wells-Barnett*; Brundage, *Lynching in the New South*; Grant, *The Anti-Lynching Movement*; and Robert L. Zangrando, *The NAACP Crusade against Lynching, 1909–1950* (Philadelphia: Temple University Press, 1980).

[9]For more information about the Freedman's Bureau, W. E. B. Du Bois, *Black Reconstruction in America, 1869–1880 with Introduction by David Levering Lewis* (New York: Free Press, 1935); Paul A. Cimbala and Randall M. Miller, *The Freedman's Bureau and Reconstruction: Reconsiderations* (New York: Fordham University Press, 1999). For more information generally about the Reconstruction Era, see Kenneth Stampp, *The Era of Reconstruction 1865–1877* (Mass Market Paperback, 1967); Eric Foner, *A Short History of Reconstruction* (HarperCollins ebooks, 2010); and Mark Wahlgren Summers, *The Ordeal of the Reunion: A New History of Reconstruction* (Chapel Hill: The University of North Carolina Press, 2014).

[10]The Civil Rights Act of 1964 forbids discrimination in the use of public facilities.

[11]For a more detailed discussion of this type of community activism, see Grant, *The Anti-Lynching Movement*.

[12]It is worth noting that after Booker T. Washington rose in prominence as the central facilitator of support for black people, Fortune became an ally.

[13]Duster, *Crusade for Justice*, 9.

[14]For more information on the yellow fever in Mississippi, see Deanne Stephens Nuwer, *Plague among the Magnolias: The 1878 Yellow Fever Epidemic in Mississippi* (Tuscaloosa: University of Alabama Press, 2015), and Khalid J. Bloom, *The Mississippi Valley's Great Yellow Fever Epidemic of 1878* (Baton Rouge: Louisiana State University Press, 1993).

[15]Gretchen Long, *Doctoring Freedom: The Politics of African American Medical Care in Slavery and Emancipation* (Chapel Hill: University of North Carolina Press, 2003).

[16]For a more detailed explanation of health policy issues and the devastating health consequences that emerged for thousands of African Americans, see W. Michael Byrd and Linda A. Clayton, *An American Health Dilemma: A Medical History of African Americans and the Problem of Race* (New York: Routledge, 2000), and Jim Downs, *Sick from Freedom: African-American Illness and Suffering during the Civil War and Reconstruction* (New York: Oxford University Press, 2012).

[17]See Stephens Nuwer, *Plague among the Magnolias*, for more details.

[18]See Paula J. Giddings, *Ida, a Sword among Lions: Ida B. Wells and the Campaign against Lynching* (New York: Amistad, 2008) for a detailed and carefully documented account of Wells and her anti-lynching campaign.

[19]One brother, Eddie, had died of spinal meningitis some time before the epidemic.

[20]Duster, *Crusade for Justice*, 13.

[21]For more information on the Memphis years, see Miriam DeCosta-Willis, *Ida B. Wells: The Memphis Diaries* (Boston: Beacon Press, 1994).

[22]Robert Church was the father of Mary Church Terrell, the first president of the National Association of Colored Women (the national network of black women's clubs that engaged actively in community development work). Terrell and Wells often competed for leadership positions in the black clubwomen's movement. Terrell usually won these contests.

[23]The name "Iola" may have resulted from a misreading of "Ida" in print. Regardless of its origins, the pen name stuck.

[24]Duster, *Crusade for Justice*, 24.

[25]For more information about the intersection of post-Reconstruction and imperialistic agenda, see John Hope Franklin and Alfred A. Moss Jr., *From Slavery to Freedom: A History of Negro Americans*, 6th ed. (New York: McGraw-Hill, 1988).

[26]Duster, *Crusade for Justice*, 69.

[27]Glenna Matthews, *The Rise of Public Woman: Woman's Power and Woman's Place in the United States, 1630–1970* (New York: Oxford University Press, 1992), 149.

[28]For more details on the entry of women into colleges and universities, see Mariam K. Chamberlain, ed., *Women in Academe: Progress and Prospects* (New York: Russell Sage Foundation, 1988), and Carol S. Pearson, Donna L. Shavlik, and Judith G. Touchton, eds., *Educating the Majority: Women Challenge Tradition in Higher Education* (New York: American Council on Education/Macmillan Publishing, 1989).

[29]For more information on African American women and organized social reform, see Dorothy Salem, *To Better Our World: Black Women in Organized Reform, 1890–1920* (New York: Carlson, 1990); Darlene Clark Hine, ed., *Black Women in America: An Historical Encyclopedia*, 2 vols. (New York: Carlson, 1993); Beverly Washington Jones, *Quest for Equality: The Life and Writings of Mary Eliza Church Terrell, 1863–1954* (New York: Carlson, 1990); and Charles Harris Wesley, *The History of the National Association of Colored Women's Clubs: A Legacy of Service* (Washington, DC: National Association of Colored Women's Clubs, 1984).

[30]Helen A. Cook was a member of a well-established African American family in Washington, DC. Mary Church Terrell was the daughter of Robert Church, a man of wealth in Memphis, Tennessee; the wife of Robert Terrell, a municipal judge in Washington, DC, a well-respected writer and orator; and the first president of the National Association of Club Women. A member of a very politically active family in Philadelphia, Charlotte Forten Grimké was the first African American member of the Port Royal Commission, a group of volunteers who went south during the Civil War to set up schools for slaves; a nationally recognized creative writer; and the wife of Francis Grimké, a renowned minister and national leader. Josephine Bruce was the wife of Blanche K. Bruce, the second African American man to be elected to the U.S. Senate. Educator Mary Jane Patterson held the distinction of being the first African American woman to be awarded a bachelor of arts degree from an established American college, Oberlin College in Ohio.

[31]Salem, *To Better Our World*, 131–32.

[32]Wells's anti-lynching pamphlets include *Southern Horrors: Lynch Law in All Its Phases* (1892); *Why the Colored American Is Not in the World's Columbian Exposition* (1893), which was co-authored; *A Red Record* (1895); *Lynch Law in Georgia* (1899); *Mob Rule in New Orleans* (1900); *The East St. Louis Massacre* (1817); and *The Arkansas Race Riot* (1920).

[33]The remaining eighty-one lynchings in the South include, among others, whites who were African American sympathizers. In the Southwest and Far West, they include Native Americans, Chicanos, Asians, African Americans, and some whites.

[34]Patricia A. Schechter, *Ida B. Wells-Barnett and American Reform, 1880–1930* (Chapel Hill: University of North Carolina Press, 2001); and Carolyn L. Karcher, "Ida B. Wells and Her Allies against Lynching: A Transnational Perspective," *Comparative American Studies* 3, no. 2 (2005): 131–51.

[35]Gail Bederman, "'Civilization,' the Decline of Middle-Class Manliness, and Ida B. Wells's Antilynching Campaign (1892–94)," *Radical History Review* 52 (1992): 5–30.

[36]See, for example, Ellen Carol Du Bois and Linda Gordon, "Seeking Ecstasy on the Battlefield: Danger and Pleasure in Nineteenth-Century Feminist Sexual Thought," *Pleasure and Danger: Exploring Female Sexuality*, edited by Carole S. Vance (Boston: Routledge & Kegan Paul, 1984), 31–49, and Martha Banta, "The Razor, the Pistol, and the Ideology of Race Etiquette." Public lecture given at Ohio State University, Columbus, Ohio, April 20, 1994.

[37]Jacquelyn Dowd Hall, *Revolt against Chivalry* (New York: Columbia University Press, 1993), xxi.

[38]See Jacqueline Jones Royster, "To Call a Thing by Its True Name: The Rhetoric of Ida B. Wells," in *Reclaiming Rhetorica: Women in the Rhetorical Tradition*, ed. Andrea A. Lunsford (Pittsburgh: University of Pittsburgh Press, 1995), 167–84.

[39]The Association of Southern Women for the Prevention of Lynching (ASWPL) was founded in 1930 by Jessie Daniel Ames, a Texas-born woman who was active in the suffrage and interracial reform movements. Along with twelve founding members, she established the ASWPL as a unit of the Atlanta-based Commission on Interracial Cooperation, which sought to educate southern whites about the causes and prevention of lynching and to persuade white women not to play a role in what the ASWPL considered to be murder and "false chivalry."

[40]See John Hope Franklin and Alfred A. Moss Jr., *From Slavery to Freedom: History of Negro Americans*, 6th ed. (New York: McGraw-Hill, 1988).

[41]In *A Red Record* (p. 87) Wells describes the savage murder of Henry Smith from Paris, Texas, and his stepson, William Butler.

[42]Proposed by Senator Henry W. Blair, Republican from New Hampshire.

[43]Note that Wells became an outsider in the NAACP. The other members were much too conservative for her tastes and much more influenced, in her view, by the perspectives of white people than by the perspectives and actual needs of the African American community.

[44]William Edward Burghardt Du Bois (1868–1963) was a preeminent African American scholar. As a professor of sociology, he is recognized for several landmark publications, including *The Souls of Black Folk* (1903). As an activist, he is probably best known for his leadership roles in the Niagara and Pan-Africanism movements, for the founding of the NAACP, and for his editing of *Crisis Magazine*, a publication of the NAACP.

[45]Thompson, *Ida B. Wells-Barnett*, 126.

[46]Leonidas Dyer, Republican from Missouri, introduced the first version of his anti-lynching bill in the House of Representatives in April 1918. This bill became the prototype for subsequent anti-lynching legislation supported by the NAACP and the NACW.

PART TWO

The Documents

SOUTHERN HORRORS.

LYNCH LAW

IN ALL

ITS PHASES

Miss IDA B. WELLS,

Price,   -   -   -   Fifteen Cents.

THE NEW YORK AGE PRINT,

1892.

PREFACE

The greater part of what is contained in these pages was published in the *New York Age* June 25, 1892, in explanation of the editorial which the Memphis whites considered sufficiently infamous to justify the destruction of my paper, *The Free Speech.*

Since the appearance of that statement, requests have come from all parts of the country that "Exiled," (the name under which it then appeared) be issued in pamphlet form. Some donations were made, but not enough for that purpose. The noble effort of the ladies of New York and Brooklyn Oct 5 have enabled me to comply with this request and give the world a true, unvarnished account of the causes of lynch law in the South.

This statement is not a shield for the despoiler of virtue, nor altogether a defense for the poor blind Afro-American Sampsons who suffer themselves to be betrayed by white Delilahs. It is a contribution to truth, an array of facts, the perusal of which it is hoped will stimulate this great American Republic to demand that justice be done though the heavens fall.

It is with no pleasure I have dipped my hands in the corruption here exposed. Somebody must show that the Afro-American race is more sinned against than sinning, and it seems to have fallen upon me to do so. The awful death-roll that Judge Lynch is calling every week is appalling, not only because of the lives it takes, the rank cruelty and outrage to the victims, but because of the prejudice it fosters and the stain it places against the good name of a weak race.

The Afro-American is not a bestial race. If this work can contribute in any way toward proving this, and at the same time arouse the conscience of the American people to a demand for justice to every citizen, and punishment by law for the lawless, I shall feel I have done my race a service. Other considerations are of minor importance.

New York City, Oct. 26, 1892.   IDA B. WELLS.

To the Afro-American women of New York and Brooklyn, whose race love, earnest zeal and unselfish effort at Lyric Hall, in the City of New York, on the night of October 5th, 1892, — made possible its publication, this pamphlet is gratefully dedicated by the author.

HON. FRED. DOUGLASS'S LETTER

Dear Miss Wells:

Let me give you thanks for your faithful paper on the lynch abomination now generally practiced against colored people in the South. There has been no word equal to it in convincing power. I have spoken, but my word is feeble in comparison. You give us what you know and testify from actual knowledge. You have dealt with the facts with cool, painstaking fidelity and left those naked and uncontradicted facts to speak for themselves.

Brave woman! you have done your people and mine a service which can neither be weighed nor measured. If American conscience were only half alive, if the American church and clergy were only half christianized, if American moral sensibility were not hardened by persistent infliction of outrage and crime against colored people, a scream of horror, shame and indignation would rise to Heaven wherever your pamphlet shall be read.

But alas! even crime has power to reproduce itself and create conditions favorable to its own existence. It sometimes seems we are deserted by earth and Heaven—yet we must still think, speak and work, and trust in the power of a merciful God for final deliverance.

Very truly and gratefully yours,

Cedar Hill, Anacostia, D.C., Oct. 25, 1892   FREDERICK DOUGLASS.

CHAPTER I.   THE OFFENSE

Wednesday evening May 24th, 1892, the city of Memphis was filled with excitement. Editorials in the daily papers of that date caused a meeting to be held in the Cotton Exchange Building; a committee was sent for the editors of the "Free Speech" an Afro-American journal published in that city, and the only reason the open threats of lynching that were made were not carried out was because they could not be found. The cause of all this commotion was the following editorial published in the "Free Speech" May 21st, 1892, the Saturday previous.

"Eight negroes lynched since last issue of the "Free Speech" one at Little Rock, Ark., last Saturday morning where the citizens broke (?)[1]

---

[1] Question marks in parentheses throughout the documents are presumably Wells's. [All footnotes in this document are the editor's.]

into the penitentiary and got their man; three near Anniston, Ala., one near New Orleans; and three at Clarksville, Ga., the last three for killing a white man, and five on the same old racket—the new alarm about raping white women. The same programme of hanging, then shooting bullets into the lifeless bodies was carried out to the letter.

Nobody in this section of the country believes the old thread bare lie that Negro men rape white women. If Southern white men are not careful, they will over-reach themselves and public sentiment will have a reaction; a conclusion will then be reached which will be very damaging to the moral reputation of their women."

"The Daily Commercial" of Wednesday following, May 25th, contained the following leader:

"Those negroes who are attempting to make the lynching of individuals of their race a means for arousing the worst passions of their kind are playing with a dangerous sentiment. The negroes may as well understand that there is no mercy for the negro rapist and little patience with his defenders. A negro organ printed in this city, in a recent issue publishes the following atrocious paragraph: 'Nobody in this section of the country believes the old thread-bare lie that negro men rape white women. If Southern white men are not careful they will over-reach themselves, and public sentiment will have a reaction; and a conclusion will be reached which will be very damaging to the moral reputation of their women.'

The fact that a black scoundrel is allowed to live and utter such loathsome and repulsive calumnies is a volume of evidence as to the wonderful patience of Southern whites. But we have had enough of it.

There are some things that the Southern white man will not tolerate, and the obscene intimations of the foregoing have brought the writer to the very outermost limit of public patience. We hope we have said enough."

The "Evening Scimitar" of same date, copied the "Commercial's" editorial with these words of comment: "Patience under such circumstances is not a virtue. If the negroes themselves do not apply the remedy without delay it will be the duty of those whom he has attacked to tie the wretch who utters these calumnies to a stake at the intersection of Main and Madison Sts., brand him in the forehead with a hot iron and perform upon him a surgical operation with a pair of tailor's shears."

Acting upon this advice, the leading citizens met in the Cotton Exchange Building the same evening, and threats of lynching were freely indulged, not by the lawless element upon which the deviltry of the South is usually saddled — but by the leading business men, in their leading business centre. Mr. Fleming, the business manager and owning a half interest [in] the Free Speech, had to leave town to escape the mob, and was afterwards ordered not to return; letters and telegrams sent me in New York where I was spending my vacation advised me that bodily harm awaited my return. Creditors took possession of the office and sold the outfit, and the "Free Speech" was as if it had never been.

The editorial in question was prompted by the many inhuman and fiendish lynchings of Afro-Americans which have recently taken place and was meant as a warning. Eight lynched in one week and five of them charged with rape! The thinking public will not easily believe freedom and education more brutalizing than slavery, and the world knows that the crime of rape was unknown during four years of civil war, when the white women of the South were at the mercy of the race which is all at once charged with being a bestial one.

Since my business has been destroyed and I am an exile from home because of that editorial, the issue has been forced, and as the writer of it I feel that the race and the public generally should have a statement of the facts as they exist. They will serve at the same time as a defense for the Afro-Americans Sampsons who suffer themselves to be betrayed by white Delilahs.

The whites of Montgomery, Ala., knew J. C. Duke sounded the keynote of the situation — which they would gladly hide from the world, when he said in his paper, "The Herald," five years ago: "Why is it that white women attract negro men now more than in former days? There was a time when such a thing was unheard of. There is a secret to this thing, and we greatly suspect it is the growing appreciation of white Juliets for colored Romeos." Mr. Duke, like the "Free Speech" proprietors, was forced to leave the city for reflecting on the "honah" of white women and his paper suppressed; but the truth remains that Afro-American men do not always rape (?) white women without their consent.

Mr. Duke, before leaving Montgomery, signed a card disclaiming any intention of slandering Southern white women. The editor of the "Free Speech" has no disclaimer to enter, but asserts instead that there are many white women in the South who would marry colored men if such an act would not place them at once beyond the pale of society and within the clutches of the law. The miscegnation laws of the South only operate against the legitimate union of the races; they leave the white man free to seduce all the colored girls he can, but it is death to the colored man who yields to the force and advances of a similar attraction in white women. White men lynch the offending Afro-American, not because he is a despoiler of virtue, but because he succumbs to the smiles of white women.

CHAPTER II.   THE BLACK AND WHITE OF IT

The "Cleveland Gazette" of January 16, 1892, publishes a case in point. Mrs. J. S. Underwood, the wife of a minister of Elyria, Ohio, accused an Afro-American of rape. She told her husband that during his absence in 1888, stumping the State for the Prohibition Party, the man came to the kitchen door, forced his way in the house and insulted her. She tried to drive him out with a heavy poker, but he overpowered and chloroformed her, and when she revived her clothing was torn and she was in a horrible condition. She did not know the man but could identify him. She pointed out William Offett, a married man, who was arrested and, being in Ohio, was granted a trial.

The prisoner vehemently denied the charge of rape, but confessed he went to Mrs. Underwood's residence at her invitation and was criminally intimate with her at her request. This availed him nothing against the sworn testimony of a minister's wife, a lady of the highest respectability. He was found guilty, and entered the penitentiary, December 14, 1888, for fifteen years. Some time afterwards the woman's remorse led her to confess to her husband that the man was innocent.

These are her words: "I met Offett at the Post Office. It was raining. He was polite to me, and as I had several bundles in my arms he offered to carry them home for me, which he did. He had a strange fascination for me, and I invited him to call on me. He called, bringing chestnuts and candy for the children. By this means we got them to leave us alone in the room. Then I sat on his lap. He made a proposal to me and I readily consented. Why I did so, I do not know, but that I did is true. He visited me several times after that and each time I was indiscreet. I did not care after the first time. In fact I could not have resisted, and had no desire to resist."

When asked by her husband why she told him she had been outraged, she said: "I had several reasons for telling you. One was the neighbors saw the fellows here, another was, I was afraid I had contracted a loathsome disease, and still another was that I feared I might give birth to a Negro baby. I hoped to save my reputation by telling you a deliberate lie." Her husband horrified by the confession had Offett, who had already served four years, released and secured a divorce.

There are thousands of such cases throughout the South, with the difference that the Southern white men in insatiate fury wreak their vengeance without intervention of law upon the Afro-Americans who consort with their women. A few instances to substantiate the assertion that some white women love the company of the Afro-American will not be out of place. Most of these cases were reported by the daily papers of the South.

In the winter of 1885–6 the wife of a practicing physician in Memphis, in good social standing whose name has escaped me, left home, husband and children, and ran away with her black coachman. She was with him a month before her husband found and brought her home. The coachman could not be found. The doctor moved his family away from Memphis, and is living in another city under an assumed name.

In the same city last year a white girl in the dusk of evening screamed at the approach of some parties that a Negro had assaulted her on the street. He was captured, tried by a white judge and jury, that acquitted him of the charge. It is needless to add if there had been a scrap of evidence on which to convict him of so grave a charge he would have been convicted.

Sarah Clark of Memphis loved a black man and lived openly with him. When she was indicted last spring for miscegenation, she swore in court that she was *not* a white woman. This she did to escape the the [sic] penitentiary and continued her illicit relation undisturbed. That she is of the lower class of whites, does not disturb the fact that she is a white woman. "The leading citizens" of Memphis are defending the "honor" of *all* white women, *demi-monde* included.

Since the manager of the "Free Speech" has been run away from Memphis by the guardians of the honor of Southern white women, a young girl living on Poplar St., who was discovered in intimate relations with a handsome mulatto young colored man, Will Morgan by name, stole her father's money to send the young fellow away from that father's wrath. She has since joined him in Chicago.

The Memphis "Ledger" for June 8th has the following; "If Lillie Bailey, a rather pretty white girl seventeen years of age, who is now at the City Hospital, would be somewhat less reserved about her disgrace there would be some very nauseating details in the story of her life. She is the mother of a little coon. The truth might reveal fearful depravity or it might reveal the evidence of a rank outrage. She will not divulge the name of the man who has left such black evidence of her disgrace, and, in fact, says it is a matter in which there can be no interest to the outside world. She came to Memphis nearly three months ago and was taken in at the Woman's Refuge in the southern part of the city. She remained there until a few weeks ago, when the child was born. The ladies in charge of the Refuge were horified. The girl was at once sent to the City Hospital, where she has been since May 30th. She is a country girl. She came to Memphis from her father's farm, a short distance from Hernando, Miss. Just when she left there she would not say. In fact she says she came to Memphis from Arkansas, and says her home is in that State. She is rather good looking, has blue eyes, a low forehead and dark red hair. The ladies at the Woman's Refuge do not know anything about the girl further than what they learned when she was an inmate of the institution; and she would not tell much. When the child was born an attempt was made to get the girl to reveal the name of the Negro who had disgraced her, she obstinately refused and it was impossible to elicit any information from her on the subject."

Note the wording. "The truth might reveal fearful depravity or rank outrage." If it had been a white child or Lillie Bailey had told a pitiful story of Negro outrage, it would have been a case of woman's weakness or assault and she could have remained at the Woman's Refuge. But a Negro child and to withhold its father's name and thus prevent the killing of another Negro "rapist." A case of "fearful depravity."

The very week the "leading citizens" of Memphis were making a spectacle of themselves in defense of all white women of every kind, an Afro-American, Mr. Stricklin, was found in a white woman's room in that city. Although she made no outcry of rape, he was jailed and would have been lynched, but the woman stated she bought curtains of him (he was a furniture dealer) and his business in her room that night was to put them up. A white woman's word was taken as absolutely in this case as when the cry of rape is made, and he was freed.

What is true of Memphis is true of the entire South. The daily papers last year reported a farmer's wife in Alabama had given birth to a Negro child. When the Negro farm hand who was plowing in the field heard it he took the mule from the plow and fled. The dispatches also told of a woman in South Carolina who gave birth to a Negro child and charged three men with being its father, *every one of whom has since disappeared.* In Tuscumbia, Ala., the colored boy who was lynched there last year for assaulting a white girl told her before his accusers that he had met her there in the woods often before.

Frank Weems of Chattanooga who was not lynched in May only because the prominent citizens became his body guard until the doors of the penitentiary closed on him, had letters in his pocket from the white woman in the case, making the appointment with him. Edward

Coy who was burned alive in Texarkana, January 1, 1892, died protesting his innocence. Investigation since as given by the Bystander in the Chicago Inter-Ocean, October 1, proves:

"1. The woman who was paraded as a victim of violence was of bad character; her husband was a drunkard and a gambler.

2. She was publicly reported and generally known to have been criminally intimate with Coy for more than a year previous.

3. She was compelled by threats, if not by violence, to make the charge against the victim[.]

4. When she came to apply the match Coy asked her if she would burn him after they had 'been sweethearting' so long.

5. A large majority of the 'superior' white men prominent in the affair are the reputed fathers of mulatto children.

These are not pleasant facts, but they are illustrative of the vital phase of the so-called 'race question,' which should properly be designated an earnest inquiry as to the best methods by which religion, science, law and political power may be employed to excuse injustice, barbarity and crime done to a people because of race and color. There can be no possible belief that these people were inspired by any consuming zeal to vindicate God's law against miscegnationists of the most practical sort. The woman was a willing partner in the victim's guilt, and being of the 'superior' race must naturally have been more guilty."

In Natchez, Miss., Mrs. Marshall, one of the *creme de la creme* of the city, created a tremendous sensation several years ago. She has a black coachman who was married, and had been in her employ several years. During this time she gave birth to a child whose color was remarked, but traced to some brunette ancestor, and one of the fashionable dames of the city was its godmother. Mrs. Marshall's social position was unquestioned, and wealth showered every dainty on this child which was idolized with its brothers and sisters by its white papa. In course of time another child appeared on the scene, but it was unmistakably dark. All were alarmed, and "rush of blood, strangulation" were the conjectures, but the doctor, when asked the cause, grimly told them it was a Negro child. There was a family conclave, the coachman heard of it and leaving his own family went West, and has never returned. As soon as Mrs. Marshall was able to travel she was sent away in deep disgrace. Her husband died within the year of a broken heart.

Ebenzer Fowler, the wealthiest colored man in Issaquena County, Miss., was shot down on the street in Mayersville, January 30, 1885, just before dark by an armed body of white men who filled his body with bullets. They charged him with writing a note to a white woman of the place, which they intercepted and which proved there was an intimacy existing between them.

Hundreds of such cases might be cited, but enough have been given to prove the assertion that there are white women in the South who love the Afro-American's company even as there are white men notorious for their preference for Afro-American women.

There is hardly a town in the South which has not an instance of the kind which is well-known, and hence the assertion is reiterated that "nobody in the South believes the old thread bare lie that negro men rape white women." Hence there is a growing demand among Afro-Americans that the guilt or innocence of parties accused of rape be fully established. They know the men of the section of the country who refuse this are not so desirous of punishing rapists as they pretend. The utterances of the leading white men show that with them it is not the crime but the *class*. Bishop Fitzgerald has become apologist for lynchers of the rapists of *white* women only. Governor Tillman, of South Carolina, in the month of June, standing under the tree in Barnwell, S.C., on which eight Afro-Americans were hung last year, declared that he would lead a mob to lynch a *negro* who raped a *white* woman[.]" So say the pulpits, officials and newspapers of the South. But when the victim is a colored woman it is different.

Last winter in Baltimore, Md., three white ruffians assaulted a Miss Camphor, a young Afro-American girl, while out walking with a young man of her own race. They held her escort and outraged the girl. It was a deed dastardly enough to arouse Southern blood, which gives its horror of rape as excuse for lawlessness, but she was an Afro-American. The case went to the courts, an Afro-American lawyer defended the men and they were acquitted.

In Nashville, Tenn., there is a white man, Pat Hanifan, who outraged a little Afro-American girl, and, from the physical injuries received, she has been ruined for life. He was jailed for six months, discharged, and is now a detective in that city. In the same city, last May, a white man outraged an Afro-American girl in a drug store. He was arrested, and released on bail at the trial. It was rumored that five hundred Afro-Americans had organized to lynch him. Two hundred and fifty white citizens armed themselves with Winchesters and guarded him. A cannon was placed in front of his home, and the Buchanan Rifles (State Militia) ordered to the scene for his protection. The Afro-American mob did not materialize. Only two weeks before Eph. Grizzard, who had only been *charged* with rape upon a white woman, had been taken from the jail, with Governor Buchanan and the police and militia standing by, dragged through the streets in broad daylight, knives plunged into him at every step, and with every fiendish cruelty a frenzied mob could devise, he was at last swung out on the bridge with hands cut to pieces as he tried to climb up the stanchions. A naked, bloody example of the blood-thirstiness of the nineteenth century civilization of the Athens of the South! No cannon or military was called out in his defense. He dared to visit a white woman.

At the very moment these civilized whites were announcing their determination "to protect their wives and daughters," by murdering Grizzard, a white man was in the same jail for raping eight-year-old Maggie Reese, an Afro-American girl. He was not harmed. The "honor" of grown women who were glad enough to be suppported by the Grizzard boys and Ed Coy, as long as the liasion was not known, needed protection; they were white. The outrage upon helpless childhood needed no avenging in this case; she was black.

A white man in Guthrie, Oklahoma Territory, two months ago inflicted such injuries upon another Afro-American child that she died. He was not punished, but an attempt was made in the same town in the month of June to lynch an Afro-American who visited a white woman.

In Memphis, Tenn., in the month of June, Ellerton L. Dorr, who is the husband of Russell Hancock's widow, was arrested for attempted rape on Mattie Cole, a neighbor's cook; he was only prevented from accomplishing his purpose, by the appearance of Mattie's employer. Dorr's friends say he was drunk and not responsible for his actions. The grand jury refused to indict him and he was discharged.

CHAPTER III.   THE NEW CRY

The appeal of Southern whites to Northern sympathy and sanction, the adroit, insiduous plea made by Bishop Fitzgerald for suspension of judgment because those "who condemn lynching express no sympathy for the *white* woman in the case," falls to the ground in the light of the foregoing.

From this exposition of the race issue in lynch law, the whole matter is explained by the well-known opposition growing out of slavery to the progress of the race. This is crystalized in the oft-repeated slogan: "This is a white man's country and the white man must rule." The South resented giving the Afro-American his freedom, the ballot box and the Civil Rights Law. The raids of the Ku-Klux and White Liners[2] to subvert reconstruction government, the Hamburg and Ellerton, S.C., the Copiah County Miss., and the Lafayette Parish, La., massacres[3] were excused as the natural resentment of intelligence against government by ignorance.

Honest white men practically conceded the necessity of intelligence murdering ignorance to correct the mistake of the general government, and the race was left to the tender mercies of the solid South. Thoughtful Afro-Americans with the strong arm of the government withdrawn and with the hope to stop such wholesale massacres urged the race to sacrifice its political rights for sake of peace. They honestly believed the race should fit itself for government, and when that should be done, the objection to race participation in politics would be removed.

But the sacrifice did not remove the trouble, nor move the South to justice. One by one the Southern States have legally (?) disfranchised the Afro-American, and since the repeal of the Civil Rights Bill nearly every Southern State has passed separate car laws with a penalty against their infringement. The race regardless of advancement is penned into filthy, stifling partitions cut off from smoking cars. All this while, although the political cause has been removed, the butcheries of black men at Barnwell, S.C., Carrolton, Miss., Waycross, Ga., and Memphis, Tenn., have gone on; also the flaying alive of a man in Kentucky, the burning of one in Arkansas, the hanging of a fifteen year old girl in Louisiana, a woman in Jackson, Tenn., and one in Hollendale, Miss., until the dark and bloody record of the South shows 728 Afro-Americans lynched during the past 8 years. Not 50 of these were for political causes; the rest were for all manner of accusations from that of rape of white women, to the case of the boy Will Lewis who was hanged at Tullahoma, Tenn., last year for being drunk and "sassy" to white folks.

These statistics compiled by the Chicago "Tribune" were given the first of this year (1892). Since then, not less than one hundred and

---

[2] Secret white supremacist societies such as the Ku Klux Klan and the White Liners flourished after 1867.

[3] Raids by armed whites, as in these three incidents cited by Wells, were typically directed against groups of African Americans rather than individuals. In the Hamburg case, several members of the African American militia were arrested on July 4, 1876, for "blocking traffic" in the course of their parade; they had refused to step aside to allow passage of two buggies driven by whites. In the ensuing riot, several African Americans were killed.

fifty have been known to have met violent death at the hands of cruel bloodthirsty mobs during the past nine months.

To palliate this record (which grows worse as the Afro-American becomes intelligent) and excuse some of the most heinous crimes that ever stained the history of a country, the South is shielding itself behind the plausible screen of defending the honor of its women. This, too, in the face of the fact that only *one-third* of the 728 victims to mobs have been *charged* with rape, to say nothing of those of that one-third who were innocent of the charge. A white correspondent of the Baltimore Sun declares that the Afro-American who was lynched in Chestertown, Md., in May for assault on a white girl was innocent; that the deed was done by a white man who had since disappeared. The girl herself maintained that her assailant was a white man. When that poor Afro-American was murdered, the whites excused their refusal of a trial on the ground that they wished to spare the white girl the mortification of having to testify in court.

This cry has had its effect. It has closed the heart, stifled the conscience, warped the judgment and hushed the voice of press and pulpit on the subject of lynch law throughout this "land of liberty." Men who stand high in the esteem of the public for christian character, for moral and physical courage, for devotion to the principles of equal and exact justice to all, and for great sagacity, stand as cowards who fear to open their mouths before this great outrage. They do not see that by their tacit encouragement, their silent acquiescence, the black shadow of lawlessness in the form of lynch law is spreading its wings over the whole country.

Men who, like Governor Tillman, start the ball of lynch law rolling for a certain crime, are powerless to stop it when drunken or criminal white toughs feel like hanging an Afro-American on any pretext.

Even to the better class of Afro-Americans the crime of rape is so revolting they have too often taken the white man's word and given lynch law neither the investigation nor condemnation it deserved.

They forget that a concession of the right to lynch a man for a certain crime, not only concedes the right to lynch any person for any crime, but (so frequently is the cry of rape now raised) it is in a fair way to stamp us a race of rapists and desperadoes. They have gone on hoping and believing that general education and financial strength would solve the difficulty, and are devoting their energies to the accumulation of both.

The mob spirit has grown with the increasing intelligence of the Afro-American. It has left the out-of-the-way places where ignorance prevails, has thrown off the mask and with this new cry stalks in broad daylight in large cities, the centres of civilization, and is encouraged by the "leading citizens" and the press.

CHAPTER IV. THE MALICIOUS AND UNTRUTHFUL WHITE PRESS

The "Daily Commercial" and "Evening Scimitar" of Memphis, Tenn., are owned by leading business men of that city, and yet, in spite of the fact that there had been no white woman in Memphis outraged by an Afro-American, and that Memphis possessed a thrifty law-abiding, property owning class of Afro-Americans the "Commercial" of May 17th, under the head of "More Rapes, More Lynchings" gave utterance to the following:

["]The lynching of three Negro scoundrels reported in our dispatches from Anniston, Ala., for a brutal outrage committed upon a white woman will be a text for much comment on "Southern barbarism" by Northern newspapers; but we fancy it will hardly prove effective for campaign purposes among intelligent people. The frequency of these lynchings calls attention to the frequency of the crimes which causes lynching. The "Southern barbarism" which deserves the serious attention of all people North and South, is the barbarism which preys upon weak and defenseless women. Nothing but the most prompt, speedy and extreme punishment can hold in check the horrible and beastial propensities of the Negro race. There is a strange similarity about a number of cases of this character which have lately occurred.

In each case the crime was deliberately planned and perpetrated by several Negroes. They watched for an opportunity when the women were left without a protector. It was not a sudden yielding to a fit of passion, but the consummation of a devilish purpose which has been seeking and waiting for the opportunity. This feature of the crime not only makes it the most fiendishly brutal, but it adds to the terror of the situation in the thinly settled country communities. No man can leave his family at night without the dread that some roving Negro ruffian is watching and waiting for this opportunity. The swift punishment which invariably follows these horrible crimes doubtless acts as a deterring effect upon the Negroes in that immediate neighborhood for a short time. But the lesson is not widely learned nor long remembered. Then such crimes, equally atrocious, have happened in quick succession, one in Tennessee, one in Arkansas, and one in Alabama. The facts of the crime appear to appeal more to the Negro's lustful imagination than the facts of the punishment do to his fears. He sets aside all fear of death in any form when opportunity is found for the gratification of his bestial desires.

There is small reason to hope for any change for the better. The commission of this crime grows more frequent every year. The generation of Negroes which have grown up since the war have lost in large measure the traditional and wholesome awe of the white race which kept the Negroes in subjection, even when their masters were in the army, and their families left unprotected except by the slaves themselves. There is no longer a restraint upon the brute passion of the Negro.

What is to be done? The crime of rape is always horrible, but the Southern man there is nothing which so fills the soul with horror, loathing and fury as the outraging of a white woman by a Negro. It is the race question in the ugliest, vilest, most dangerous aspect. The Negro as a political factor can be controlled. But neither laws nor lynchings can subdue his lusts. Sooner or later it will force a crisis. We do not know in what form it will come."

In its issue of June 4th, the Memphis "Evening Scimitar" gives the following excuse for lynch law:

"Aside from the violation of white women by Negroes, which is the outcropping of a bestial perversion of instinct, the chief cause of trouble between the races in the South is the Negro's lack of manners. In the state of slavery he learned politeness from association with white people, who took pains to teach him. Since the emancipation came and the tie of mutual interest and regard between master and servant was broken, the Negro has drifted away into a state which is neither freedom nor bondage. Lacking the proper inspiration of the one and the restraining force of the other he has taken up the idea that boorish insolence is independence, and the exercise of a decent degree of breeding toward white people is identical with servile submission. In consequence of the prevalence of this notion there are many Negroes who use every opportunity to make themselves offensive, particularly when they think it can be done with impunity.

We have had too many instances right here in Memphis to doubt this, and our experience is not exceptional. *The white people won't stand this sort of thing, and whether they be insulted as individuals [or] as a race, the response will be prompt and effectual.* The bloody riot of 1866,[4]

---

[4]This Memphis riot, one of the bloodiest of the Reconstruction era, resulted in the deaths of forty-six African Americans (men, women, and children), the injury of many more, and the burning of ninety-one houses, twelve schools, and four churches. The riot

in which so many Negroes perished, was brought on principally by the outrageous conduct of the blacks toward the whites on the streets. It is also a remarkable and discouraging fact that the majority of such scoundrels are Negroes who have received educational advantages at the hands of the white taxpayers. They have got just enough of learning to make them realize how hopelessly their race is behind the other in everything that makes a great people, and they attempt to "get even" by insolence, which is ever the resentment of inferiors. There are well-bred Negroes among us, and it is truly unfortunate that they should have to pay, even in part, the penalty of the offenses committed by the baser sort, but this is the way of the world. The innocent must suffer for the guilty. If the Negroes as a people possessed a hundredth part of the self-respect which is evidenced by the courteous bearing of some that the "Scimitar" could name, the friction between the races would be reduced to a minimum. It will not do to beg the question by pleading that many white men are also stirring up strife. The Caucasian blackguard simply obeys the promptings of a depraved disposition, and he is seldom deliberately rough or offensive toward strangers or unprotected women.

The Negro tough, on the contrary, is given to just that kind of offending, and he almost invariably singles out white people as his victims."

On March 9th, 1892, there were lynched in this same city three of the best specimens of young since-the-war Afro-American manhood. They were peaceful, law-abiding citizens and energetic business men.

They believed the problem was to be solved by eschewing politics and putting money in the purse. They owned a flourishing grocery business in a thickly populated suburb of Memphis, and a white man named Barrett had one on the opposite corner. After a personal difficulty which Barrett sought by going into the "People's Grocery" drawing a pistol and was thrashed by Calvin McDowell, he (Barrett) threatened to "clean them out." These men were a mile beyond the city limits and police protection; hearing that Barrett's crowd was coming to attack them Saturday night, they mustered forces and prepared to defend themselves against the attack.

When Barrett came he led a *posse* of officers, twelve in number, who afterward claimed to be hunting a man for whom they had a warrant. That twelve men in citizen's clothes should think it necessary to go in the night to hunt one man who had never before been arrested, or made

---

was touched off when African American soldiers from Fort Pickering freed a prisoner from the custody of the Memphis police.

any record as a criminal has never been explained. When they entered the back door the young men thought the threatened attack was on, and fired into them. Three of the officers were wounded, and when the *defending* party found it was officers of the law upon whom they had fired, they ceased and got away.

Thirty-one men were arrested and thrown in jail as "conspirators," although they all declared more than once they did not know they were firing on officers. Excitement was at fever heat until the morning papers, two days after, announced that the wounded deputy sheriffs were out of danger. This hindered rather than helped the plans of the whites. There was no law on the statute books which would execute an Afro-American for wounding a white man, but the "unwritten law" did. Three of these men, the president, the manager and clerk of the grocery—"the leaders of the conspiracy"—were secretly taken from jail and lynched in a shockingly brutal manner. "The Negroes are getting too independent," they say, "we must teach them a lesson."

What lesson? The lesson of subordination. "Kill the leaders and it will cow the Negro who dares to shoot a white man, even in self-defense."

Although the race was wild over the outrage, the mockery of law and justice which disarmed men and locked them up in jails where they could be easily and safely reached by the mob—the Afro-American ministers, newspapers and leaders counselled obedience to the law which did not protect them.

Their counsel was heeded and not a hand was uplifted to resent the outrage; following the advice of the "Free Speech," people left the city in great numbers.

The dailies and associated press reports heralded these men to the country as "toughs," and "Negro desperadoes who kept a low dive." This same press service printed that the Negro who was lynched at Indianola, Miss., in May, had outraged the sheriff's eight-year-old daughter[.] The girl was more than eighteen years old, and was found by her father in this man's room, who was a servant on the place.

Not content with misrepresenting the race, the mob-spirit was not to be satisfied until the paper which was doing all it could to counteract this impression was silenced. The colored people were resenting their bad treatment in a way to make itself felt, yet gave the mob no excuse for further murder, until the appearance of the editorial which is construed as a reflection on the "honor" of the Southern white women. It is not half so libelous as that of the "Commercial" which appeared four days before, and which has been given in these pages. They would have lynched the manager of the "Free Speech" for exercising the right of free speech if they had found him as quickly as they would have hung a rapist, and glad of the excuse to do so. The owners were ordered not to return, "The Free Speech" was suspended with as little compunction as the business of the "People's Grocery" broken up and the proprietors murdered.

CHAPTER V.   THE SOUTH'S POSITION

Henry W. Grady[5] in his well-remembered speeches in New England and New York pictured the Afro-American as incapable of self-government. Through him and other leading men the cry of the South to the country has been "Hands off! Leave us to solve our problem." To the Afro-American the South says, "the white man must and will rule." There is little difference between the Ante-bellum South and the New South.

Her white citizens are wedded to any method however revolting, any measure however extreme, for the subjugation of the young manhood of the race. They have cheated him out of his ballot, deprived him of civil rights or redress therefor in the civil courts, robbed him of the fruits of his labor, and are still murdering, burning and lynching him.

The result is a growing disregard of human life. Lynch law has spread its insidious influence till men in New York State, Pennsylvania and on the free Western plains feel they can take the law in their own hands with impunity, especially where an Afro-American is concerned. The South is brutalized to a degree not realized by its own inhabitants, and the very foundation of government, law and order, are imperilled.

Public sentiment has had a slight "reaction" though not sufficient to stop the crusade of lawlessness and lynching. The spirit of christianity of the great M. E. Church was aroused to the frequent and revolting crimes against a weak people, enough to pass strong condemnatory resolutions at its General Conference in Omaha last May. The spirit of justice of the grand old party asserted itself sufficiently to secure a denunciation of the wrongs, and a feeble declaration of the belief in human rights in the Republican platform at Minneapolis, June 7th. Some of the great dailies and weeklies have swung into line declaring that lynch law must go. The President of the United States[6] issued a proclamation that it be

---

[5]Henry Grady, nationally renowned journalist and orator, was part owner and editor of the *Atlanta Constitution*.
[6]Benjamin Harrison, a Republican from Ohio.

not tolerated in the territories over which he has jurisdiction. Governor Northern and Chief Justice Bleckley of Georgia have proclaimed against it. The citizens of Chattanooga, Tenn., have set a worthy example in that they not only condemn lynch law, but her public men demanded a trial for Weems, the accused rapist, and guarded him while the trial was in progress. The trial only lasted ten minutes, and Weems chose to plead guilty and accept twenty-one years sentence, than invite the certain death which awaited him outside that cordon of police if he had told the truth and shown the letters he had from the white woman in the case.

Col. A. S. Colyar, of Nashville, Tenn., is so overcome with the horrible state of affairs that he addressed the following earnest letter to the Nashville "American." "Nothing since I have been a reading man has so impressed me with the decay of manhood among the people of Tennessee [*sic*] as the dastardly submission to the mob reign. We have reached the unprecedented low level; the awful criminal depravity of substituting the mob for the court and jury, of giving up the jail keys to the mob whenever they are demanded. We do it in the largest cities and in the country towns; we do it in midday; we do it after full, not to say formal, notice, and so thoroughly and generally is it acquiesced in that the murderers have discarded the formula of masks. They go into the town where everybody knows them, sometimes under the gaze of the governor, in the presence of the courts, in the presence of the sheriff and his deputies, in the presence of the entire police force, take out the prisoner, take his life, often with fiendish glee, and often with acts of cruelty and barbarism which impress the reader with a degeneracy rapidly approaching savage life. That the State is disgraced but faintly expresses the humiliation which has settled upon the once proud people of Tennessee. The State, in its majesty, through its organized life, for which the people pay liberally, makes but one record, but one note, and that a criminal falsehood, 'was hung by persons to the jury unknown.' The murder at Shelbyville is only a verification of what every intelligent man knew would come, because with a mob a rumor is as good as a proof."

These efforts brought forth apologies and a short halt, but the lynching mania was raged again through the past three months with unabated fury.

The strong arm of the law must be brought to bear upon lynchers in severe punishment, but this cannot and will not be done unless a healthy public sentiment demands and sustains such action.

The men and women in the South who disapprove of lynching and remain silent on the perpetration of such outrages, are particeps criminis, accomplices, accessories before and after the fact, equally guilty with the actual law-breakers who would not persist if they did not know that neither the law nor militia would be employed against them.

CHAPTER VI. SELF HELP

In the creation of this healthier public sentiment, the Afro-American can do for himself what no one else can do for him. The world looks on with wonder that we have conceded so much and remain law-abiding under such great outrage and provocation.

To Northern capital and Afro-American labor the South owes its rehabilitation. If labor is withdrawn capital will not remain. The Afro-American is thus the backbone of the South. A thorough knowledge and judicious exercise of this power in lynching localities could many times effect a bloodless revolution. The white man's dollar is his god, and to stop this will be to stop outrages in many localities.

The Afro Americans of Memphis denounced the lynching of three of their best citizens, and urged and waited for the authorities to act in the matter and bring the lynchers to justice. No attempt was made to do so, and the black men left the city by thousands, bringing about great stagnation in every branch of business. Those who remained so injured the business of the street car company by staying off the cars, that the superintendent, manager and treasurer called personally on the editor of the "Free Speech," asked them to urge our people to give them their patronage again. Other business men became alarmed over the situation and the "Free Speech" was run away that the colored people might be more easily controlled. A meeting of white citizens in June, three months after the lynching, passed resolutions for the first time, condemning it. *But they did not punish the lynchers.* Every one of them was known by name, because they had been selected to do the dirty work, by some of the very citizens who passed these resolutions. Memphis is fast losing her black population, who proclaim as they go that there is no protection for the life and property of any Afro-American citizen in Memphis who is not a slave.

The Afro-American citizens of Kentucky, whose intellectual and financial improvement has been phenomenal, have never had a separate car law until now. Delegations and petitions poured into the Legislature against it, yet the bill passed and the Jim Crow Car of Kentucky is a legalized institution. Will the great mass of Negroes continue to patronize the railroad? A special from Covington, Ky., says:

Covington, June 13th. — The railroads of the State are beginning to feel very markedly, the effects of the separate coach bill recently passed by the Legislature. No class of people in the State have so many and so largely attended excursions as the blacks. All these have been abandoned, and regular travel is reduced to a minimum. A competent authority says the loss to the various roads will reach $1,000,000 this year.

A call to a State Conference in Lexington, Ky., last June had delegates from every county in the State. Those delegates, the ministers, teachers, heads of secret and others orders, and the head of every every [sic] family should pas[s] the word around for every member of the race in Kentucky to stay off railroads unless obliged to ride[.] If they did so, and their advice was followed persistently the convention would not need to petition the Legislature to repeal the law or raise money to file a suit. The railroad corporations would be so effected they would in self-defense lobby to have the separate car law repealed. On the other hand, as long as the railroads can get Afro-American excursions they will always have plenty of money to fight all the suits brought against them. They will be aided in so doing by the same partisan public sentiment which passed the law. White men passed the law, and white judges and juries would pass upon the suits against the law, and render judgment in line with their prejudices and in deference to the greater financial power.

The appeal to the white man's pocket has ever been more effectual than all the appeals ever made to his conscience. Nothing, absolutely nothing, is to be gained by a further sacrifice of manhood and self-respect. By the right exercise of his power as the industrial factor of the South, the Afro-American can demand and secure his rights, the punishment of lynchers, and a fair trial for accused rapists.

Of the many inhuman outrages of this present year, the only case where the proposed lynching did *not* occur, was where the men armed themselves in Jacksonville, Fla., and Paducah, Ky., and prevented it. The only times an Afro-American who was assaulted got away has been when he had a gun and used it in self-defense.

The lesson this teaches and which every Afro American should ponder well, is that a Winchester rifle should have a place of honor in every black home, and it should be used for that protection which the law refuses to give. When the white man who is always the aggressor knows he runs as great risk of biting the dust every time his Afro-American victim does, he will have greater respect for Afro-American life. The more the Afro-American yields and cringes and begs, the more he has to do so, the more he is insulted, outraged and lynched.

The assertion has been substantiated throughout these pages that the press contains unreliable and doctored reports of lynchings, and one of the most necessary things for the race to do is to get these facts before the public. The people must know before they can act, and there is no educator to compare with the press.

The Afro-American papers are the only ones which will print the truth, and they lack means to employ agents and detectives to get at the facts. The race must rally a mighty host to the support of their journals, and thus enable them to do much in the way of investigation.

A lynching occurred at Port Jarvis, N.Y., the first week in June. A white and colored man were implicated in the assault upon a white girl. It was charged that the white man paid the colored boy to make the assault, which he did on the public highway in broad day time, and was lynched. This, too was done by "parties unknown." The white man in the case still lives. He was imprisoned and promises to fight the case on trial. At the preliminary examination, it developed that he had been a suitor of the girl's. She had repulsed and refused him, yet had given him money, and he had sent threatening letters demanding more.

The day before this examination she was so wrought up, she left home and wandered miles away. When found she said she did so because she was afraid of the man's testimony. Why should she be afraid of the prisoner? Why should she yield to his demands for money if not to prevent him exposing something he knew? It seems explainable only on the hypothesis that a *liason* existed between the colored boy and the girl, and the white man knew of it. The press is singularly silent. Has it a motive? We owe it to ourselves to find out.

The story comes from Larned, Kansas, Oct. 1st, that a young white lady held at bay until daylight, without alarming any one in the house, "a burly Negro" who entered her room and bed. The "burly Negro" was promptly lynched without investigation or examination of inconsistent stories.

A house was found burned down near Montgomery, Ala., in Monroe County, Oct. 13th, a few weeks ago; also the burned bodies of the owners and melted piles of gold and silver.

These discoveries led to the conclusion that the awful crime was not prompted by motives of robbery. The suggestion of the whites was that "brutal lust was the incentive, and as there are nearly 200 Negroes living within a radius of five miles of the place the conclusion was inevitable that some of them were the perpetrators."

Upon this "suggestion" probably made by the real criminal, the mob acted upon the "conclusion" and arrested ten Afro-Americans, four of whom, they tell the world, confessed to the deed of murdering Richard L. Johnson and outraging his daughter, Jeanette. These four men, Berrell Jones, Moses Johnson, Jim and John Packer, none of them 25 years of age, upon this conclusion, were taken from jail, hanged, shot, and burned while yet alive the night of Oct. 12th. The same report says Mr. Johnson was on the best of terms with his Negro tenants.

The race thus outraged must find out the facts of this awful hurling of men into eternity on supposition, and give them to the indifferent and apathetic country. We feel this to be a garbled report, but how can we prove it?

Near Vicksburg, Miss., a murder was committed by a gang of burglars. Of course it must have been done by Negroes, and Negroes were arrested for it. It is believed that 2 men, Smith Tooley and John Adams belonged to a gang controlled by white men and, fearing exposure, on the night of July 4th, they were hanged in the Court House yard by those interested in silencing them. Robberies since committed in the same vicinity have been known to be by white men who had their faces blackened. We strongly believe in the innocence of these murdered men, but we have no proof. No other news goes out to the world save that which stamps us as a race of cut-throats, robbers and lustful wild beasts. So great is Southern hate and prejudice, they legally (?) hung poor little thirteen year old Mildrey Brown at Columbia, S.C., Oct. 7th, on the circumstantial evidence that she poisoned a white infant. If her guilt had been proven unmistakably, had she been white, Mildrey Brown would never have been hung.

The country would have been aroused and South Carolina disgraced forever for such a crime. The Afro American himself did not know as he should have known as his journals should be in a position to have him know and act.

Nothing is more definitely settled than he must act for himself. I have shown how he may employ the boycott, emigration and the press, and I feel that by a combination of all these agencies can be effectually stamped out lynch law, that last relic of barbarism and slavery. "The gods help those who help themselves."

A RED RECORD.

Tabulated Statistics and Alleged Causes of

Lynchings in the United States,

1892–1893–1894.

Respectfully submitted to the Nineteenth Century
civilization in "the Land of the Free and
the Home of the Brave."

BY
Miss IDA B. WELLS,
128 Clark Street,
CHICAGO.

PREFACE

Hon. Frederick Douglass' Letter[1]

Dear Miss Wells:

Let me give you thanks for your faithful paper on the lynch abomination now generally practiced against colored people in the South. There has been no word equal to it in convincing power. I have spoken, but my word is feeble in comparison. You give us what you know and testify from actual knowledge. You have dealt with the facts with cool, painstaking fidelity, and left those naked and uncontradicted facts to speak for themselves.

Brave woman! you have done your people and mine a service which can neither be weighed nor measured. If the American conscience were only half alive, if the American church and clergy were only half Christianized, if American moral sensibility were not hardened by persistent infliction of outrage and crime against colored people, a scream of horror, shame, and indignation would rise to Heaven wherever your pamphlet shall be read.

But alas! even crime has power to reproduce itself and create conditions favorable to its own existence. It sometimes seems we are deserted by earth and Heaven — yet we must still think, speak and work, and trust in the power of a merciful God for final deliverance.

Very truly and gratefully yours,

Cedar Hill, Anacostia, D.C. Frederick Douglass.

CONTENTS

---

[1]This letter was originally written for *Southern Horrors*; Wells reprinted it in *A Red Record*.

CHAPTER I. THE CASE STATED

The student of American sociology will find the year 1894 marked by a pronounced awakening of the public conscience to a system of anarchy and outlawry which had grown during a series of ten years to be so common, that scenes of unusual brutality failed to have any visible effect upon the humane sentiments of the people of our land.

Beginning with the emancipation of the Negro, the inevitable result of unbribled power exercised for two and a half centuries, by the white man over the Negro, began to show itself in acts of conscienceless outlawry. During the slave regime, the Southern white man owned the Negro body and soul. It was to his interest to dwarf the soul and preserve the body. Vested with unlimited power over his slave, to subject him to any and all kinds of physical punishment, the white man was still restrained from such punishment as tended to injure the slave by abating his physical powers and thereby reducing his financial worth. While slaves were scourged mercilessly, and in countless cases inhumanly treated in other respects, still the white owner rarely permitted his anger to go so far as to take a life, which would entail upon him a loss of several hundred dollars. The slave was rarely killed, he was too valuable; it was easier and quite as effective, for discipline or revenge, to sell him "Down South."

But Emancipation came and the vested interests of the white man in the Negro's body were lost. The white man had no right to scourge the emancipated Negro, still less has he a right to kill him. But the Southern white people had been educated so long in that school of practice, in which might makes right, that they disdained to draw strict lines of action in dealing with the Negro. In slave times the Negro was kept subservient and submissive by the frequency and severity of the scourging, but, with freedom, a new system of intimidation came into vogue; the Negro was not only whipped and scourged; he was killed.

Not all nor nearly all of the murders done by white men, during the past thirty years in the South, have come to light, but the statistics as gathered and preserved by white men, and which have not been questioned, show that during these years more than ten thousand Negroes have been killed in cold blood, without the formality of judicial trial and legal execution. And yet, as evidence of the absolute impunity with which the white man dares to kill a Negro, the same record shows that during all these years, and for all these murders only three white men have been tried, convicted, and executed. As no white man has been lynched for the murder of colored people, these three executions are the only instances of the death penalty being visited upon white men for murdering Negroes.

Naturally enough the commission of these crimes began to tell upon the public conscience, and the Southern white man, as a tribute to the nineteenth century civilization, was in a manner compelled to give excuses for his barbarism. His excuses have adapted themselves to the emergency, and are aptly outlined by that greatest of all Negroes, Frederick Douglass, in an article of recent date, in which he shows that there have been three distinct eras of Southern barbarism, to account for which three distinct excuses have been made.

The first excuse given to the civilized world for the murder of unoffending Negroes was the necessity of the white man to repress and stamp out alleged "race riots." For years immediately succeeding the war there was an appalling slaughter of colored people, and the wires usually conveyed to northern people and the world the intelligence, first, that an insurrection was being planned by Negroes, which, a few hours later, would prove to have been vigorously resisted by white men, and controlled with a resulting loss of several killed and wounded. It was always a remarkable feature in these insurrections and riots that only Negroes were killed during the rioting, and that all the white men escaped unharmed.

From 1865 to 1872, hundreds of colored men and women were mercilessly murdered and the almost invariable reason assigned was that they met their death by being alleged participants in an insurrection or riot. But this story at last wore itself out. No insurrection ever materialized; no Negro rioter was ever apprehended and proven guilty, and no dynamite ever recorded the black man's protest against oppression and wrong. It was too much to ask thoughtful people to believe this transparent story, and the southern white people at last made up their minds that some other excuse must be had.

Then came the second excuse, which had its birth during the turbulent times of reconstruction. By an amendment to the Constitution the Negro was given the right of franchise, and, theoretically at least, his ballot became his invaluable emblem of citizenship. In a government "of the people, for the people, and by the people," the Negro's vote became an important factor in all matters of state and national politics. But this did not last long. The southern white man would not consider that the Negro had any right which a white man was bound to respect, and the idea of a republican form of government in the southern states grew into general contempt. It was maintained that "This is a white man's government," and regardless of numbers the white man should rule. "No

Negro domination" became the new legend on the sanguinary banner of the sunny South, and under it rode the Ku Klux Klan, the Regulators, and the lawless mobs, which for any cause chose to murder one man or a dozen as suited their purpose best. It was a long, gory campaign; the blood chills and the heart almost loses faith in Christianity when one thinks of Yazoo, Hamburg, Edgefield, Copiah, and the countless massacres of defenseless Negroes, whose only crime was the attempt to exercise their right to vote.

But it was a bootless strife for colored people. The government which had made the Negro a citizen found itself unable to protect him. It gave him the right to vote, but denied him the protection which should have maintained that right. Scourged from his home; hunted through the swamps; hung by midnight raiders, and openly murdered in the light of day, the Negro clung to his right of franchise with a heroism which would have wrung admiration from the hearts of savages. He believed that in that small white ballot there was a subtle something which stood for manhood as well as citizenship, and thousands of brave black men went to their graves, exemplifying the one by dying for the other.

The white man's victory soon became complete by fraud, violence, intimidation and murder. The franchise vouchsafed to the Negro grew to be a "barren ideality," and regardless of numbers, the colored people found themselves voiceless in the councils of those whose duty it was to rule. With no longer the fear of "Negro Domination" before their eyes, the white man's second excuse became valueless. With the Southern governments all subverted and the Negro actually eliminated from all participation in state and national elections, there could be no longer an excuse for killing Negroes to prevent "Negro Domination."

Brutality still continued; Negroes were whipped, scourged, exiled, shot and hung whenever and wherever it pleased the white man so to treat them, and as the civilized world with increasing persistency held the white people of the South to account for its outlawry, the murderers invented the third excuse—that Negroes had to be killed to avenge their assaults upon women. There could be framed no possible excuse more harmful to the Negro and more unanswerable if true in its sufficiency for the white man.

Humanity abhors the assailant of womanhood, and this charge upon the Negro at once placed him beyond the pale of human sympathy. With such unanimity, earnestness and apparent candor was this charge made and reiterated that the world has accepted the story that the Negro is a monster which the Southern white man has painted him. And to-day, the Christian world feels, that while lynching is a crime, and lawlessness and anarchy the certain precursors of a nation's fall, it can not by word or deed, extend sympathy or help to a race of outlaws, who might mistake their plea for justice and deem it an excuse for their continued wrongs.

The Negro has suffered much and is willing to suffer more. He recognizes that the wrongs of two centuries can not be righted in a day, and he tries to bear his burden with patience for to-day and be hopeful for to-morrow. But there comes a time when the veriest worm will turn, and the Negro feels to-day that after all the work he has done, all the sacrifices he has made, and all the suffering he has endured, if he did not, now, defend his name and manhood from this vile accusation, he would be unworthy even of the contempt of mankind. It is to this charge he now feels he must make answer.

If the Southern people in defense of their lawlessness, would tell the truth and admit that colored men and women are lynched for almost any offense, from murder to a misdemeanor, there would not now be the necessity for this defense. But when they intentionally, maliciously and constantly belie the record and bolster up these falsehoods by the words of legislators, preachers, governors and bishops, then the Negro must give to the world his side of the awful story.

A word as to the charge itself. In considering the third reason assigned by the Southern white people for the butchery of blacks, the question must be asked, what the white man means when he charges the black man with rape. Does he mean the crime which the statutes of the civilized states describe as such? Not by any means. With the Southern white man, any mesalliance existing between a white woman and a colored man is a sufficient foundation for the charge of rape. The Southern white man says that it is impossible for a voluntary alliance to exist between a white woman and a colored man, and therefore, the fact of an alliance is a proof of force. In numerous instances where colored men have been lynched on the charge of rape, it was positively known at the time of lynching, and indisputably proven after the victim's death, that the relationship sustained between the man and woman was voluntary and clandestine, and that in no court of law could even the charge of assault have been successfully maintained.

It was for the assertion of this fact, in the defense of her own race, that the writer hereof became an exile; her property destroyed and her return to her home forbidden under penalty of death, for writing the following editorial which was printed in her paper, the Free Speech, in Memphis, Tenn., May 21, 1892:

"Eight Negroes lynched since last issue of the 'Free Speech' one at Little Rock, Ark., last Saturday morning where the citizens broke (?)

into the penitentiary and got their man; three near Anniston, Ala., one near New Orleans; and three at Clarksville, Ga., the last three for killing a white man, and five on the same old racket—the new alarm about raping white women. The same programme of hanging, then shooting bullets into the lifeless bodies was carried out to the letter. Nobody in this section of the country believes the old threadbare lie that Negro men rape white women. If Southern white men are not careful, they will over-reach themselves and public sentiment will have a reaction; a conclusion will then be reached which will be very damaging to the moral reputation of their women."

But threats cannot suppress the truth, and while the Negro suffers the soul deformity, resultant from two and a half centuries of slavery, he is no more guilty of this vilest of all vile charges than the white man who would blacken his name.

During all the years of slavery, no such charge was ever made, not even during the dark days of the rebellion, when the white man, following the fortunes of war went to do battle for the maintenance of slavery. While the master was away fighting to forge the fetters upon the slave, he left his wife and children with no protectors save the Negroes themselves. And yet during those years of trust and peril, no Negro proved recreant to his trust and no white man returned to a home that had been dispoiled.

Likewise during the period of alleged "insurrection," and alarming "race riots," it never occurred to the white man, that his wife and children were in danger of assault. Nor in the Reconstruction era, when the hue and cry was against "Negro Domination," was there ever a thought that the domination would ever contaminate a fireside or strike to death the virtue of womanhood. It must appear strange indeed, to every thoughtful and candid man, that more than a quarter of a century elapsed before the Negro began to show signs of such infamous degeneration.

In his remarkable apology for lynching, Bishop Haygood,[2] of Georgia, says: "No race, not the most savage, tolerates the rape of woman, but it may be said without reflection upon any other people that the Southern people are now and always have been most sensitive concerning the honor of their women—their mothers, wives, sisters and daughters." It is not the purpose of this defense to say one word against the white women of the South. Such need not be said, but it is their misfortune that the chivalrous white men of that section, in order to

---

[2]Atticus G. Haygood was president of Emory University when he was named a bishop of the Methodist Church in 1890.

escape the deserved execration of the civilized world, should shield themselves by their cowardly and infamously false excuse, and call into question that very honor about which their distinguished priestly apologist claims they are most sensitive. To justify their own barbarism they assume a chivalry which they do not possess. True chivalry respects all womanhood, and no one who reads the record, as it is written in the faces of the million mulattoes in the South, will for a minute conceive that the southern white man had a very chivalrous regard for the honor due the women of his own race or respect for the womanhood which circumstances placed in his power. That chivalry which is "most sensitive concerning the honor of women" can hope for but little respect from the civilized world, when it confines itself entirely to the women who happen to be white. Virtue knows no color line, and the chivalry which depends upon complexion of skin and texture of hair can command no honest respect.

When emancipation came to the Negroes, there arose in the northern part of the United States an almost divine sentiment among the noblest, purest and best white women of the North, who felt called to a mission to educate and Christianize the millions of southern ex-slaves. From every nook and corner of the North, brave young white women answered that call and left their cultured homes, their happy associations and their lives of ease, and with heroic determination went to the South to carry light and truth to the benighted blacks. It was a heroism no less than that which calls for volunteers for India, Africa and the Isles of the sea. To educate their unfortunate charges; to teach them the Christian virtues and to inspire in them the moral sentiments manifest in their own lives, these young women braved dangers whose record reads more like fiction than fact. They became social outlaws in the South. The peculiar sensitiveness of the southern white men for women, never shed its protecting influence about them. No friendly word from their own race cheered them in their work; no hospitable doors gave them the companionship like that from which they had come. No chivalrous white man doffed his hat in honor or respect. They were "Nigger teachers"—unpardonable offenders in the social ethics of the South, and were insulted, persecuted and ostracised, not by Negroes, but by the white manhood which boasts of its chivalry toward women.

And yet these northern women worked on, year after year, unselfishly, with a heroism which amounted almost to martyrdom. Threading their way through dense forests, working in schoolhouse, in the cabin and in the church, thrown at all times and in all places among the unfortunate and lowly Negroes, whom they had come to find and to serve, these northern women, thousands and thousands of them, have spent more than a quarter of a century in giving to the colored people their splendid lessons for home and heart and soul. Without protection, save that which innocence gives to every good woman, they went about their work, fearing no assault and suffering none. Their chivalrous protectors were hundreds of miles away in their northern homes, and yet they never feared any "great dark faced mobs," they dared night or day to "go beyond their own roof trees." They never complained of assaults, and no mob was ever called into existence to avenge crimes against them. Before the world adjudges the Negro a moral monster, a vicious assailant of womanhood and a menace to the sacred precincts of home, the colored people ask the consideration of the silent record of gratitude, respect, protection and devotion of the millions of the race in the South, to the thousands of northern white women who have served as teachers and missionaries since the war.

The Negro may not have known what chivalry was, but he knew enough to preserve inviolate the womanhood of the South which was entrusted to his hands during the war. The finer sensibilities of his soul may have been crushed out by years of slavery, but his heart was full of gratitude to the white women of the North, who blessed his home and inspired his soul in all these years of freedom. Faithful to his trust in both of these instances, he should now have the impartial ear of the civilized world, when he dares to speak for himself as against the infamy wherewith he stands charged.

It is his regret, that, in his own defense, he must disclose to the world that degree of dehumanizing brutality which fixes upon America the blot of a national crime. Whatever faults and failings other nations may have in their dealings with their own subjects or with other people, no other civilized nation stands condemned before the world with a series of crimes so peculiarly national. It becomes a painful duty of the Negro to reproduce a record which shows that a large portion of the American people avow anarchy, condone murder and defy the contempt of civilization.

These pages are written in no spirit of vindictiveness, for all who give the subject consideration must concede that far too serious is the condition of that civilized government in which the spirit of unrestrained outlawry constantly increases in violence, and casts its blight over a continually growing area of territory. We plead not for the colored people alone, but for all victims of the terrible injustice which puts men and women to death without form of law. During the year 1894, there were

132 persons executed in the United States by due form of law, while in the same year, 197 persons were put to death by mobs who gave the victims no opportunity to make a lawful defense. No comment need be made upon a condition of public sentiment responsible for such alarming results.

The purpose of the pages which follow shall be to give the record which has been made, not by colored men, but that which is the result of compilations made by white men, of reports sent over the civilized world by white men in the South. Out of their own mouths shall the murderers be condemned. For a number of years the Chicago Tribune, admittedly one of the leading journals of America, has made a specialty of the compilation of statistics touching upon lynching. The data compiled by that journal and published to the world January 1st, 1894, up to the present time has not been disputed. In order to be safe from the charge of exaggeration, the incidents hereinafter reported have been confined to those vouched for by the Tribune.

CHAPTER II.   LYNCH LAW STATISTICS

From the record published in the Chicago Tribune, January 1, 1894, the following computation of lynching statistics is made referring only to the colored victims of Lynch Law during the year 1893:

ARSON

Sept. 15, Paul Hill, Carrollton, Ala.; Sept. 15, Paul Archer, Carrollton, Ala.; Sept. 15, William Archer, Carrollton, Ala.; Sept. 15, Emma Fair, Carrollton, Ala.

SUSPECTED ROBBERY

Dec. 23, unknown negro, Fannin, Miss.

ASSAULT

Dec. 25, Calvin Thomas, near Brainbridge, Ga.

ATTEMPTED ASSAULT

Dec. 28, Tillman Green, Columbia, La.

INCENDIARISM

Jan. 26, Patrick Wells, Quincy, Fla.; Feb. 9, Frank Harrell, Dickery, Miss.; Feb. 9, William Filder, Dickery, Miss.

ATTEMPTED RAPE

Feb. 21, Richard Mays, Springville, Mo.; Aug. 14, Dug Hazleton, Carrollton, Ga.; Sept. 1, Judge McNeil, Cadiz, Ky.; Sept. 11, Frank Smith, Newton, Miss.; Sept. 16, William Jackson, Nevada, Mo.; Sept. 19, Riley Gulley, Pine Apple, Ala.; Oct. 9, John Davis, Shorterville, Ala.; Nov. 8, Robert Kennedy, Spartansburg, S.C.

BURGLARY

Feb. 16, Richard Forman, Granada, Miss.

WIFE BEATING

Oct. 14, David Jackson, Covington, La.

ATTEMPTED MURDER

Sept. 21, Thomas Smith, Roanoke, Va.

ATTEMPTED ROBBERY

Dec. 12, four unknown negroes, near Selma, Ala.

RACE PREJUDICE

Jan. 30, Thomas Carr, Kosciusko, Miss.; Feb. 7, William Butler, Hickory Creek, Texas; Aug. 27, Charles Tart, Lyons Station, Miss.; Dec. 7, Robert Greenwood, Cross county, Ark.; July 14, Allen Butler, Lawrenceville, Ill.

THIEVES

Oct. 24, two unknown negroes, Knox Point, La.

ALLEGED BARN BURNING

Nov. 4, Edward Wagner, Lynchburg, Va.; Nov. 4, William Wagner, Lynchburg, Va.; Nov. 4, Samuel Motlow, Lynchburg, Va.; Nov. 4, Eliza Motlow, Lynchburg, Va.

ALLEGED MURDER

Jan. 21, Robert Landry, St. James Parish, La.; Jan. 21, Chicken George, St. James Parish, La.; Jan. 21, Richard Davis, St. James Parish, La.; Dec. 8, Benjamin Menter, Berlin, Ala.; Dec. 8, Robert Wilkins, Berlin, Ala.; Dec. 8, Joseph Gevhens, Berlin, Ala.

ALLEGED COMPLICITY IN MURDER

Sept. 16, Valsin Julian, Jefferson Parish, La.; Sept. 16, Basil Julian, Jefferson Parish, La.; Sept. 16, Paul Julian, Jefferson Parish, La.; Sept. 16, John Willis, Jefferson Parish, La.

MURDER

June 29, Samuel Thorp, Savannah, Ga.; June 29, George S. Riechen, Waynesboro, Ga.; June 30, Joseph Bird, Wilberton, I. T.;[3] July 1, James Lamar, Darien, Ga.; July 28, Henry Miller, Dallas, Texas; July 28, Ada Hiers, Walterboro, S.C.; July 28, Alexander Brown, Bastrop, Texas; July 30, W. G. Jamison, Quincy, Ill.; Sept. 1, John Ferguson, Lawrens, S.C.; Sept. 1, Oscar Johnston, Berkeley, S.C.; Sept. 1, Henry Ewing, Berkeley, S.C.; Sept. 8, William Smith, Camden, Ark.; Sept. 15, Staples Green, Livingston, Ala.; Sept. 29, Hiram Jacobs, Mount Vernon, Ga.; Sept. 29, Lucien Mannet, Mount Vernon, Ga.; Sept. 29, Hire Bevington, Mount Vernon, Ga.; Sept. 29, Weldon Gordon, Mount Vernon, Ga.; Sept. 29, Parse Strickland, Mount Vernon, Ga.; Oct. 20, William Dalton, Cartersville, Ga.; Oct. 27, M. B. Taylor, Wise Court House, Va.; Oct. 27, Isaac Williams, Madison, Ga.; Nov. 10, Miller Davis, Center Point, Ark.; Nov. 14, John Johnston, Auburn, N.Y.

Sept. 27, Calvin Stewart, Langley, S.C.; Sept. 29, Henry Coleman, Benton, La.; Oct. 18, William Richards, Summerfield, Ga.; Oct. 18, James Dickson, Summerfield, Ga.; Oct. 27, Edward Jenkins, Clayton county, Ga.; Nov. 9, Henry Boggs, Fort White, Fla.; Nov. 14, three unknown negroes, Lake City Junction, Fla.; Nov. 14, D. T. Nelson, Varney, Ark.; Nov. 29, Newton Jones, Baxley, Ga.; Dec. 2, Lucius Holt, Concord, Ga.; Dec. 10, two unknown negroes, Richmond, Ala.; July 12, Henry Fleming, Columbus, Miss.; July 17, unknown negro, Briar Field, Ala.; July 18, Meredith Lewis, Roseland, La.; July 29, Edward Bill, Dresden, Tenn.; Aug. 1, Henry Reynolds, Montgomery, Tenn.; Aug. 9, unknown negro, McCreery, Ark.; Aug. 12, unknown negro, Brantford, Fla.; Aug. 18, Charles Walton, Morganfield, Ky.; Aug. 21, Charles Tait, near Memphis, Tenn.; Aug. 28, Leonard Taylor, New Castle, Ky.; Sept. 8, Benjamin Jackson, Quincy, Miss.; Sept. 14, John Williams, Jackson, Tenn.

SELF DEFENSE

July 30, unknown negro[,] Wingo, Ky.

---

[3]*I. T.*, Indian Territory.

POISONING WELLS

Aug. 18, two unknown negroes, Franklin Parish, La.

ALLEGED WELL POISONING

Sept. 15, Benjamin Jackson, Jackson, Miss.; Sept. 15, Mahala Jackson, Jackson, Miss.; Sept. 15, Louisa Carter, Jackson, Miss.; Sept. 15, W. A. Haley, Jackson, Miss.; Sept. 15, Rufus Bigley, Jackson, Miss.

INSULTING WHITES

Feb. 18, John Hughes, Moberly, Mo.; June 2, Isaac Lincoln, Fort Madison, S.C.

MURDEROUS ASSAULT

April 20, Daniel Adams, Selina, Kan.

NO OFFENSE

July 21, Charles Martin, Shelby Co., Tenn.; July 30, William Steen, Paris, Miss.; August 31, unknown negro, Yarborough, Tex.; Sept. 30, unknown negro, Houston, Tex.; Dec. 28, Mack Segars, Brantley, Ala.

ALLEGED RAPE

July 7, Charles T. Miller, Bardwell, Ky.; Aug. 10, Daniel Lewis, Waycross, Ga.; Aug. 10, James Taylor, Waycross, Ga.; Aug. 10, John Chambers, Waycross, Ga.

ALLEGED STOCK POISONING

Dec. 16, Henry G. Givens, Nebro, Ky.

SUSPECTED MURDER

Dec. 23, Sloan Allen, West Mississippi.

SUSPICION OF RAPE

Feb. 14, Andy Blount, Chattanooga, Tenn.

TURNING STATE'S EVIDENCE

Dec. 19, William Ferguson, Adele, Ga.

RAPE

Jan. 19, James Williams, Pickens Co., Ala.; Feb. 11, unknown negro, Forest Hill, Tenn.; Feb. 26, Joseph Hayne, or Paine, Jellico, Tenn.; Nov. 1,

Abner Anthony, Hot Springs, Va.; Nov. 1, Thomas Hill, Spring Place, Ga.; April 24, John Peterson, Denmark, S.C.; May 6, Samuel Gaillard, ——, S.C.; May 10, Haywood Banks, or Marksdale, Columbia, S.C.; May 12, Israel Halliway, Napoleonville, La.; May 12, unknown negro, Wytheville, Va.; May 31, John Wallace, Jefferson Springs, Ark.; June 3, Samuel Bush, Decatur, Ill.; June 8, L. C. Dumas, Gleason, Tenn.; June 13, William Shorter, Winchester, Va.; June 14, George Williams, near Waco, Tex.; June 24, Daniel Edwards, Selina or Selma, Ala.; June 27, Ernest Murphy, Daleville, Ala.; July 6, unknown negro, Poplar Head, La.; July 6, unknown negro, Poplar Head, La.; July 12, Robert Larkin, Oscola, Tex.; July 17, Warren Dean, Stone Creek, Ga.; July 21, unknown negro, Brantford, Fla.; July 17, John Cotton, Connersville, Ark.; July 22, Lee Walker, New Albany, Miss.; July 26, —— Handy, Suansea, S.C.; July 30, William Thompson, Columbia, S.C.; July 28, Isaac Harper, Calera, Ala.; July 30, Thomas Preston, Columbia, S.C.; July 30, Handy Kaigler, Columbia, S.C.; Aug. 13, Monroe Smith, Springfield, Ala.; Aug. 19, negro tramp, near Paducah, Ky.; Aug. 21, John Nilson, near Leavenworth, Kan.; Aug. 23, Jacob Davis, Green Wood, S.C.; Sept. 2, William Arkinson, McKenney, Ky.; Sept. 16, unknown negro, Centerville, Ala.; Sept. 16, Jessie Mitchell, Amelia C. H., Va.; Sept 25, Perry Bratcher, New Boston, Tex.; Oct. 9, William Lacey, Jasper, Ala.; Oct. 22, John Gamble, Pikesville, Tenn.

OFFENSES CHARGED ARE AS FOLLOWS

Rape, 39; attempted rape, 8; alleged rape, 4; suspicion of rape, 1; murder, 44; alleged murder, 6; alleged complicity in murder, 4; murderous assault, 1; attempted murder, 1; attempted robbery, 4; arson, 4; incendiarism, 3; alleged stock poisoning, 1; poisoning wells, 2; alleged poisoning wells, 5; burglary, 1; wife beating, 1; self defense, 1; suspected robbery, 1; assault and battery, 1; insulting whites, 2; malpractice, 1; alleged barn burning, 4; stealing, 2; unknown offense, 4; no offense, 1; race prejudice, 4; total, 159.

LYNCHINGS BY STATES

Alabama, 25; Arkansas, 7; Florida, 7; Georgia, 24; Indian Territory, 1; Illinois, 3; Kansas, 2; Kentucky, 8; Louisiana, 18; Mississippi, 17; Missouri, 3; New York, 1; South Carolina, 15; Tennessee, 10; Texas, 8; Virginia, 10.

RECORD FOR THE YEAR 1892

While it is intended that the record here presented shall include specially the lynchings of 1893, it will not be amiss to give the record for the year preceding. The facts contended for will always appear manifest—that not one-third of the victims lynched were charged with rape, and further that the charges made embraced a range of offenses from murders to misdemeanors.

In 1892 there were 241 persons lynched. The entire number is divided among the following states:

Alabama, 22; Arkansas, 25; California, 3; Florida, 11; Georgia, 17; Idaho, 8; Illinois, 1; Kansas, 3; Kentucky, 9; Louisiana, 29; Maryland, 1; Mississippi, 16; Missouri, 6; Montana, 4; New York, 1; North Carolina, 5; North Dakota, 1; Ohio, 3; South Carolina, 5; Tennessee, 28; Texas, 15; Virginia, 7; West Virginia, 5; Wyoming, 9; Arizona Territory, 3; Oklahoma, 2.

Of this number 160 were of Negro descent. Four of them were lynched in New York, Ohio and Kansas; the remainder were murdered in the South. Five of this number were females. The charges for which they were lynched cover a wide range. They are as follows:

Rape, 46; murder, 58; rioting, 3; race prejudice, 6; no cause given, 4; incendiarism, 6; robbery, 6; assault and battery, 1; attempted rape, 11; suspected robbery, 4; larceny, 1; self defense, 1; insulting women, 2; desperadoes, 6; fraud, 1; attempted murder, 2; no offense stated, boy and girl, 2.

In the case of the boy and girl above referred to, their father, named Hastings, was accused of the murder of a white man; his fourteen-year-old daughter and sixteen-year-old son were hanged and their bodies filled with bullets, then the father was also lynched. This was in November, 1892, at Jonesville, Louisiana.

CHAPTER III.   LYNCHING IMBECILES

(An Arkansas Butchery)

The only excuse which capital punishment attempts to find is upon the theory that the criminal is past the power of reformation and his life is a constant menace to the community. If, however, he is mentally unbalanced, irresponsible for his acts, there can be no more inhuman act conceived of than the wilful sacrifice of his life. So thoroughly is that principle grounded in the law, that all civilized society surrounds human life with a safeguard, which prevents the execution of a criminal who is insane, even if sane at the time of his criminal act. Should he become insane after its commission the law steps in and protects him during the period of his insanity. But Lynch Law has no such regard for human life. Assuming for itself an absolute supremacy over the law of the land, it has time and again dyed its hands in the blood of men who were imbeciles. Two or three noteworthy cases will suffice to show with what inhuman ferocity irresponsible men have been put to death by this system of injustice.

An instance occurred during the year 1892 in Arkansas, a report of which is given in full in the Arkansas Democrat, published at Little Rock, in that state, on the 11th day of February of that year. The paper mentioned is perhaps one of the leading weeklies in that state and the account given in detail has every mark of a careful and conscientious investigation. The victims of this tragedy were a colored man, named Hamp Biscoe, his wife and a thirteen year-old son. Hamp Biscoe, it appears, was a hard working, thrifty farmer, who lived near England, Arkansas, upon a small farm with his family. The investigation of the tragedy was conducted by a resident of Arkansas named R. B. Carlee, a white man, who furnished the account to the Arkansas Democrat over his own signature. He says the original trouble which led to the lynching was a quarrel between Biscoe and a white man about a debt. About six years after Biscoe pre-empted his land, a white man made a demand of $100 upon him for services in showing him the land and making the sale. Biscoe denied the service and refused to pay the demand. The white man, however, brought suit, obtained judgment for the hundred dollars and Biscoe's farm was sold to pay the judgment.

The suit, judgment and subsequent legal proceedings appear to have driven Biscoe almost crazy and brooding over his wrongs he grew to be a confirmed imbecile. He would allow but few men[,] white or colored, to come upon his place, as he suspected every stranger to be planning to steal his farm. A week preceding the tragedy, a white man named Venable, whose farm adjoined Biscoe's, let down the fence and proceeded to drive through Biscoe's field. The latter saw him; grew very excited, cursed him and drove him from his farm with bitter oaths and violent threats. Venable went away and secured a warrant for Biscoe's arrest. This warrant was placed in the hands of a constable named John Ford, who took a colored deputy and two white men out to Biscoe's farm to make the arrest. When they arrived at the house Biscoe refused to be arrested and warned them he would shoot if they persisted in their attempt to arrest him. The warning was unheeded by Ford, who entered upon the premises, when Biscoe, true to his word, fired upon him. The load tore a part of his clothes from his body, one shot going through his arm and entering his breast. After he had fallen, Ford drew his revolver and shot Biscoe in the head and his wife through the arm. The Negro deputy then began firing and struck Biscoe in the small of the back.

Ford's wound was not dangerous and in a few days he was able to be around again. Biscoe, however, was so severely shot that he was unable to stand after the firing was over.

Two other white men hearing the exchange of shots went to the rescue of the officers, forced open the door of Biscoe's cabin and arrested him, his wife and thirteen-year-old son, and took them, together with a babe at the breast, to a small frame house near the depot and put them under guard. The subsequent proceedings were briefly told by Mr. Carlee in the columns of the Arkansas Democrat above mentioned, from whose account the following excerpt is taken:

"It was rumored here that the Negroes were to be lynched that night, but I do not think it was generally credited, as it was not believed that Ford was greatly hurt and the Negro was held to be fatally injured and crazy at that. But that night, about 8 o'clock, a party of perhaps twelve or fifteen men, a number of whom were known to the guards, came to the house and told the Negro guards they would take care of the prisoners now, and for them to leave; as they did not obey at once they were persuaded to leave with words that did not admit of delay.

"The woman began to cry and said, 'You intend to kill us to get our money.' They told her to hush (she was heavy with child and had a child at her breast) as they intended to give her a nice present. The guards heard no more, but hastened to a Negro church near by and urged the preacher to go up and stop the mob. A few minutes after, the shooting began, perhaps about forty shots being fired. The white men then left rapidly and the Negroes went to the house. Hamp Biscoe and his wife were killed, the baby had a slight wound across the upper lip; the boy was still alive and lived until after midnight, talking rationally and telling who did the shooting.

"He said when they came in and shot his father, he attempted to run out of doors and a young man shot him in the bowels and that he fell. He saw another man shoot his mother and a taller young man, whom he did not know, shoot his father. After they had killed them, the young man who had shot his mother pulled off her stockings and took $220 in currency that she had hid there. The men then came to the door where the boy was lying and one of them turned him over and put his pistol to his breast and shot him again. This is the story the dying boy told as near as I can get it. It is quite singular that the guards and those who had conversed with him were not required to testify. The woman was known to have the money as she had exposed it that day. She also had $36 in silver, which the plunderer of the body did not get. The Negro was undoubtedly insane and had been for several years. The citizens of this community condemn the murder and have no sympathy with it. The Negro was a well to do farmer, but had become crazed because he was convinced some plot had been made to steal his land and only a few days ago declared that he expected to die in defense of his home in a short time and he did not care how soon. The killing of a woman with the child at her breast and in her condition, and also a young boy, was extremely brutal. As for Hamp Biscoe he was dangerous and should long have been confined in the insane asylum. Such were the facts as near as I can get them and you can use them as you see fit, but I would prefer you would suppress the names charged by the Negroes with the killing."

Perhaps the civilized world will think, that with all these facts laid before the public, by a writer who signs his name to his communication, in a land where grand juries are sworn to investigate, where judges and juries are sworn to administer the law and sheriffs are paid to execute the decrees of the courts, and where, in fact, every instrument of civilization is supposed to work for the common good of all citizens, that this matter was duly investigated, the criminals apprehended and the punishment meted out to the murderers. But this is a mistake; nothing of the kind was done or attempted. Six months after the publication, above referred to, an investigator, writing to find out what had been done in the matter, received the following reply:

OFFICE OF
S. S. GLOVER,
SHERIFF AND COLLECTOR,
LONOKE COUNTY.

Lonoke, Ark., 9-12-1892.

Geo. Washington, Esq.,
Chicago, Ill.

DEAR SIR: — The parties who killed Hamp Briscoe February the 9th, have never been arrested. The parties are still in the county. It was done by some of the citizens, and those who know will not tell.

S. S. GLOVER, Sheriff.

Thus acts the mob with the victim of its fury, conscious that it will never be called to an account. Not only is this true, but the moral support of those who are chosen by the people to execute the law, is frequently given to the support of lawlessness and mob violence. The press and even the pulpit, in the main either by silence or open apology, have condoned and encouraged this state of anarchy.

Tortured and Burned in Texas

Never in the history of civilization has any Christian people stooped to such shocking brutality and indescribable barbarism as that which characterized the people of Paris, Texas, and adjacent communities on the 1st of February, 1893. The cause of this awful outbreak of human passion was the murder of a four year old child, daughter of a man named Vance. This man, Vance, had been a police officer in Paris for years, and was known to be a man of bad temper, overbearing manner and given to harshly treating the prisoners under his care. He had arrested Smith and, it is said, cruelly mistreated him. Whether or not the murder of his child was an act of fiendish revenge, it has not been shown, but many persons who know of the incident have suggested that the secret of the attack on the child lay in a desire for revenge against its father.

In the same town there lived a Negro, named Henry Smith, a well known character, a kind of roustabout, who was generally considered a harmless, weak-minded fellow, not capable of doing any important work, but sufficiently able to do chores and odd jobs around the houses of the white people who cared to employ him. A few days before the final tragedy, this man, Smith, was accused of murdering Myrtle Vance. The crime of murder was of itself bad enough, and to prove that against Smith would have been amply sufficient in Texas to have committed him to the gallows, but the finding of the child so exasperated the father and his friends, that they at once shamefully exaggerated the facts and declared that the babe had been ruthlessly assaulted and then killed. The truth was bad enough, but the white people of the community made it a point to exaggerate every detail of the awful affair, and to inflame the public mind so that nothing less than immediate and violent death would satisfy the populace. As a matter of fact, the child was not brutally assaulted as the world has been told in excuse for the awful barbarism of that day. Persons who saw the child after its death, have stated, under the most solemn pledge to truth, that there was no evidence of such an assault as was published at that time, only a slight abrasion and discoloration was noticeable and that mostly about the neck. In spite of this fact, so eminent a man as Bishop Haygood[4] deliberately and, it must also appear, maliciously falsified the fact by stating that the child was torn limb from limb, or to quote his own words, "First outraged with demoniacal cruelty and then taken by her heels and torn asunder in the mad wantonness of gorilla ferocity."

[4]See note p. 75.

Nothing is farther from the truth than that statement. It is a cold blooded, deliberate, brutal falsehood which this Christian (?) Bishop uses to bolster up the infamous plea that the people of Paris were driven to insanity by learning that the little child had been viciously assaulted, choked to death, and then torn to pieces by a demon in human form. It was a brutal murder, but no more brutal than hundreds of murders which occur in this country, and which have been equalled every year in fiendishness and brutality, and for which the death penalty is prescribed by law and inflicted only after the person has been legally adjudged guilty of the crime. Those who knew Smith, believe that Vance had at some time given him cause to seek revenge and that this fearful crime was the outgrowth of his attempt to avenge himself of some real or fancied wrong. That the murderer was known as an imbecile, had no effect whatever upon the people who thirsted for his blood. They determined to make an example of him and proceeded to carry out their purpose with unspeakably greater ferocity than that which characterized the half crazy object of their revenge.

For a day or so after the child was found in the woods, Smith remained in the vicinity as if nothing had happened, and when finally becoming aware that he was suspected, he made an attempt to escape. He was apprehended, however, not far from the scene of his crime and the news flashed across the country that the white Christian people of Paris, Texas and the communities thereabout had deliberately determined to lay aside all forms of law and inaugurate an entirely new form of punishment for the murder. They absolutely refused to make any inquiry as to the sanity or insanity of their prisoner, but set the day and hour when in the presence of assembled thousands they put their helpless victim to the stake, tortured him, and then burned him to death for the delectation and satisfaction of Christian people.

Lest it might be charged that any description of the deeds of that day are exaggerated, a white man's description which was published in the white journals of this country is used. The New York Sun of February 2d, 1893, contains an account, from which we make the following excerpt:

PARIS, Tex., Feb. 1, 1893.—Henry Smith, the negro ravisher of 4-year-old Myrtle Vance, has expiated in part his awful crime by death at the stake. Ever since the perpetration of his awful crime this city and the entire surrounding country has been in a wild frenzy of excitement. When the news came last night that he had been captured at Hope, Ark., that he had been identified by B. B. Sturgeon, James T. Hicks, and many other of the Paris searching party, the city was wild with joy over the apprehension of the brute. Hundreds of people poured into the city from the adjoining country and the word passed from lip to lip that the punishment of the fiend should fit the crime—that death by fire was the penalty Smith should pay for the most atrocious murder and terrible outrage in Texas history. Curious and sympathizing alike, they came on train and wagons, on horse, and on foot to see if the frail mind of a man could think of a way to sufficiently punish the perpetrator of so terrible a crime. Whisky shops were closed, unruly mobs were dispersed, schools were dismissed by a proclamation from the mayor, and everything was done in a businesslike manner.

Meeting of Citizens

About 2 o'clock Friday a mass meeting was called at the courthouse and captains appointed to search for the child. She was found mangled beyond recognition, covered with leaves and brush as above mentioned. As soon as it was learned upon the recovery of the body that the crime was so atrocious the whole town turned out in the chase. The railroads put up bulletins offering free transportation to all who would join in the search. Posses went in every direction, and not a stone was left unturned. Smith was tracked to Detroit on foot, where he jumped on a freight train and left for his old home in Hempstead county, Arkansas. To this county he was tracked and yesterday captured at Clow, a flag station on the Arkansas & Louisiana railway about twenty miles north of Hope. Upon being questioned the fiend denied everything, but upon being stripped for examination his undergarments were seen to be spattered with blood and a part of his shirt was torn off. He was kept under heavy guard at Hope last night, and later on confessed the crime.

This morning he was brought through Texarkana, where 5,000 people awaited the train, anxious to see a man who had received the fate of Ed. Coy. At that place speeches were made by prominent Paris citizens, who asked that the prisoner be not molested by Texarkana people, but that the guard be allowed to deliver him up to the outraged and indignant citizens of Paris. Along the road the train gathered strength from the various towns, the people crowded upon the platforms and tops of coaches anxious to see the lynching and the negro who was soon to be delivered to an infuriated mob.

Burned at the Stake

Arriving here at 12 o'clock the train was met by a surging mass of humanity 10,000 strong. The negro was placed upon a carnival float in mockery of a king upon his throne, and, followed by an immense crowd, was escorted through the city so that all might see the most inhuman monster known in current history. The line of march was up Main street to the square, around the square down Clarksville street to Church street, thence to the open prairies about 300 yards from the Texas & Pacific depot. Here Smith was placed upon a scaffold, six feet square and ten feet high, securely bound, within the view of all beholders. Here the victim was tortured for fifty minutes by red-hot iron brands thrust against his quivering body. Commencing at the feet the brands were placed against him inch by inch until they were thrust against the face. Then, being apparently dead, kerosene was poured upon him, cottonseed hulls placed beneath him and set on fire. In less time than it takes to relate it, the tortured man was wafted beyond the grave to another fire, hotter and more terrible than the one just experienced.

Curiosity seekers have carried away already all that was left of the memorable event, even to pieces of charcoal. The cause of the crime was that Henry Vance when a deputy policeman, in the course of his duty was called to arrest Henry Smith for being drunk and disorderly. The Negro was unruly, and Vance was forced to use his club. The Negro swore vengeance, and several times assaulted Vance. In his greed for revenge, last Thursday, he grabbed up the little girl and committed the crime. The father is prostrated with grief and the mother now lies at death's door, but she has lived to see the slayer of her innocent babe suffer the most horrible death that could be conceived.

Torture beyond Description

Words to describe the awful torture inflicted upon Smith cannot be found. The Negro, for a long time after starting on the journey to Paris, did not realize his plight. At last when he was told that he must die by slow torture he begged for protection. His agony was awful. He pleaded and writhed in bodily and mental pain. Scarcely had the train reached Paris than this torture commenced. His clothes were torn off piecemeal and scattered in the crowd, people catching the shreds and putting them away as mementos. The child's father, her brother, and two uncles then gathered about the Negro as he lay fastened to the torture platform and thrust hot irons into his quivering flesh. It was horrible — the man dying by slow torture in the midst of smoke from his own burning flesh. Every groan from the fiend, every contortion of his body was cheered by the thickly packed crowd of 10,000 persons. The mass of beings 600 yards in diameter, the scaffold being the center. After burning the feet and legs, the hot irons — plenty of fresh ones being at hand — were rolled up and down Smith's stomach, back, and arms. Then the eyes were burned out and irons were thrust down his throat.

The men of the Vance family having wreaked vengeance, the crowd piled all kinds of combustible stuff around the scaffold, poured oil on it and set it afire. The Negro rolled and tossed out of the mass, only to be pushed back by the people nearest him. He tossed out again, and was roped and pulled back. Hundreds of people turned away, but the vast crowd still looked calmly on. People were here from every part of this section. They came from Dallas, Fort Worth, Sherman, Denison, Bonham, Texarkana, Fort Smith, Ark., and a party of fifteen came from Hempstead county, Arkansas, where he was captured. Every train that came in was loaded to its utmost capacity, and there were demands at many points for special trains to bring the people here to see the unparalleled punishment for an unparalleled crime. When the news of the burning went over the country like wildfire, at every country town anvils boomed forth the announcement.

Should Have Been in an Asylum

It may not be amiss in connection with this awful affair, in proof of our assertion that Smith was an imbecile, to give the testimony of a well known colored minister, who lived at Paris, Texas, at the time of the lynching. He was a witness of the awful scenes there enacted, and attempted, in the name of God and humanity, to interfere in the programme. He barely escaped with his life, was driven out of the city and became an exile because of his actions. Reverend King was in New York about the middle of February, and he was there interviewed for a daily paper for that city, and we quote his account as an eye witness of the affair. Said he:

"I was ridden out of Paris on a rail because I was the only man in Lamar county to raise my voice against the lynching of Smith. I opposed the illegal measures before the arrival of Henry Smith as a prisoner, and I was warned that I might meet his fate if I was not careful; but the sense of justice made me bold, and when I saw the poor wretch trembling with fear, and got so near him that I could hear his teeth chatter, I determined to stand by him to the last.

"I hated him for his crime, but two crimes do not make a virtue; and in the brief conversation I had with Smith I was more firmly convinced than ever that he was irresponsible.

"I had known Smith for years, and there were times when Smith was out of his head for weeks. Two years ago I made an effort to have him put in an asylum, but the white people were trying to fasten the murder of a young colored girl upon him, and would not listen. For days before the murder of the little Vance girl, Smith was out of his head and dangerous. He had just undergone an attack of delirium tremens and was in no condition to be allowed at large. He realized his condition, for I spoke with him not three weeks ago, and in answer to my exhortations, he promised to reform. The next time I saw him was on the day of his execution.

"'Drink did it! drink did it,' he sobbed. Then bowing his face in his hands, he asked: 'Is it true, did I kill her? Oh, my God, my God!' For a moment he seemed to forget the awful fate that awaited him, and his body swayed to and fro with grief. Some one seized me by the shoulder and hurled me back, and Smith fell writhing to the ground in terror as four men seized his arms to drag him to the float on which he was to be exhibited before he was finally burned at the stake.

"I followed the procession and wept aloud as I saw little children of my own race follow the unfortunate man and taunt him with jeers. Even at the stake, children of both sexes and colors gathered in groups, and when the father of the murdered child raised the hissing iron with which he was about to torture the helpless victim, the children became as frantic as the grown people and struggled forward to obtain places of advantage.

"It was terrible. One little tot scarcely older than little Myrtle Vance clapped her baby hands as her father held her on his shoulders above the heads of the people.

"'For God's sake,' I shouted, 'send the children home.'

"'No, no,' shouted a hundred maddened voices; 'let them learn a lesson.'

"I love children, but as I looked about the little faces distorted with passion and the bloodshot eyes of the cruel parents who held them high in their arms, I thanked God that I have none of my own.

"As the hot iron sank deep into poor Henry's flesh a hideous yell rent the air, and, with a sound as terrible as the cry of lost souls on judgment day, 20,000 maddened people took up the victim's cry of agony and a prolonged howl of maddened glee rent the air.

"No one was himself now. Every man, woman and child in that awful crowd was worked up to a greater frenzy than that which actuated Smith's horrible crime. The people were capable of any new atrocity now, and as Smith's yells became more and more frequent, it was difficult to hold the crowd back, so anxious were the savages to participate in the sickening tortures.

"For half an hour I tried to pray as the beads of agony rolled down my forehead and bathed my face.

"For an instant a hush spread over the people. I could stand no more, and with a superhuman effort dashed through the compact mass of humanity and stood at the foot of the burning scaffold.

"'In the name of God,' I cried, 'I command you to cease this torture.'

"The heavy butt of a Winchester rifle descended on my head and I fell to the ground. Rough hands seized me and angry men bore me away, and I was thankful.

"At the outskirts of the crowd I was attacked again, and then several men, no doubt glad to get away from the fearful place, escorted me to my home, where I was allowed to take a small amount of clothing. A jeering crowd gathered without, and when I appeared at the door ready hands seized me and I was placed upon a rail, and, with curses and oaths, taken to the railway station and placed upon a train. As the train moved out some one thrust a roll of bills into my hand and said, 'God bless you, but it was no use.'"

When asked if he should ever return to Paris, Mr. King said: "I shall never go south again. The impressions of that awful day will stay with me forever."

CHAPTER IV.   LYNCHING OF INNOCENT MEN

(Lynched on Account of Relationship)

If no other reason appealed to the sober sense of the American people to check the growth of Lynch Law, the absolute unreliability and recklessness of the mob in inflicting punishment for crimes done, should do so. Several instances of this spirit have occurred in the year past. In Louisiana, near New Orleans, in July, 1893, Roselius Julian, a colored man, shot and killed a white judge, named Victor Estopinal. The cause of the shooting has never been definitely ascertained. It is claimed that the Negro resented an insult to his wife, and the killing of the white man was an act of a Negro (who dared) to defend his home. The judge was killed in the court house, and Julian, heavily armed, made his escape to the swamps near the city. He has never been apprehended, nor has any information ever been gleaned as to his whereabouts. A mob determined to secure the fugitive murderer and burn him alive. The swamps were hunted through and through in vain, when, being unable to wreak their revenge upon the murderer, the mob turned its attention to his unfortunate relatives. Dispatches from New Orleans, dated September 19, 1893, described the affair as follows:

"Posses were immediately organized and the surrounding country was scoured, but the search was fruitless so far as the real criminal was concerned. The mother, three brothers and two sisters of the Negro were arrested yesterday at the Black Ridge in the rear of the city by the police and taken to the little jail on Judge Estopinal's place about Southport, because of the belief that they were succoring the fugitive.

"About 11 o'clock twenty-five men, some armed with rifles and shotguns, came up to the jail. They unlocked the door and held a conference among themselves as to what they should do. Some were in favor of hanging the five, while others insisted that only two of the brothers should be strung up. This was finally agreed to, and the two doomed negroes were hurried to a pasture one hundred yards distant, and there asked to take their last chance of saving their lives by making a confession, but the Negroes made no reply. They were then told to kneel down and pray. One did so, the other remained standing, but both prayed fervently. The taller Negro was then hoisted up. The shorter Negro stood gazing at the horrible death of his brother without flinching. Five minutes later he was also hanged. The mob decided to take the remaining brother out to Camp Parapet and hang him there. The other two were to be taken out and flogged, with an order to get out of the parish in less than half an hour. The third brother, Paul, was taken out to the camp, which is about a mile distant in the interior, and there he was hanged to a tree."

Another young man, who was in no way related to Julian, who perhaps did not even know the man and who was entirely innocent of any offense in connection therewith, was murdered by the same mob. The same paper says:

"During the search for Julian on Saturday one branch of the posse visited the house of a Negro family in the neighborhood of Camp Parapet, and failing to find the object of their search, tried to induce John Willis, a young Negro, to disclose the whereabouts of Julian. He refused to do so, or could not do so, and was kicked to death by the gang."

An Indiana Case

Almost equal to the ferocity of the mob which killed the three brothers, Julian and the unoffending, John Willis, because of the murder of Judge Estopinal, was the action of a mob near Vincennes, Ind. In this case a wealthy colored man, named Allen Butler, who was well known in the community, and enjoyed the confidence and respect of the entire country, was made the victim of a mob and hung because his son had become unduly intimate with a white girl who was a servant around his house. There was no pretense that the facts were otherwise than as here stated. The woman lived at Butler's house as a servant, and she and Butler's son fell in love with each other, and later it was found that the girl was in a delicate condition. It was claimed, but with how much truth no one has ever been able to tell, that the father had procured an abortion, or himself had operated on the girl, and that she had left the house to go back to her home. It was never claimed that the father was in any way responsible for the action of his son, but the authorities procured the arrest of both father and son, and at the preliminary examination the father gave bail to appear before the Grand Jury when it should convene. On the same night, however, the mob took the matter in hand and with the intention of hanging the son. It assembled near Sumner, while the boy, who had been unable to give bail, was lodged in jail at Lawrenceville. As it was impossible to reach Lawrenceville and hang the son, the leaders of the mob concluded they would go to Butler's house and hang him. Butler was found at his home, taken out by the mob and hung to a tree. This was in the law-abiding state of Indiana, which furnished the United States its last president and which claims all the honor, pride and glory of northern civilization. None of the leaders of the mob were apprehended, and no steps whatever were taken to bring the murderers to justice.

Killed for His Stepfather's Crime

An account has been given of the cremation of Henry Smith, at Paris, Texas, for the murder of the infant child of a man named Vance. It would appear that human ferocity was not sated when it vented itself upon a human being by burning his eyes out, by thrusting a red hot iron down his throat, and then by burning his body to ashes. Henry Smith, the victim of these savage orgies, was beyond all the power of torture, but a few miles outside of Paris, some members of the community concluded that it would be proper to kill a stepson named William Butler as a partial penalty for the original crime. This young man, against whom no word has ever been said, and who was in fact an orderly, peaceable boy, had been watched with the severest scrutiny by members of the mob who believed he knew something of the whereabouts of Smith. He declared from the very first that he did not know where his stepfather was, which statement was well proven to be a fact after the discovery of Smith in

Arkansas, whence he had fled through swamps and woods and unfrequented places. Yet Butler was apprehended, placed under arrest, and on the night of February 6th, taken out on Hickory Creek, five miles southeast of Paris, and hung for his stepfather's crime. After his body was suspended in the air, the mob filled it with bullets.

Lynched Because the Jury Acquitted Him

The entire system of the judiciary of this country is in the hands of white people. To this add the fact of the inherent prejudice against colored people, and it will be clearly seen that a white jury is certain to find a Negro prisoner guilty if there is the least evidence to warrant such a finding.

Meredith Lewis was arrested in Roseland, La., in July of last year. A white jury found him not guilty of the crime of murder wherewith he stood charged. This did not suit the mob. A few nights after the verdict was rendered, and he declared to be innocent, a mob gathered in his vicinity and went to his house. He was called, and suspecting nothing, went outside. He was seized and hurried off to a convenient spot and hanged by the neck until he was dead for the murder of a woman of which the jury had said he was innocent.

Lynched as a Scapegoat

Wednesday, July 5th, about 10 o'clock in the morning, a terrible crime was committed within four miles of Wickliffe, Ky. Two girls, Mary and Ruby Ray, were found murdered a short distance from their home. The news of this terrible cowardly murder of two helpless young girls spread like wild fire, and searching parties scoured the territory surrounding Wickliffe and Bardwell. Two of the searching party, the Clark brothers, saw a man enter the Dupoyster cornfield; they got their guns and fired at the fleeing figure, but without effect; he got away, but they said he was a white man or nearly so. The search continued all day without effect, save the arrest of two or three strange Negroes. A bloodhound was brought from the penitentiary and put on the trail which he followed from the scene of the murder to the river and into the boat of a fisherman named Gordon. Gordon stated that he had ferried one man and only one across the river about about [sic] half past six the evening of July 5th; that his passenger sat in front of him, and he was a white man or a very bright mulatto, who could not be told from a white man. The bloodhound was put across the river in the boat, and he struck a trail again at Bird's Point on the Missouri side, ran about three hundred yards to the cottage of a white farmer named Grant and there lay down refusing to go further.

Thursday morning a brakesman on a freight train going out of Sikeston, Mo., discovered a Negro stealing a ride; he ordered him off and had hot words which terminated in a fight. The brakesman had the Negro arrested. When arrested, between 11 and 12 o'clock, he had on a dark woolen shirt, light pants and coat, and no vest. He had twelve dollars in paper, two silver dollars and ninety-five cents in change; he had also four rings in his pockets, a knife and a razor which were rusted and stained. The Sikeston authorities immediately jumped to the conclusion that this man was the murderer for whom the Kentuckians across the river were searching. They telegraphed to Bardwell that their prisoner had on no coat, but wore a blue vest and pants which would perhaps correspond with the coat found at the scene of the murder, and that the names of the murdered girls were in the rings found in his possession.

As soon as this news was received, the sheriffs of Ballard and Carlisle counties and a posse (?) of thirty well armed and determined Kentuckians, who had pledged their word the prisoner should be taken back to the scene of the supposed crime, to be executed there if proved to be the guilty man, chartered a train and at nine o'clock Thursday night started for Sikeston. Arriving there two hours later, the sheriff at Sikeston, who had no warrant for the prisoner's arrest and detention, delivered him into the hands of the mob without authority for so doing, and accompanied them to Bird's Point. The prisoner gave his name as Miller, his home at Springfield, and said he had never been in Kentucky in his life, but the sheriff turned him over to the mob to be taken to Wickliffe, that Frank Gordon, the fisherman, who had put a man across the river might identify him.

In other words, the protection of the law was withdrawn from C. J. Miller, and he was given to a mob by this sheriff at Sikeston, who knew that the prisoner's life depended on one man's word. After an altercation with the train men, who wanted another $50 for taking the train back to Bird's Point, the crowd arrived there at three o'clock, Friday morning. Here was anchored "The Three States," a ferry boat plying between Wickliffe, Ky., Cairo, Ill., and Bird's Point, Mo. This boat left Cairo at twelve o'clock, Thursday, with nearly three hundred of Cairo's best (?) citizens and thirty kegs of beer on board. This was consumed while the crowd and the bloodhound waited for the prisoner.

When the prisoner was on board "The Three States" the dog was turned loose, and after moving aimlessly around followed the crowd to where Miller sat handcuffed and there stopped. The crowd closed in on the pair and insisted that the brute had identified him because of that action. When the boat reached Wickliffe, Gordon, the fisherman, was called on to say whether the prisoner was the man he ferried over the river the day of the murder.

The sheriff of Ballard county informed him, sternly that if the prisoner was not the man, he (the fisherman) would be held responsible as knowing who the guilty man was. Gordon stated before, that the man he ferried across was a white man or a bright colored man; Miller was a dark brown skinned man, with kinky hair, "neither yellow nor black," says the Cairo Evening Telegram of Friday, July 7th. The fisherman went up to Miller from behind, looked at him without speaking for fully five minutes, then slowly said, "Yes, that's the man I crossed over." This was about six o'clock, Friday morning, and the crowd wished to hang Miller then and there. But Mr. Ray, the father of the girls, insisted that he be taken to Bardwell, the county seat of Ballard, and twelve miles inland. He said he thought a white man committed the crime, and that he was not satisfied that was the man. They took him to Bardwell and at ten o'clock, this same excited, unauthorized mob undertook to determine Miller's guilt. One of the Clark brothers who shot at a fleeing man in the Dupoyster cornfield, said the prisoner was the same man; the other said he was not, but the testimony of the first was accepted. A colored woman who had said she gave breakfast to a colored man clad in a blue flannel suit the morning of the murder, said positively that she had never seen Miller before. The gold rings found in his possession had no names in them, as had been asserted, and Mr. Ray said they did not belong to his daughters. Meantime a funeral pyre for the purpose of burning Miller to death had been erected in the center of the village. While the crowd swayed by passion was clamoring that he be burnt, Miller stepped forward and made the following statement: "My name is C. J. Miller. I am from Springfield, Ill.; my wife lives at 716 N. 2d street. I am here among you today, looked upon as one of the most brutal men before the people. I stand here surrounded by men who are excited, men who are not willing to let the law take its course, and as far as the crime is concerned, I have committed no crime, and certainly no crime gross enough to deprive me of my life and liberty to walk upon the green earth."

A telegram was sent to the chief of the police at Springfield, Ill., asking if one C. J. Miller lived there. An answer in the negative was returned. A few hours after, it was ascertained that a man named Miller, and his wife, did live at the number the prisoner gave in his speech, but

Lynching of C. J. Miller, at Bardwell, Kentucky, July 7th, 1893. [This and all subsequent images were part of the original pamphlets. — ED.]

the information came to Bardwell too late to do the prisoner any good. Miller was taken to jail, every stitch of clothing literally torn from his body and examined again. On the lower left side of the bosom of his shirt was found a dark reddish spot about the size of a dime. Miller said it was paint which he had gotten on him at Jefferson Barracks. This spot was only on the right side, and could not be seen from the under side at all, thus showing it had not gone through the cloth as blood or any liquid substance would do.

Chief-of-Police Mahaney, of Cairo, Ill., was with the prisoner, and he took his knife and scraped at the spot, particles of which came off in his hand. Miller told them to take his clothes to any expert, and if the spot was shown to be blood, they might do anything they wished with him. They took his clothes away and were gone some time. After a while they were brought back and thrown into the cell without a word. It is needless to say that if the spot had been found to be blood, that fact would have been announced, and the shirt retained as evidence. Meanwhile numbers of rough, drunken men crowded into the cell and tried to force a confession of the deed from the prisoner's lips. He refused to talk save to reiterate his innocence. To Mr. Mahaney, who talked seriously and kindly to him, telling him the mob meant to burn and torture him at three o'clock, Miller said: "Burning and torture here lasts but a little while, but if I die with a lie on my soul, I shall be tortured forever. I am innocent." For more than three hours, all sorts of pressure in the way of threats, abuse and urging, was brought to bear to force him to confess to the murder and thus justify the mob in its deed of murder. Miller remained firm; but as the hour drew near, and the crowd became more impatient, he asked for a priest. As none could be procured, he then asked for a Methodist minister, who came, prayed with the doomed man, baptized him and exhorted Miller to confess. To keep up the flagging spirits of the dense crowd around the jail, the rumor went out more than once, that Miller had confessed. But the solemn assurance of the minister, chief-of-police, and leading editor—who were with Miller all along—is that this rumor is absolutely false.

At three o'clock the mob rushed to the jail to secure the prisoner. Mr. Ray had changed his mind about the promised burning; he was still in doubt as to the prisoner's guilt. He again addressed the crowd to that effect, urging them not to burn Miller, and the mob heeded him so far, that they compromised on hanging instead of burning, which was agreed to by Mr. Ray. There was a loud yell, and a rush was made for the prisoner. He was stripped naked, his clothing literally torn from his body, and his shirt was tied around his loins. Some one declared the rope was a "white man's death," and a log-chain, nearly a hundred feet in length, weighing over one hundred pounds, was placed round Miller's neck and body, and he was led and dragged through the streets of the village in that condition followed by thousands of people. He fainted from exhaustion several times, but was supported to the platform where they first intended burning him.

The chain was hooked around his neck, a man climbed the telegraph pole and the other end of the chain was passed up to him and made fast to the cross-arm. Others brought a long forked stick which Miller was made to straddle. By this means he was raised several feet from the ground and then let fall. The first fall broke his neck, but he was raised in this way and let fall a second time. Numberless shots were fired into the dangling body, for most of that crowd were heavily armed, and had been drinking all day.

Miller's body hung thus exposed from three to five o'clock, during which time, several photographs of him as he hung dangling at the end of the chain were taken, and his toes and fingers were cut off. His body was taken down, placed on the platform, the torch applied, and in a few moments there was nothing left of C. J. Miller save a few bones and ashes. Thus perished another of the many victims of Lynch Law, but it is the honest and sober belief of many who witnessed the scene that an innocent man has been barbarously and shockingly put to death in the glare of the 19th century civilization, by those who profess to believe in Christianity, law and order.

CHAPTER V.   LYNCHED FOR ANYTHING OR NOTHING

(Lynched for Wife Beating)

In nearly all communities wife beating is punishable with a fine, and in no community is it made a felony. Dave Jackson, of Abita, La., was a colored man who had beaten his wife. He had not killed her, nor seriously wounded her, but as Louisiana lynchers had not filled out their quota of crimes, his case was deemed of sufficient importance to apply the method of that barbarous people. He was in the custody of the officials, but the mob went to the jail and took him out in front of the prison and hanged him by the neck until he was dead. This was in Nov. 1893.

Hanged for Stealing Hogs

Details are very meagre of a lynching which occurred near Knox Point, La., on the 24th of October, 1893. Upon one point, however, there was no uncertainty, and that is, that the persons lynched were Negroes. It was claimed that they had been stealing hogs, but even this claim had not been subjected to the investigation of a court. That matter was not considered necessary. A few of the neighbors who had lost hogs suspected these men were responsible for their loss, and made up their minds to furnish an example for others to be warned by. The two men were secured by a mob and hanged.

Lynched for No Offense

Perhaps the most characteristic feature of this record of lynch law for the year 1893, is the remarkable fact that five human beings were lynched and that the matter was considered of so little importance that the powerful press bureaus of the country did not consider the matter of enough importance to ascertain the causes for which they were hanged. It tells the world, with perhaps greater emphasis than any other feature of the record, that Lynch Law has become so common in the United States that the finding of the dead body of a Negro, suspended between heaven and earth to the limb of a tree, is of so slight importance that neither the civil authorities nor press agencies consider the matter worth investigating. July 21st, in Shelby county, Tenn., a colored man by the name of Charles Martin was lynched. July 30th, at Paris, Mo., a colored man named William Steen shared the same fate. December 28th, Mack Segars was announced to have been lynched at Brantley, Alabama. August 31st, at Yarborough, Texas, and on September 19th, at Houston, a colored man was found lynched, but so little attention was paid to the matter that not only was no record made as to why these last two men were lynched, but even their names were not given. The dispatches simply stated that an unknown Negro was found lynched in each case.

There are friends of humanity who feel their souls shrink from any compromise with murder, but whose deep and abiding reverence for womanhood causes them to hesitate in giving their support to this crusade against Lynch Law, out of fear that they may encourage the miscreants whose deeds are worse than murder. But to these friends it must appear certain that these five men could not have been guilty of any terrible crime. They were simply lynched by parties of men who had it in their power to kill them, and who chose to avenge some fancied wrong by murder, rather than submit their grievances to court.

Lynched Because They Were Saucy

At Moberly, Mo., February 18th and at Fort Madison, S.C., June 2d, both in 1892, a record was made in the line of lynching which should certainly appeal to every humanitarian who has any regard for the sacredness of human life. John Hughes, of Moberly, and Isaac Lincoln, of Fort Madison, and Will Lewis in Tullahoma, Tenn., suffered death for no more serious charge than that they "were saucy to white people." In the days of slavery it was held to be a very serious matter for a colored person to fail to yield the sidewalk at the demand of a white person, and it will not be surprising to find some evidence of this intolerance existing in the days of freedom. But the most that could be expected as a penalty for acting or speaking saucily to a white person would be a slight physical chastisement to make the Negro "know his place" or an arrest and fine. But Missouri, Tennessee and South Carolina chose to make precedents in their cases and as a result both men, after being charged with their offense and apprehended, were taken by a mob and lynched. The civil authorities, who in either case would have been very quick to satisfy the aggrieved white people had they complained and brought the prisoners to court, by imposing proper penalty upon them, did not feel it their duty to make any investigation after the Negroes were killed. They were dead and out of the way and as no one would be called upon to render an account for their taking off, the matter was dismissed from the public mind.

Lynched for a Quarrel

One of the most notable instances of lynching for the year 1893, occurred about the 20th of September. It was notable for the fact that the mayor of the city exerted every available power to protect the victim of the lynching from the mob. In his splendid endeavor to uphold the law, the mayor called out the troops, and the result was a deadly fight between the militia and mob, nine of the mob being killed.

The trouble occurred at Roanoke, Va. It is frequently claimed that lynchings occur only in sparsely settled districts, and, in fact, it is a favorite plea of governors and reverend apologists to couple two arrant falsehoods, stating that lynchings occur only because of assaults upon white women, and that these assaults occur and the lynchings follow in thinly inhabited districts where the power of the law is entirely inadequate to meet the emergency. This Roanoke case is a double refutation, for it not only disproves the alleged charge that the Negro assaulted a white woman, as was telegraphed all over the country at the time, but it also shows conclusively that even in one of the largest cities of the old state of Virginia, one of the original thirteen colonies, which prides itself of being the mother of presidents, it was possible for a lynching to occur in broad daylight under circumstances of revolting savagery.

When the news first came from Roanoke of the contemplated lynching, it was stated that a big burly Negro had assaulted a white woman, that he had been apprehended and that the citizens were determined to summarily dispose of his case. Mayor Trout was a man who believed in maintaining the majesty of the law, and who at once gave notice that no lynching would be permitted in Roanoke, and that the Negro, whose name was Smith, being in the custody of the law, should be dealt with according to law; but the mob did not pay any attention to the brave words of the mayor. It evidently thought that it was only another case of swagger, such as frequently characterizes lynching episodes. Mayor Trout, finding immense crowds gathering about the city, and fearing an attempt to lynch Smith, called out the militia and stationed them at the jail.

It was known that the woman refused to accuse Smith of assaulting her, and that his offense consisted in quarreling with her about the change of money in a transaction in which he bought something from her market booth. Both parties lost their temper, and the result was a row from which Smith had to make his escape. At once the old cry was sounded that the woman had been assaulted, and in a few hours all the town was wild with people thirsting for the assailant's blood. The further incidents of that day may well be told by a dispatch from Roanoke under date of the 21st of September and published in the Chicago Record. It says:

"It is claimed by members of the military company that they frequently warned the mob to keep away from the jail, under penalty of being shot. Capt. Bird told them he was under orders to protect the prisoner whose life the mob so eagerly sought, and come what may he would not allow him to be taken by the mob. To this the crowd replied with hoots and derisive jeers. The rioters appeared to become frenzied at the determined stand taken by the men and Captain Bird, and finally a crowd of excited men made a rush for the side door of the jail. The captain directed his men to drive the would-be lynchers back.

"At this moment the mob opened fire on the soldiers. This appeared for a moment to startle the captain and his men. But it was only for a moment. Then he coolly gave the command: 'Ready! aim! fire!' The company obeyed to the instant, and poured a volley of bullets into that part of the mob which was trying to batter down the side door of the jail.

"The rioters fell back before the fire of the militia, leaving one man writhing in the agonies of death at the doorstep. There was a lull for a moment. Then the word was quickly passed through the throng in front of the jail and down the street that a man was killed. Then there was an awful rush toward the little band of soldiers. Excited men were yelling like demons.

"The fight became general, and ere it was ended nine men were dead and more than forty wounded."

This stubborn stand on behalf of law and order disconcerted the crowd and it fell back in disorder. It did not long remain inactive but assembled again for a second assault. Having only a small band of militia, and knowing they would be absolutely at the mercy of the thousands who were gathering to wreak vengeance upon them, the mayor ordered them to disperse and go to their homes, and he himself, having been wounded, was quietly conveyed out of the city.

The next day the mob grew in numbers and its rage increased in its intensity. There was no longer any doubt that Smith, innocent as he was of any crime, would be killed, for with the mayor out of the city and the governor of the state using no effort to control the mob, it was only a question of a few hours when the assault would be repeated and its victim put to death. All this happened as per programme. The description of that morning's carnival appeared in the paper above quoted and reads as follows:

"A squad of twenty men took the negro Smith from three policemen just before five o'clock this morning and hanged him to a hickory limb on Ninth avenue, in the residence section of the city. They riddled his body with bullets and put a placard on it saying: 'This is Mayor Trout's friend.' A coroner's jury of Bismel was summoned and viewed the body and rendered a verdict of death at the hands of unknown men. Thousands of persons visited the scene of the lynching between daylight and eight o'clock when the body was cut down. After the jury had completed its work the body was placed in the hands of officers, who were unable to keep back the mob. Three hundred men tried to drag the body through the streets of the town, but the Rev. Dr. Campbell of the First Presbyterian church and Capt. R. B. Moorman, with pleas and by force prevented them.

"Capt. Moorman hired a wagon and the body was put in it. It was then conveyed to the bank of the Roanoke, about two miles from the scene of the lynching. Here the body was dragged from the wagon by ropes for about 200 yards and burned. Piles of dry brushwood were brought, and the body was placed upon it, and more brushwood piled on the body, leaving only the head bare. The whole pile was then saturated with coal oil and a match was applied. The body was consumed within an hour. The cremation was witnessed by several thousand people. At one time the mob threatened to burn the Negro in Mayor Trout's yard."

Thus did the people of Roanoke, Va., add this measure of proof to maintain our contention that it is only necessary to charge a Negro with a crime in order to secure his certain death. It was well known in the city before he was killed that he had not assaulted the woman with whom he had had the trouble, but he dared to have an altercation with a white woman, and he must pay the penalty. For an offense which would not in any civilized community have brought upon him a punishment greater than a fine of a few dollars, this unfortunate Negro was hung, shot and burned.

Suspected, Innocent and Lynched

Five persons, Benjamin Jackson, his wife, Mahala Jackson, his mother-in-law, Lou Carter, Rufus Bigley, were lynched near Quincy, Miss., the charge against them being suspicion of well poisoning. It appears from the newspaper dispatches at that time that a family by the name of Woodruff was taken ill in September of 1892. As a result of their illness one or more of the family are said to have died, though that matter is not stated definitely. It was suspected that the cause of their illness was the existence of poison in the water, some miscreant having placed poison in the well. Suspicion pointed to a colored man named Benjamin Jackson who was at once arrested. With him also were arrested his wife and mother-in-law and all were held on the same charge.

The matter came up for judicial investigation, but as might have been expected, the white people concluded it was unnecessary to wait the result of the investigation—that it was preferable to hang the accused first and try him afterward. By this method of procedure, the desired result was always obtained—the accused was hanged. Accordingly Benjamin Jackson was taken from the officers by a crowd of about two hundred people, while the inquest was being held, and hanged. After the killing of Jackson, the inquest was continued to ascertain the possible connection of the other persons charged with the crime. Against the wife and mother-in-law of the unfortunate man there was not the slightest evidence and the coroner's jury was fair enough to give them their liberty. They were declared innocent and returned to their homes. But this did not protect the women from the demands of the Christian white people of that section of the country. In any other land and with any other people, the fact that these two accused persons were women would have pleaded in their favor for protection and fair play, but that had no weight with the Mississippi Christians nor the further fact that a jury of white men had declared them innocent. The hanging of one victim on an unproven charge did not begin to satisfy the mob in its bloodthirsty demands and the result was that even after the women had been discharged, they were at once taken in charge by a mob, which hung them by the neck until they were dead.

Still the mob was not satisfied. During the coroner's investigation the name of a fourth person, Rufus Bigley, was mentioned. He was acquainted with the Jacksons and that fact, together with some testimony adduced at the inquest, prompted the mob to decide that he should die also. Search was at once made for him and the next day he was apprehended. He was not given over into the hands of the civil authorities for trial nor did the coroner's inquest find that he was guilty, but the mob was quite sufficient in itself. After finding Bigley, he was strung up to a tree and his body left hanging, where it was found next day. It may be remarked here in passing that this instance of the moral degradation of the people of Mississippi did not excite any interest in the public at large. American Christianity heard of this awful affair and read of its details and neither press nor pulpit gave the matter more than a passing comment. Had it occurred in the wilds of interior Africa, there would have been an outcry from the humane people of this country against the savagery which would so mercilessly put men and women to death. But it was an evidence of American civilization to be passed by unnoticed, to be denied or condoned as the requirements of any future emergency might determine.

Lynched for an Attempted Assault

With only a little more aggravation than that of Smith who quarreled at Roanoke with the market woman, was the assault which operated as the incentive to a most brutal lynching in Memphis, Tenn. Memphis is one of the queen cities of the south, with a population of about seventy thousand souls—easily one of the twenty largest, most progressive and wealthiest cities of the United States. And yet in its streets there occurred a scene of shocking savagery which would have disgraced the Congo. No woman was harmed, no serious indignity suffered. Two women driving to town in a wagon, were suddenly accosted by Lee Walker. He claimed that he demanded something to eat. The women claimed that he attempted to assault them. They gave such an alarm that he ran away. At once the dispatches spread over the entire country that a big, burly Negro had brutally assaulted two women. Crowds began to search for the alleged fiend. While hunting him they shot another Negro dead in his tracks for refusing to stop when ordered to do so. After a few days Lee Walker was found, and put in jail in Memphis until the mob there was ready for him.

The Memphis Commercial of Sunday, July 23, contains a full account of the tragedy from which the following extracts are made:

At 12 o'clock last night, Lee Walker, who attempted to outrage Miss Mollie McCadden, last Tuesday morning, was taken from the county jail and hanged to a telegraph pole just north of the prison. All day rumors were afloat that with nightfall an attack would be made upon the jail, and as everyone anticipated that a vigorous resistance would be made, a conflict between the mob and the authorities was feared.

At 10 o'clock Capt. O'Haver, Sergt. Horan and several patrolmen were on hand, but they could do nothing with the crowd. An attack by the mob was made on the door in the south wall, and it yielded. Sheriff McLendon and several of his men threw themselves into the breach, but two or three of the storming party shoved by. They were seized by the police, but were not subdued, the officers refraining from using their clubs. The entire mob might at first have been dispersed by ten policemen who would use their clubs, but the sheriff insisted that no violence be done.

The mob got an iron rail and used it as a battering ram against the lobby doors. Sheriff McLendon tried to stop them, and some one of the mob knocked him down with a chair. Still he counseled moderation and would not order his deputies and the police to disperse the crowd by force. The pacific policy of the sheriff impressed the mob with the idea that the officers were afraid, or at least would do them no harm, and they redoubled their efforts, urged on by a big switchman. At 12 o'clock the door of the prison was broken in with a rail.

As soon as the rapist was brought out of the door calls were heard for a rope; then some one shouted, "Burn him!" But there was no time to make a fire. When Walker got into the lobby a dozen of the men began beating and stabbing him. He was half dragged, half carried to the corner of Front street and the alley between Sycamore and Mill, and hung to a telegraph pole.

Walker made a desperate resistance. Two men entered his cell first and ordered him to come forth. He refused, and they failing to drag him out, others entered. He scratched and bit his assailants, wounding several of them severely with his teeth. The mob retaliated by striking and cutting him with fists and knives. When he reached the steps leading down to the door he made another stand and was stabbed again and again. By the time he reached the lobby his power to resist was gone, and he was shoved along through the mob of yelling, cursing men and boys, who beat, spat upon and slashed the wretch-like demon. One of the leaders of the mob fell, and the crowd walked ruthlessly over him. He was badly hurt—a jawbone fractured and internal injuries inflicted. After the lynching friends took charge of him.

The mob proceeded north on Front street with the victim, stopping at Sycamore street to get a rope from a grocery. "Take him to the iron bridge on Main street," yelled several men. The men who had hold of the Negro were in a hurry to finish the job, however, and when they reached the telephone pole at the corner of Front street and the first alley north of Sycamore they stopped. A hastily improvised noose was slipped over the Negro's head, and several young men mounted a pile of lumber near the pole and threw the rope over one of the iron stepping pins. The Negro was lifted up until his feet were three feet above the ground, the rope was made taut, and a corpse dangled in midair. A big fellow who helped lead the mob pulled the Negro's legs until his neck cracked. The wretch's clothes had been torn off, and, as he swung, the man who pulled his legs mutilated the corpse.

One or two knife cuts, more or less, made little difference in the appearance of the dead rapist, however, for before the rope was around his neck his skin was cut almost to ribbons. One pistol shot was fired while the corpse was hanging. A dozen voices protested against the use of firearms, and there was no more shooting. The body was permitted to hang for half an hour, then it was cut down and the rope divided among those who lingered around the scene of the tragedy. Then it was suggested that the corpse be burned, and it was done. The entire performance, from the assault on the jail to the burning of the dead Negro was witnessed by a score or so of policemen and as many deputy sheriffs, but not a hand was lifted to stop the proceedings after the jail door yielded.

As the body hung to the telegraph pole, blood streaming down from the knife wounds in his neck, his hips and lower part of his legs also slashed with knives, the crowd hurled expletives at him, swung the body so that it was dashed against the pole, and, so far from the ghastly sight proving trying to the nerves, the crowd looked on with complaisance, if not with real pleasure. The Negro died hard. The neck was not broken, as the body was drawn up without being given a fall, and death came by strangulation. For fully ten minutes after he was strung up the chest heaved occasionally, and there were convulsive movements of the limbs. Finally he was pronounced dead, and a few minutes later Detective Richardson climbed on a pile of staves and cut the rope. The body fell in a ghastly heap, and the crowd laughed at the sound and crowded around the prostrate body, a few kicking the inanimate carcass.

Detective Richardson, who is also a deputy coroner, then proceeded to impanel the following jury of inquest: J. S. Moody, A. C. Waldran, B. J. Childs, J. N. House, Nelson Bills, T. L. Smith, and A. Newhouse. After viewing the body the inquest was adjourned without any testimony being taken until 9 o'clock this morning. The jury will meet at the coroner's office, 51 Beale street, up stairs, and decide on a verdict. If no witnesses are forthcoming, the jury will be able to arrive at a verdict just the same, as all members of it saw the lynching. Then some one raised the cry of "Burn him!" It was quickly taken up and soon resounded from a hundred throats. Detective Richardson, for a long time, single-handed, stood the crowd off. He talked and begged the men not to bring disgrace on the city by burning the body, arguing that all the vengeance possible had been wrought.

While this was going on a small crowd was busy starting a fire in the middle of the street. The material was handy. Some bundles of staves were taken from the adjoining lumber yard for kindling. Heavier wood was obtained from the same source, and coal oil from a neighboring grocery. Then the cries of "Burn him! Burn him!" were redoubled.

Half a dozen men seized the naked body. The crowd cheered. They marched to the fire, and giving the body a swing, it was landed in the middle of the fire. There was a cry for more wood, as the fire had begun to die owing to the long delay. Willing hands procured the wood, and it was piled up on the Negro, almost, for a time, obscuring him from view. The head was in plain view, as also were the limbs, and one arm which stood out high above the body, the elbow crooked, held in that position by a stick of wood. In a few moments the hands began to swell, then came great blisters over all the exposed parts of the body; then in places the flesh was burned away and the bones began to show through. It was a horrible sight, one which, perhaps, none there had ever witnessed before. It proved too much for a large part of the crowd and the majority of the mob left very shortly after the burning began.

But a large number stayed, and were not a bit set back by the sight of a human body being burned to ashes. Two or three white women, accompanied by their escorts, pushed to the front to obtain an unobstructed view, and looked on with astonishing coolness and nonchalance. One man and woman brought a little girl, not over 12 years old, apparently their daughter, to view a scene which was calculated to drive sleep from the child's eyes for many nights, if not to produce a permanent injury to her nervous system. The comments of the crowd were varied. Some remarked on the efficacy of this style of cure for rapists, others rejoiced that men's wives and daughters were now safe from this wretch. Some laughed as the flesh cracked and blistered, and while a large number pronounced the burning of a dead body as a useless episode, not in all that throng was a word of sympathy heard for the wretch himself.

The rope that was used to hang the Negro, and also that which was used to lead him from the jail, were eagerly sought by relic hunters. They almost fought for a chance to cut off a piece of rope, and in an incredibly short time both ropes had disappeared and were scattered in the pockets of the crowd in sections of from an inch to six inches long. Others of the relic hunters remained until the ashes cooled to obtain such ghastly relics as the teeth, nails, and bits of charred skin of the immolated victim of his own lust. After burning the body the mob tied a rope around the charred trunk and dragged it down Main street to the court house, where it was hanged to a center pole. The rope broke and the corpse dropped with a thud, but it was again hoisted, the charred legs barely touching the ground. The teeth were knocked out and the finger nails cut off as souvenirs. The crowd made so much noise that the police interfered. Undertaker Walsh was telephoned for, who took charge of the body and carried it to his establishment, where it will be prepared for burial in the potter's field today.

A prelude to this exhibition of 19th century barbarism was the following telegram received by the Chicago Inter Ocean, at 2 o'clock, Saturday afternoon — ten hours before the lynching:

"MEMPHIS, TENN., July 22, To Inter-Ocean, Chicago.

"Lee Walker, colored man, accused of raping white women, in jail here, will be taken out and burned by whites to-night. Can you send Miss Ida Wells to write it up? Answer. R. M. Martin, with Public Ledger."

The Public Ledger is one of the oldest evening daily papers in Memphis, and this telegram shows that the intentions of the mob were well known long before they were executed. The personnel of the mob is given by the Memphis Appeal-Avalanche. It says, "At first it seemed as if a crowd of roughs were the principals, but as it increased in size, men in all walks of life figured as leaders, although the majority were young men."

This was the punishment meted out to a Negro, charged, not with rape, but attempted assault, and without any proof as to his guilt, for the women were not given a chance to identify him. It was only a little less horrible than the burning alive of Henry Smith, at Paris, Texas, February 1st, 1893, or that of Edward Coy, in Texarkana, Texas, February 20, 1892. Both were charged with assault on white women, and both were tied to the stake and burned while yet alive, in the presence of ten thousand persons. In the case of Coy, the white woman in the case, applied the match, even while the victim protested his innocence.

The cut which is here given [p. 114] is the exact reproduction of the photograph taken at the scene of the lynching at Clanton, Alabama, August, 1891. The cause for which the man was hanged is given in the words of the mob which were written on the back of the photograph, and they are also given. This photograph was sent to Judge A. W. Tourgee, of Mayville, N.Y.

In some of these cases the mob affects to believe in the Negro's guilt. The world is told that the white woman in the case identifies him, or the prisoner "confesses." But in the lynching which took place in Barnwell County, South Carolina, April 24, 1893, the mob's victim, John Peterson, escaped and placed himself under Governor Tillman's protection; not only did he declare his innocence, but offered to prove an alibi, by white witnesses. Before his witnesses could be brought, the mob arrived at the Governor's mansion and demanded the prisoner. He was given up, and although the white woman in the case said he was not the man, he was hanged 24 hours after, and over a thousand bullets fired into his body, on the declaration that "a crime had been committed and some one had to hang for it."

CHAPTER VI.   HISTORY OF SOME CASES OF RAPE

It has been claimed that the Southern white women have been slandered because, in defending the Negro race from the charge that all colored men, who are lynched, only pay penalty for assaulting women. It is certain that lynching mobs have not only refused to give the Negro a chance to defend himself, but have killed their victim with a full knowledge that the relationship of the alleged assailant with the woman who accused him, was voluntary and clandestine. As a matter of fact, one of the prime causes of the Lynch Law agitation has been a necessity for defending the Negro from this awful charge against him. This defense has been necessary because the apologists for outlawry insist that in no case has the accusing woman been a willing consort of her paramour, who is lynched because overtaken in wrong. It is well known, however, that such is the case. In July of this year, 1894, John Paul Bocock, a Southern white man living in New York, and assistant editor of the New York Tribune, took occasion to defy the publication of any instance where the lynched Negro was the victim of a white woman's falsehood. Such cases are not rare, but the press and people conversant with the facts, almost invariably suppress them.

The New York Sun of July 30th, 1894, contained a synopsis of interviews with leading congressmen and editors of the South. Speaker Crisp, of the House of Representatives, who was recently a Judge of the Supreme Court of Georgia, led in declaring that lynching seldom or never took place, save for vile crime against women and children. Dr. Hoss, editor of the leading organ of the Methodist Church South, published in its columns that it was his belief that more than three hundred women had been assaulted by Negro men within three months. When asked to prove his charges, or give a single case upon which his "belief" was founded, he said that he could do so, but the details were unfit for publication. No other evidence but his "belief" could be adduced to substantiate this grave charge, yet Bishop Haygood,[5] in the Forum of October, 1893, quotes this "belief" in apology for lynching, and voluntarily adds: "It is my opinion that this is an underestimate." The "opinion" of this man, based upon a "belief," had greater weight coming from a man who has posed as a friend to "Our Brother in Black," and was accepted as authority. An interview of Miss Frances E. Willard, the great apostle of temperance, the daughter of abolitionists and a personal friend and helper of many individual colored people, has been quoted in support of the utterance of this calumny against a weak and defenseless race. In the New York Voice of October 23, 1890, after a tour in the South, where she was told all these things by the "best white people," she said: "The grogshop is the Negro's center of power. Better whisky and more of it is the rallying cry of great, dark-faced mobs. The colored race multiplies like the locusts of Egypt. The grogshop is its center of power. The safety of woman, of childhood, the home, is menaced in a thousand localities at this moment, so that men dare not go beyond the sight of their own roof-tree."

These charges so often reiterated, have had the effect of fastening the odium upon the race of a peculiar propensity for this foul crime. The Negro is thus forced to a defense of his good name, and this chapter will be devoted to the history of some of the cases where assault upon white women by Negroes is charged. He is not the aggressor in this fight, but the situation demands that the facts be given, and they will speak for themselves. Of the 1,115 Negro men, women and children hanged, shot and roasted alive from January 1st, 1882, to January 1st, 1894, inclusive, only 348 of that number were charged with rape. Nearly 700 of these persons were lynched for any other reason which could be manufactured by a mob wishing to indulge in a lynching bee.

[5]See note p. 75.

Scene of lynching at Clanton, Alabama, August 1891.

A White Woman's Falsehood

The Cleveland, Ohio, Gazette, January 16, 1892, gives an account of one of these cases of "rape."

Mrs. J. C. Underwood, the wife of a minister of Elyria, Ohio, accused an Afro-American of rape. She told her husband that during his absence in 1888, stumping the state for the Prohibition Party, the man came to the kitchen door, forced his way in the house and insulted her. She tried to drive him out with a heavy poker, but he overpowered and chloroformed her, and when she revived her clothing was torn and she was in a horrible condition. She did not know the man, but could identify him. She subsequently pointed out William Offett, a married man, who was arrested, and, being in Ohio, was granted a trial.

Facsimile of the back of the photograph.

The prisoner vehemently denied the charge of rape, but confessed he went to Mrs. Underwood's residence at her invitation and was criminally intimate with her at her request. This availed him nothing against the sworn testimony of a minister's wife, a lady of the highest respectability. He was found guilty, and entered the penitentiary, December 14, 1888, for fifteen years. Sometime afterwards the woman's remorse led her to confess to her husband that the man was innocent. These are her words: "I met Offett at the postoffice. It was raining. He was polite to me, and as I had several bundles in my arms he offered to carry them home for me, which he did. He had a strange fascination for me, and I invited him to call on me. He called, bringing chestnuts and candy for the children. By this means we got them to leave us alone in the room. Then I sat on his lap. He made a proposal to me and I readily consented. Why I did so I do not know, but that I did is true. He visited me several times after that and each time I was indiscreet. I did not care after the first time. In fact I could not have resisted, and had no desire to resist."

When asked by her husband why she told him she had been outraged, she said: "I had several reasons for telling you. One was the neighbors saw the fellow here, another was, I was afraid I had contracted a loathsome disease, and still another was that I feared I might give birth to a Negro baby. I hoped to save my reputation by telling you a deliberate lie." Her husband, horrified by the confession, had Offett, who had already served four years, released and secured a divorce.

There have been many such cases throughout the South, with the difference that the Southern white men in insensate fury wreak their vengeance without intervention of law upon the Negro who consorts with their women.

Tried to Manufacture an Outrage

The Memphis (Tenn.) Ledger, of June 8, 1892, has the following: "If Lillie Bailey, a rather pretty white girl, seventeen years of age, who is now at the city hospital, would be somewhat less reserved about her disgrace there would be some very nauseating details in the story of her life. She is the mother of a little coon. The truth might reveal fearful depravity or the evidence of a rank outrage. She will not divulge the name of the man who has left such black evidence of her disgrace, and in fact says it is a matter in which there can be no interest to the outside world. She came to Memphis nearly three months ago, and was taken in at the Woman's Refuge in the southern part of the city. She remained there until a few weeks ago when the child was born. The ladies in charge of the Refuge were horrified. The girl was at once sent to the city hospital, where she has been since May 30th. She is a country girl. She came to Memphis from her father's farm, a short distance from Hernando, Miss. Just when she left there she would not say. In fact she says she came to Memphis from Arkansas, and says her home is in that state. She is rather good looking, has blue eyes, a low forehead and dark red hair. The ladies at the Woman's Refuge do not know anything about the girl further than what they learned when she was an inmate of the institution; and she would not tell much. When the child was born an attempt was made to get the girl to reveal the name of the Negro who had disgraced her, she obstinately refused and it was impossible to elicit any information from her on the subject."

Note the wording: "The truth might reveal fearful depravity or rank outrage." If it had been a white child or if Lillie Bailey had told a pitiful story of Negro outrage, it would have been a case of woman's weakness or assault and she could have remained at the Woman's Refuge. But a Negro child and to withhold its father's name and thus prevent the killing of another Negro "rapist" was a case of "fearful depravity." Had she revealed the father's name, he would have been lynched and his taking off charged to an assault upon a white woman.

Burned Alive for Adultery

In Texarkana, Arkansas, Edward Coy was accused of assaulting a white woman. The press dispatches of February 18, 1892, told in detail how he was tied to a tree, the flesh cut from his body by men and boys, and after coal oil was poured over him, the woman he had assaulted gladly set fire to him, and 15,000 persons saw him burn to death. October 1st, the Chicago Inter Ocean contained the following account of that horror from the pen of the "Bystander"—Judge Albion W. Tourgee—as the result of his investigations:

"1. The woman who was paraded as victim of violence was of bad character; her husband was a drunkard and a gambler.
"2. She was publicly reported and generally known to have been criminally intimate with Coy for more than a year previous.
"3. She was compelled by threats, if not by violence, to make the charge against the victim.
"4. When she came to apply the match Coy asked her if she would burn him after they had 'been sweethearting' so long.
"5. A large majority of the 'superior' white men prominent in the affair are the reputed fathers of mulatto children.

"These are not pleasant facts, but they are illustrative of the vital phase of the so-called 'race question,' which should properly be designated an earnest inquiry as to the best methods by which religion, science, law and political power may be employed to excuse injustice, barbarity and crime done to a people because of race and color. There can be no possible belief that these people were inspired by any consuming zeal to vindicate God's law against miscegenationists of the most practical sort. The woman was a willing partner in the victim's guilt, and being of the 'superior' race must naturally have been more guilty."

Not Identified but Lynched

February 11th, 1893, there occurred in Shelby county, Tennessee, the fourth Negro lynching within fifteen months. The three first were lynched in the city of Memphis for firing on white men in self-defense. This Negro, Richard Neal, was lynched a few miles from the city limits, and the following is taken from the Memphis (Tenn.) Scimitar:

"As the Scimitar stated on Saturday the Negro, Richard Neal, who raped Mrs. Jack White near Forest Hill, in this county, was lynched by a mob of about 200 white citizens of the neighborhood. Sheriff McLendon, accompanied by Deputies Perkins, App and Harvey and a Scimitar reporter, arrived on the scene of the execution about 3:30 in the afternoon. The body was suspended from the first limb of a post oak tree by a new quarter inch grass rope. A hangman's knot, evidently tied by an expert, fitted snugly under the left ear of the corpse, and a new hame string pinioned, the victim's arms behind him. His legs were not tied. The body was perfectly limber when the Sheriff's posse cut it down and retained enough heat to warm the feet of Deputy Perkins, whose road cart was converted into a hearse. On arriving with the body at Forest Hill the Sheriff made a bargain with a stalwart young man with a blonde mustache and deep blue eyes, who told the Scimitar reporter that he was the leader of the mob, to haul the body to Germantown for $3.

"When within half-a-mile of Germantown the Sheriff and posse were overtaken by Squire McDonald of Collierville, who had come down to hold the inquest. The Squire had his jury with him, and it was agreed for the convenience of all parties that he should proceed with the corpse to Germantown and conduct the inquiry as to the cause of death. He did so, and a verdict of death from hanging by parties unknown was returned in due form.

"The execution of Neal was done deliberately and by the best people of the Collierville, Germantown and Forest Hill neighborhoods, without passion or exhibition of anger.

"He was arrested on Friday about ten o'clock, by Constable Bob Cash, who carried him before Mrs. White. She said: 'I think he is the man. I am almost certain of it. If he isn't the man he is exactly like him.'

"The Negro's coat was torn also, and there were other circumstances against him. The committee returned and made its report, and the chairman put the question of guilt or innocence to a vote.

"All who thought the proof strong enough to warrant execution were invited to cross over to the other side of the road. Everybody but four or five negroes crossed over.

"The committee then placed Neal on a mule with his arms tied behind him, and proceeded to the scene of the crime, followed by the mob. The rope, with a noose already prepared, was tied to the limb nearest the spot where the unpardonable sin was committed, and the doomed man's mule was brought to a standstill beneath it.

"Then Neal confessed. He said he was the right man, but denied that he used force or threats to accomplish his purpose. It was a matter of purchase, he claimed, and said the price paid was twenty-five cents. He warned the colored men present to beware of white women and resist temptation, for to yield to their blandishments or to the passions of men, meant death.

"While he was speaking, Mrs. White came from her home and calling Constable Cash to one side, asked if he could not save the Negro's life. The reply was, 'No,' and Mrs. White returned to the house.

"When all was in readiness, the husband of Neal's victim leaped upon the mule's back and adjusted the rope around the Negro's neck. No cap was used, and Neal showed no fear, nor did he beg for mercy. The mule was struck with a whip and bounded out from under Neal, leaving him suspended in the air with his feet about three feet from the ground."

Delivered to the Mob
by the Governor of the State

John Peterson, near Denmark, S.C., was suspected of rape, but escaped, went to Columbia, and placed himself under Gov. Tillman's protection, declaring he too could prove an alibi by white witnesses. A white reporter hearing his declaration volunteered to find these witnesses, and telegraphed the governor that he would be in Columbia with them on Monday. In the meantime the mob at Denmark, learning Peterson's whereabouts, went to the governor and demanded the prisoner. Gov. Tillman, who had during his canvass for re-election the year before, declared that he would lead a mob to lynch a Negro that assaulted a white woman, gave Peterson up to the mob. He was taken back to Denmark, and the white girl in the case as positively declared that he was not the man. But the verdict of the mob was that "the crime had been committed and somebody had to hang for it, and if he, Peterson, was not guilty of that he was of some other crime," and he was hung, and his body riddled with 1,000 bullets.

Lynched as a Warning

Alabama furnishes a case in point. A colored man named Daniel Edwards, lived near Selma, Alabama, and worked for a family of a farmer near that place. This resulted in an intimacy between the young man and a daughter of the householder, which finally developed in the disgrace of the girl. After the birth of the child, the mother disclosed the fact that Edwards was its father. The relationship had been sustained for more than a year, and yet this colored man was apprehended, thrown into jail from whence he was taken by a mob of one hundred neighbors and hung to a tree and his body riddled with bullets. A dispatch which describes the lynching, ends as follows. "Upon his back was found pinned this morning the following: Warning to all Negroes that are too intimate with white girls. This the work of one hundred best citizens of the South Side.'"

There can be no doubt from the announcement made by this "one hundred best citizens" that they understood full well the character of the relationship which existed between Edwards and the girl, but when the dispatches were sent out, describing the affair, it was claimed that Edwards was lynched for rape.

Suppressing the Truth

In a county in Mississippi during the month of July the Associated Press dispatches sent out a report that the sheriff's eight year old daughter had been assaulted by a big, black, burly brute who had been promptly lynched. The facts which have since been investigated show that the girl was more than eighteen years old and that she was discovered by her father in this young man's room who was a servant on the place. But these facts the Associated Press has not given to the world, nor did the same agency acquaint the world with the fact that a Negro youth who was lynched in Tuscumbia, Ala., the same year on the same charge told the white girl who accused him before the mob, that he had met her in the woods often by appointment. There is a young mulatto in one of the State prisons of the South to-day who is there by charge of a young white woman to screen herself. He is a college graduate and had been corresponding with, and clandestinely visiting her until he was surprised and run out of her room en deshabille[6] by her father. He was put in prison in another town to save his life from the mob and his lawyer advised that it were better to save his life by pleading guilty to charges made and being sentenced for years, than to attempt a defense by exhibiting the letters written him by this girl. In the latter event, the mob would surely murder him, while there was a chance for his life by adopting the former course. Names, places and dates are not given for the same reason.

The excuse has come to be so safe, it is not surprising that a Philadelphia girl, beautiful and well educated, and of good family, should make a confession published in all the daily papers of that city October, 1894, that she had been stealing for some time, and that to cover one of her thefts, she had said she had been bound and gagged in her father's house by a colored man, and money stolen therefrom by him. Had this been done in many localities, it would only have been necessary for her to "identify" the first Negro in that vicinity, to have brought about another lynching bee[.]

A Vile Slander with Scant Retraction

The following published in the Cleveland (Ohio) Leader of Oct. 23d, 1894, only emphasizes our demand that a fair trial shall be given those accused of crime, and the protection of the law be extended until time for a defense be granted.

"The sensational story sent out last night from Hicksville that a Negro had outraged a little four-year-old girl proves to be a base canard. The correspondents who went into the details should have taken the pains to investigate, and the officials should have known more of the matter before they gave out such grossly exaggerated information.

"The Negro, Charles O'Neil, had been working for a couple of women and, it seems, had worked all winter without being remunerated. There is a little girl, and the girl's mother and grandmother evidently started the story with idea of frightening the Negro out of the country and thus balancing accounts. The town was considerably wrought up and for a time things looked serious. The accused had a preliminary hearing today and not an iota of evidence was produced to indicate that such a crime had been committed, or that he had even attempted such an outrage. The village marshal was frightened nearly out of his wits and did little to quiet the excitement last night.

[6]*En deshabille*: undressed.

"The affair was an outrage on the Negro, at the expense of innocent childhood, a brainless fabrication from start to finish."

The original story was sent throughout this country and England, but the Cleveland Leader, so far as known, is the only journal which has published these facts in refutation of the slander so often published against the race.

Not only is it true that many of the alleged cases of rape against the Negro, are like the foregoing, but the same crime committed by white men against Negro women and girls, is never punished by mob or the law. A leading journal in South Carolina openly said some months ago that "it is not the same thing for a white man to assault a colored woman as for a colored man to assault a white woman, because the colored woman had no finer feelings nor virtue to be outraged!" Yet colored women have always had far more reason to complain of white men in this respect than ever white women have had of Negroes.

Illinois Has a Lynching

In the month of June, 1893, the proud commonwealth of Illinois joined the ranks of Lynching States. Illinois, which gave to the world the immortal heroes, Lincoln, Grant and Logan,[7] trailed its banner of justice in the dust—dyed its hands red in the blood of a man not proven guilty of crime.

June 3, 1893, the country about Decatur, one of the largest cities of the state was startled with the cry that a white woman had been assaulted by a colored tramp. Three days later a colored man named Samuel Bush was arrested and put in jail. A white man testified that Bush, on the day of the assault, asked him where he could get a drink and he pointed to the house where the farmer's wife was subsequently said to have been assaulted. Bush said he went to the well but did not go near the house, and did not assault the woman. After he was arrested the alleged victim did not see him to identify him—he was presumed to be guilty.

The citizens determined to kill him. The mob gathered, went to the jail, met with no resistance, took the suspected man, dragged him out tearing every stitch of clothing from his body, then hanged him to a telegraph pole. The grand jury refused to indict the lynchers though the names of over twenty persons who were leaders in the mob were well

[7]John Alexander Logan (1826–1886) was a Union general in the Civil War who went on to serve in both houses of Congress. As a Radical Republican congressman he was active in the impeachment trial of President Andrew Johnson.

known. In fact twenty-two persons were indicted, but the grand jurors and the prosecuting attorney disagreed as to the form of the indictments, which caused the jurors to change their minds. All indictments were reconsidered and the matter was dropped. Not one of the dozens of men prominent in that murder have suffered a whit more inconvenience for the butchery of that man, than they would have suffered for shooting a dog.

Color Line Justice

In Baltimore, Maryland, a gang of white ruffians assaulted a respectable colored girl who was out walking with a young man of her own race. They held her escort and outraged the girl. It was a deed dastardly enough to arouse Southern blood, which gives its horror of rape as excuse for lawlessness, but she was a colored woman. The case went to the courts and they were acquitted.

In Nashville, Tennessee, there was a white man, Pat Hanifan, who outraged a little colored girl, and from the physical injuries received she was ruined for life. He was jailed for six months, discharged, and is now a detective in that city. In the same city, last May, a white man outraged a colored girl in a drug store. He was arrested and released on bail at the trial. It was rumored that five hundred colored men had organized to lynch him. Two hundred and fifty white citizens armed themselves with Winchesters and guarded him. A cannon was placed in front of his home, and the Buchanan Rifles (State Militia) ordered to the scene for his protection. The colored mob did not show up. Only two weeks before, Eph. Grizzard, who had only been charged with rape upon a white woman, had been taken from the jail, with Governor Buchanan and the police and militia standing by, dragged through the streets in broad daylight, knives plunged into him at every step, and with every fiendish cruelty that a frenzied mob could devise, he was at last swung out on the bridge with hands cut to pieces as he tried to climb up the stanchions. A naked, bloody example of the bloodthirstiness of the nineteenth century civilization of the Athens of the South! No cannon nor military were called out in his defense. He dared to visit a white woman.

At the very moment when these civilized whites were announcing their determination "to protect their wives and daughters," by murdering Grizzard, a white man was in the same jail for raping eight-year-old Maggie Reese, a colored girl. He was not harmed. The "honor" of grown women who were glad enough to be supported by the Grizzard boys and Ed Coy, as long as the liaison was not known, needed protection; they were white. The outrage upon helpless childhood needed no avenging in this case; she was black.

A white man in Guthrie, Oklahoma Territory, two months after inflicted such injuries upon another colored girl that she died. He was not punished, but an attempt was made in the same town in the month of June to lynch a colored man who visited a white woman.

In Memphis, Tennessee, in the month of June, Ellerton L. Dorr, who is the husband of Russell Hancock's widow, was arrested for attempted rape on Mattie Cole, a neighbor's cook; he was only prevented from accomplishing his purpose by the appearance of Mattie's employer. Dorr's friends say he was drunk and not responsible for his actions. The grand jury refused to indict him and he was discharged.

In Tallahassee, Florida, a colored girl, Charlotte Gilliam, was assaulted by white men. Her father went to have a warrant for their arrest issued, but the judge refused to issue it.

In Bowling Green, Virginia, Moses Christopher, a colored lad, was charged with assault, September 10. He was indicted, tried, convicted and sentenced to death in one day. In the same state at Danville, two weeks before—August 29, Thomas J. Penn, a white man, committed a criminal assault upon Lina Hanna, a twelve-year-old colored girl, but he has not been tried, certainly not killed either by the law or the mob.

In Surrey county, Virginia, C. L. Brock, a white man, criminally assaulted a ten-year-old colored girl, and threatened to kill her if she told. Notwithstanding, she confessed to her aunt, Mrs. Alice Bates, and the white brute added further crime by killing Mrs. Bates when she upbraided him about his crime upon her niece. He emptied the contents of his revolver into her body as she lay. Brock has never been apprehended, and no effort has been made to do so by the legal authorities.

But even when punishment is meted out by law to white villians for this horrible crime, it is seldom or never that capital punishment is invoked. Two cases just clipped from the daily papers will suffice to show how this crime is punished when committed by white offenders and black.

LOUISVILLE, KY., October 19.—Smith Young, colored, was to-day sentenced to be hanged. Young criminally assaulted a six-year-old child about six months ago.

Jacques Blucher, the Pontiac Frenchman who was arrested at that place for a criminal assault on his daughter Fanny on July 29 last, pleaded nolo contendere when placed on trial at East Greenwich, near Providence, R.I., Tuesday, and was sentenced to five years in State Prison.

Charles Wilson was convicted of assault upon seven-year-old Mamie Keys in Philadelphia, in October, and sentenced to ten years in prison. He was white. Indianapolis courts sentenced a white man in September to eight years in prison for assault upon a twelve-year old white girl.

April 24, 1893, a lynching was set for Denmark, S.C., on the charge of rape. A white girl accused a Negro of assault, and the mob was about to lynch him. A few hours before the lynching three reputable white men rode into the town and solemnly testified that the accused Negro was at work with them 25 miles away on the day and at the hour the crime had been committed. He was accordingly set free. A white person's word is taken as absolutely for as against a Negro.

CHAPTER VII.   THE CRUSADE JUSTIFIED

(Appeal from America to the World)

It has been urged in criticism of the movement appealing to the English people for sympathy and support in our crusade against Lynch Law that our action was unpatriotic, vindictive and useless. It is not a part of the plan of this pamphlet to make any defense for that crusade nor to indict any apology for the motives which led to the presentation of the facts of American lynchings to the world at large. To those who are not willfully blind and unjustly critical, the record of more than a thousand lynchings in ten years is enough to justify any peaceable movement tending to ameliorate the conditions which led to this unprecedented slaughter of human beings.

If America would not hear the cry of men, women and children whose dying groans ascended to heaven praying for relief, not only for them but for others who might soon be treated as they, then certainly no fair-minded person can charge disloyalty to those who make an appeal to the civilization of the world for such sympathy and help as it is possible to extend. If stating the facts of these lynchings, as they appeared from time to time in the white newspapers of America—the news gathered by white correspondents, compiled by white press bureaus and disseminated among white people—shows any vindictiveness, then the mind which so charges is not amenable to argument.

But it is the desire of this pamphlet to urge that the crusade started and thus far continued has not been useless, but has been blessed with the most salutary results. The many evidences of the good results can not here be mentioned, but the thoughtful student of the situation can himself find ample proof. There need not here be mentioned the fact that for the first time since lynching began, has there been any occasion for the governors of the several states to speak out in reference to these crimes against law and order.

No matter how heinous the act of the lynchers may have been, it was discussed only for a day or so and then dismissed from the attention of the public. In one or two instances the governor has called attention to the crime, but the civil processes entirely failed to bring the murderers to justice. Since the crusade against lynching was started, however, governors of states, newspapers, senators and representatives and bishops of churches have all been compelled to take cognizance of the prevalence of this crime and to speak in one way or another in the defense of the charge against this barbarism in the United States. This has not been because there was any latent spirit of justice voluntarily asserting itself, especially in those who do the lynching, but because the entire American people now feel, both North and South, that they are objects in the gaze of the civilized world and that for every lynching humanity asks that America render its account to civilization and itself.

Awful Barbarism Ignored

Much has been said during the months of September and October of 1894 about the lynching of six colered men who on suspicion of incendiarism were made the victims of a most barbarous massacre. They were arrested, one by one, by officers of the law; they were handcuffed and chained together and by the officers of the law loaded in a wagon and deliberately driven into an ambush where a mob of lynchers awaited them. At the time and upon the chosen spot, in the darkness of the night and far removed from the habitation of any human soul, the wagon was halted and the mob fired upon the six manacled men, shooting them to death as no humane person would have shot dogs. Chained together as they were, in their awful struggles after the first volley, the victims tumbled out of the wagon upon the ground and there in the mud, struggling in their death throes, the victims were made the target of the murderous shotguns, which fired into the writhing, struggling, dying mass of humanity, until every spark of life was gone. Then the officers of the law who had them in charge, drove away to give the alarm and to tell the world that they had been waylaid and their prisoners forcibly taken from them and killed.

It has been claimed that the prompt, vigorous and highly commendable steps of the governor of the State of Tennessee and the judge having jurisdiction over the crime, and of the citizens of Memphis generally, was the natural revolt of the humane conscience in that section of the country, and the determination of honest and honorable men to rid the community of such men as those who were guilty of this terrible massacre. It has further been claimed that this vigorous uprising of the people and this most commendably prompt action of the civil authorities, is ample proof that the American people will not tolerate the lynching of innocent men, and that in cases where brutal lynchings have not been promptly dealt with, the crimes on the part of the victims were such as to put them outside the pale of humanity and that the world considered their death a necessary sacrifice for the good of all.

But this line of argument can in no possible way be truthfully sustained. The lynching of the six men in 1894, barbarous as it was, was in no way more barbarous than took nothing more than a passing notice. It was only the other lynchings which preceded it, and of which the public[8] fact that the attention of the civilized world has been called to lynching in America which made the people of Tennessee feel the absolute necessity for a prompt, vigorous and just arraignment of all the murderers connected with that crime. Lynching is no longer "Our Problem," it is the problem of the civilized world, and Tennessee could not afford to refuse the legal measures which Christianity demands shall be used for the punishment of crime.

Memphis Then and Now

Only two years prior to the massacre of the six men near Memphis, that same city took part in a massacre in every way as bloody and brutal as that of September last. It was the murder of three young colored men and who were known to be among the most honorable, reliable, worthy and peaceable colored citizens of the community. All of them were engaged in the mercantile business, being members of a corporation which conducted a large grocery store, and one of the three being a letter carrier in the employ of the government. These three men were arrested for resisting an attack of a mob upon their store, in which melee none of the assailants, who had armed themselves for their devilish deeds by securing court processes, were killed or even seriously injured. But

---

[8]For sense, the preceding sentence should read: The lynching of the six men in 1894, barbarous as it was, was in no way more barbarous than other lynchings which preceded it, and of which the public took nothing more than a passing notice. It was only the fact . . .

these three men were put in jail, and on three or four nights after their incarceration a mob of less than a dozen men, by collusion with the civil authorities, entered the jail, took the three men from the custody of the law and shot them to death. Memphis knew of this awful crime, knew then and knows today who the men were who committed it, and yet not the first step was ever taken to apprehend the guilty wretches who walk the streets today with the brand of murder upon their foreheads, but as safe from harm as the most upright citizen of that community. Memphis would have been just as calm and complacent and self-satisfied over the murder of the six colored men in 1894 as it was over these three colored men in 1892, had it not recognized the fact that to escape the brand of barbarism it had not only to speak its denunciation but to act vigorously in vindication of its name.

An Alabama Horror Ignored

A further instance of this absolute disregard of every principle of justice and the indifference to the barbarism of Lynch Law may be cited here, and is furnished by white residents in the city of Carrolton, Alabama. Several cases of arson had been discovered, and in their search for the guilty parties, suspicion was found to rest upon three men and a woman. The four suspects were Paul Hill, Paul Archer, William Archer, his brother, and a woman named Emma Fair. The prisoners were apprehended, earnestly asserted their innocence, but went to jail without making any resistance. They claimed that they could easily prove their innocence upon trial.

One would suspect that the civilization which defends itself against the barbarisms of Lynch Law by stating that it lynches human beings only when they are guilty of awful attacks upon women and children, would have been very careful to have given these four prisoners, who were simply charged with arson, a fair trial, to which they were entitled upon every principle of law and humanity. Especially would this seem to be the case when it is considered that one of the prisoners charged was a woman, and if the Nineteenth Century has shown any advancement upon any lines of human action, it is pre-eminently shown in its reverence, respect and protection of its womanhood. But the people of Alabama failed to have any regard for womanhood whatever.

The three men and the woman were put in jail to await trial. A few days later it was rumored that they were to be subjects of Lynch Law, and, sure enough, at night a mob of lynchers went to the jail, not to avenge any awful crime against womanhood, but to kill four people who had been suspected of setting a house on fire. They were caged in their cells, helpless and defenseless; they were at the mercy of civilized white Americans, who, armed with shotguns, were there to maintain the majesty of American law. And most effectively was their duty done by these splendid representatives of Governor Fishback's brave and honorable white southerners, who resent "outside interference." They lined themselves up in the most effective manner and poured volley after volley into the bodies of their helpless, pleading victims, who in their bolted prison cells could do nothing but suffer and die. Then these lynchers went quietly away and the bodies of the woman and three men were taken out and buried with as little ceremony as men would bury hogs.

No one will say that the massacre near Memphis in 1894 was any worse than this bloody crime of Alabama in 1892. The details of this shocking affair were given to the public by the press, but public sentiment was not moved to action in the least; it was only a matter of a day's notice and then went to swell the list of murders which stand charged against the noble, Christian people of Alabama.

America Awakened

But there is now an awakened conscience throughout the land, and Lynch Law can not flourish in the future as it has in the past. The close of the year 1894 witnessed an aroused interest, an assertative humane principle which must tend to the extirpation of that crime. The awful butchery last mentioned failed to excite more than a passing comment in 1894, but far different is it today. Gov. Jones, of Alabama, in 1893 dared to speak out against the rule of the mob in no uncertain terms. His address indicated a most helpful result of the present agitation. In face of the many denials of the outrages on the one hand and apologies for lynchers on the other, Gov. Jones admits the awful lawlessness charged and refuses to join in the infamous plea made to condone the crime. No stronger nor more effective words have been said than those following from Gov. Jones.

"While the ability of the state to deal with open revolts against the supremacy of its laws has been ably demonstrated, I regret that deplorable acts of violence have been perpetrated, in at least four instances, within the past two years by mobs, whose sudden work and quick dispersions rendered it impossible to protect their victims. Within the past two years nine prisoners, who were either in jail or in the custody of the officers, have been taken from them without resistance, and put to death. There was doubt of the guilt of the defendants in most of these cases, and few of them were charged with capital offenses. None of them involved the crime of rape. The largest rewards allowed by law were offered for the apprehension of the offenders, and officers were charged to a vigilant performance of their duties, and aided in some instances by the services of skilled detectives; but not a single arrest has been made and the grand juries in these counties have returned no bills of indictment. This would indicate either that local public sentiment approved these acts of violence or was too weak to punish them, or that the officers charged with that duty were in some way lacking in their performance. The evil cannot be cured or remedied by silence as to its existence. Unchecked, it will continue until it becomes a reproach to our good name, and a menace to our prosperity and peace; and it behooves you to exhaust all remedies within your power to find better preventives for such crimes."

A Friendly Warning

From England comes a friendly voice which must give to every patriotic citizen food for earnese thought. Writing from London, to the Chicago Inter Ocean, Nov. 25, 1894, the distinguished compiler of our last census, Hon. Robert P. Porter, gives the American people a most interesting review of the anti-lynching crusade in England, submitting editorial opinions from all sections of England and Scotland, showing the consensus of British opinion on this subject. It hardly need be said, that without exception, the current of English thought deprecates the rule of mob law, and the conscience of England is shocked by the revelation made during the present crusade. In his letter Mr. Porter says:

"While some English journals have joined certain American journals in ridiculing the well-meaning people who have formed the anti-lynching committee, there is a deep under current on this subject which is injuring the Southern States far more than those who have not been drawn into the question of English investment for the South as I have can surmise. This feeling is by no means all sentiment. An Englishman whose word and active co-operation could send a million sterling to any legitimate Southern enterprise said the other day: "I will not invest a farthing in States where these horrors occur. I have no particular sympathy with the anti-lynching committee, but such outrages indicate to my mind that where life is held to be of such little value there is even less assurance that the laws will protect property. As I understand it the States, not the national government, control in such matters, and where those laws are strongest there is the best field for British capital."

Probably the most bitter attack on the anti-lynching committee has come from the London Times. Those Southern Governors who had their bombastic letters published in the Times, with favorable editorial comment, may have had their laugh at the anti-lynchers here too soon. A few days ago, in commenting on an interesting communication from Richard H. Edmonds, editor of the Manufacturer's Record, setting forth the industrial advantages of the Southern States, which was published in its columns, the Times says: "Without in any way countenancing the impertinence of 'anti-lynching' committee, we may say that a state of things in which the killing of Negroes by blood-thirsty mobs is an incident of not unfrequent occurrence is not conducive to success in industry. Its existence, however, is a serious obstacle to the success of the South in industry; for even now Negro labor, which means at best inefficient labor, must be largely relied on there, and its efficiency must be still further diminished by spasmodic terrorism.

"Those interested in the development of the resources of the Southern States, and no one in proportion to his means has shown more faith in the progress of the South than the writer of this article, must take hold of this matter earnestly and intelligently. Sneering at the anti-lynching committee will do no good. Back of them, in fact, if not in form, is the public opinion of Great Britain. Even the Times cannot deny this. It may not be generally known in the United States, but while the Southern and some of the Northern newspapers are making a target of Miss Wells, the young colored woman who started this English movement, and cracking their jokes at the expense of Miss Florence Balgarnie, who, as honorable secretary, conducts the committee's correspondence, the strongest sort of sentiment is really at the back of the movement. Here we have crystallized every phase of political opinion. Extreme Unionists like the Duke of Argyll and advanced home rulers such as Justin McCarthy; Thomas Burt, the labor leader; Herbert Burrows, the Socialist, and Tom Mann, representing all phases of the Labor party, are co-operating with conservatives like Sir T. Eldon Gorst. But the real strength of this committee is not visible to the casual observer. As a matter of fact it represents many of the leading and most powerful British journals. A. E. Fletcher is editor of the London Daily Chronicle; P. W. Clayden is prominent in the counsels of the London Daily News; Professor James Stuart is Gladstone's[9] great friend and editor of the London Star; William Byles

---

[9]A highly respected statesman, William Ewart Gladstone served as prime minister of Great Britain on four occasions: 1868–1874, 1880–1885, 1886, and 1892–1894 (during the time of Wells's speaking tours of Great Britain).

is editor and proprietor of the Bradford Observer; Sir Hugh Gilzen Reid is a leading Birmingham editor; in short, this committee has secured if not the leading editors, certainly important and warm friends, representing the Manchester Guardian, the Leeds Mercury, the Plymouth Western News, Newcastle Leader, the London Daily Graphic, the Westminster Gazette, the London Echo, a host of minor papers all over the kingdom, and practically the entire religious press of the kingdom.

"The greatest victory for the anti-lynchers comes this morning in the publication in the London Times of William Lloyd Garrison's letter. This letter will have immense effect here. It may have been printed in full in the United States, but nevertheless I will quote a paragraph which will strengthen the anti-lynchers greatly in their crusade here:

"'A year ago the South derided and resented Northern protests; today it listens, explains and apologizes for its uncovered cruelties. Surely a great triumph for a little woman to accomplish! It is the power of truth simply and unreservedly spoken, for her language was inadequate to describe the horrors exposed.'

"If the Southern states are wise, and I say this with the earnestness of a friend and one who has built a home in the mountain regions of the South and thrown his lot in with them, they will not only listen, but stop lawlessness of all kinds. If they do, and thus secure the confidence of Englishmen, we may in the next decade realize some of the hopes for the new South we have so fondly cherished."

CHAPTER VIII.   MISS WILLARD'S ATTITUDE

No class of American citizens stands in greater need of the humane and thoughtful consideration of all sections of our country than do the colored people, nor does any class exceed us in the measure of grateful regard for acts of kindly interest in our behalf. It is, therefore, to us, a matter of keen regret that a Christian organization so large and influential as the Woman's Christian Temperance Union, should refuse to give its sympathy and support to our oppressed people who ask no further favor than the promotion of public sentiment which shall guarantee to every person accused of crime the safeguard of a fair and impartial trial, and protection from butchery by brutal mobs. Accustomed as we are to the indifference and apathy of Christian people, we would bear this instance of ill fortune in silence, had not Miss Willard gone out of her way to antagonize the cause so dear to our hearts by including in her

Annual Address to the W. C. T. U. Convention at Cleveland, November 5, 1894, a studied, unjust and wholly unwarranted attack upon our work.

In her address Miss Willard said:

The zeal for her race of Miss Ida B. Wells, a bright young colored woman, has, it seems to me, clouded her perception as to who were her friends and well-wishers in all high-minded and legitimate efforts to banish the abomination of lynching and torture from the land of the free and the home of the brave. It is my firm belief that in the statements made by Miss Wells concerning white women having taken the initiative in nameless acts between the races she has put an imputation upon half the white race in this country that is unjust, and, save in the rarest exceptional instances, wholly without foundation. This is the unanimous opinion of the most disinterested and observant leaders of opinion whom I have consulted on the subject, and I do not fear to say that the laudable efforts she is making are greatly handicapped by statements of this kind, nor to urge her as a friend and well-wisher to banish from her vocabulary all such allusions as a source of weakness to the cause she has at heart.

This paragraph, brief as it is, contains two statements which have not the slightest foundation in fact. At no time, nor in any place, have I made statements "concerning white women having taken the initiative in nameless acts between the races." Further, at no time, or place nor under any circumstance, have I directly or inferentially "put an imputation upon half the white race in this country" and I challenge this "friend and well-wisher" to give proof of the truth of her charge. Miss Willard protests against lynching in one paragraph and then, in the next, deliberately misrepresents my position in order that she may criticise a movements [sic], whose only purpose is to protect our oppressed race from vindictive slander and Lynch Law.

What I have said and what I now repeat—in answer to her first charge—is, that colored men have been lynched for assault upon women, when the facts were plain that the relationship between the victim lynched and the alleged victim of his assault was voluntary, clandestine and illicit. For that very reason we maintain, that, in every section of our land, the accused should have a fair, impartial trial, so that a man who is colored shall not be hanged for an offense, which, if he were white, would not be adjudged a crime. Facts cited in another chapter—"History of Some Cases of Rape"—amply maintain this position. The publication of these facts in defense of the good name of the race casts no "imputation upon half the white race in this country" and no such imputation can be inferred except by persons deliberately determined to be unjust.

But this is not the only injury which this cause has suffered at the hands of our "friend and well-wisher." It has been said that the Women's Christian Temperance Union, the most powerful organization of women in America, was misrepresented by me while I was in England. Miss Willard was in England at the time and knowing that no such misrepresentation came to her notice, she has permitted that impression to become fixed and widespread, when a word from her would have made the facts plain.

I never at any time or place or in any way misrepresented that organization. When asked what concerted action had been taken by churches and great moral agencies in America to put down Lynch Law, I was compelled in truth to say that no such action had occurred, that pulpit, press and moral agencies in the main were silent and for reasons known to themselves, ignored the awful conditions which to the English people appeared so abhorrent. Then the question was asked what the great moral reformers like Miss Frances Willard and Mr. Moody[10] had done to suppress Lynch Law and again I answered—nothing. That Mr. Moody had never said a word against lynching in any of his trips to the South, or in the North either, so far as was known, and that Miss Willard's only public utterance on the situation had condoned lynching and other unjust practices of the South against the Negro. When proof of these statements was demanded, I sent a letter containing a copy of the New York Voice, Oct. 23, 1890, in which appeared Miss Willard's own words of wholesale slander against the colored race and condonation of Southern white people's outrages against us. My letter in part reads as follows:

But Miss Willard, the great temperance leader, went even further in putting the seal of her approval upon the southerners' method of dealing with the Negro. In October, 1890, the Women's Christian Temperance Union held its national meeting at Atlanta, Georgia. It was the first time in the history of the organization that it had gone south for a national meeting, and met the southerners in their own homes. They were welcomed with open arms. The governor of the state and the legislature gave special audiences in the halls of state legislation to the temperance workers. They set out to capture the northerners to their way of seeing

---

[10]Rev. Dwight L. Moody, an internationally recognized evangelist from Northfield, Massachusetts, is perhaps best known as the founder of the Chicago Bible Institute (now the Moody Bible Institute).

things, and without troubling to hear the Negro side of the question, these temperance people accepted the white man's story of the problem with which he had to deal. State organizers were appointed that year, who had gone through the southern states since then, but in obedience to southern prejudices have confined their work to white persons only. It is only after Negroes are in prison for crimes that efforts of these temperance women are exerted without regard to "race, color, or previous condition." No "ounce of prevention" is used in their case; they are black, and if these women went among the Negroes for this work, the whites would not receive them. Except here and there, are found no temperance workers of the Negro race; "the great dark-faced mobs" are left the easy prey of the saloonkeepers.

There was pending in the National Congress at this time a Federal Election Bill, the object being to give the National Government control of the national elections in the several states. Had this bill become a law, the Negro, whose vote has been systematically suppressed since 1875 in the southern states, would have had the protection of the National Government, and his vote counted. The South would have been no longer "solid"; the Southerners saw that the balance of power which they unlawfully held in the House of Representatives and the Electoral College, based on the Negro population, would be wrested from them. So they nick-named the pending elections law the "Force Bill"—probably because it would force them to disgorge their ill-gotten political gains—and defeated it. While it was being discussed, the question was submitted to Miss Willard: "What do you think of the race problem and the Force Bill?"

Said Miss Willard: "Now, as to the 'race problem' in its minified, current meaning, I am a true lover of the southern people—have spoken and worked in, perhaps, 200 of their towns and cities; have been taken into their love and confidence at scores of hospitable firesides; have heard them pour out their hearts in the splendid frankness of their impetuous natures. And I have said to them at such times: 'When I go North there will be wafted to you no word from pen or voice that is not loyal to what we are saying here and now.' Going South, a woman, a temperance woman, and a Northern temperance woman—three great barriers to their good will yonder—I was received by them with a confidence that was one of the most delightful surprises of my life. I think we have wronged the South, though we did not mean to do so. The reason was, in part, that we had irreparably wronged ourselves by putting no safeguards on the ballot box at the North that would sift out alien illiterates. They rule our cities today; the saloon is their palace, and the toddy stick their sceptre. It is not fair that they should vote, nor is it fair that a plantation Negro, who can neither read nor write, whose ideas are bounded by the fence of his own field and the price of his own mule, should be entrusted with the ballot. We ought to have put an educational test upon that ballot from the first. The Anglo-Saxon race will never submit to be dominated by the Negro so long as his altitude reaches no higher than the personal liberty of the saloon, and the power of appreciating the amount of liquor that a dollar will buy. New England would no more submit to this than South Carolina. 'Better whisky and more of it' has been the rallying cry of great dark-faced mobs in the Southern localities where local option was snowed under by the colored vote. Temperance has no enemy like that, for it is unreasoning and unreasonable. Tonight it promises in a great congregation to vote for temperance at the polls tomorrow; but tomorrow twenty-five cents changes that vote in favor of the liquor-seller.

"I pity the southerners, and I believe the great mass of them are as conscientious and kindly-intentioned toward the colored man as an equal number of white church-members of the North. Would-be demagogues lead the colored people to destruction. Half-drunken white roughs murder them at the polls, or intimidate them so that they do not vote. But the better class of people must not be blamed for this, and a more thoroughly American population than the Christian people of the South does not exist. They have the traditions, the kindness, the probity, the courage of our forefathers. The problem on their hands is immeasurable. The colored race multiplies like the locusts of Egypt. The grog-shop is its center of power. 'The safety of woman, of childhood, of the home, is menaced in a thousand localities at this moment, so that the men dare not go beyond the sight of their own roof-tree.' How little we know of all this, seated in comfort and affluence here at the North, descanting upon the rights of every man to cast one vote and have it fairly counted; that well-worn shibboleth invoked once more to dodge a living issue.

"The fact is that illiterate colored men will not vote at the South until the white population chooses to have them do so; and under similar conditions they would not at the North." Here we have Miss Willard's words in full, condoning fraud, violence, murder, at the ballot box; rapine, shooting, hanging and burning; for all these things are done and being done now by the Southern white people. She does not stop there, but goes a step further to aid them in blackening the good name of an entire race, as shown by the sentences quoted in the paragraph above. These utterances, for which the colored people have never forgiven Miss Willard, and which Frederick Douglass has denounced as false, are to be found in full in the Voice of October 23, 1890, a temperance organ published at New York city.

This letter appeared in the May number of Fraternity, the organ of the first Anti-Lynching society of Great Britain. When Lady Henry Somerset learned through Miss Florence Balgarnie that this letter had been published she informed me that if the interview was published she would take steps to let the public know that my statements must be received with caution. As I had no money to pay the printer to suppress the edition which was already published and these ladies did not care to do so, the May number of Fraternity was sent to its subscribers as usual. Three days later there appeared in the daily Westminster Gazette an "interview" with Miss Willard, written by Lady Henry Somerset, which was so subtly unjust in its wording that I was forced to reply in my own defense. In that reply I made only statements which, like those concerning Miss Willard's Voice interview, have not been and cannot be denied. It was as follows:

Lady Henry Somerset's Interview with Miss Willard

To the Editor of the Westminster Gazette: Sir—The interview published in your columns today hardly merits a reply, because of the indifference to suffering manifested. Two ladies are represented sitting under a tree at Reigate, and, after some preliminary remarks on the terrible subject of lynching, Miss Willard laughingly replies by cracking a joke. And the concluding sentence of the interview shows the object is not to determine how best they may help the Negro who is being hanged, shot and burned, but "to guard Miss Willard's reputation."

With me it is not myself nor my reputation, but the life of my people, which is at stake, and I affirm that this is the first time to my knowledge that Miss Willard has said a single word in denunciation of lynching or demand for law. The year 1890, the one in which the interview appears, had a larger lynching record than any previous year, and the number and territory have increased, to say nothing of the human beings burnt alive.

If so earnest as she would have the English public believe her to be, why was she silent when five minutes were given me to speak last June at Princes' Hall, and in Holborn Town Hall this May? I should say it was as President of the Women's Christian Temperance Union of America she is timid, because all these unions in the South emphasize the hatred of the Negro by excluding him. There is not a single colored woman admitted to the Southern W. C. T. U., but still Miss Willard blames the Negro for the defeat of Prohibition in the South. Miss Willard quotes from Fraternity, but forgets to add my immediate recognition of her presence on the platform at Holborn Town Hall, when, amidst many other resolutions on temperance and other subjects in which she is interested, time was granted to carry an anti-lynching resolution. I was so thankful for this crumb of her speechless presence that I hurried off to the editor of Fraternity and added a postscript to my article blazoning forth that fact.

Any statements I have made concerning Miss Willard are confirmed by the Hon. Frederick Douglass (late United States minister to Hayti) in a speech delivered by him in Washington in January of this year, which has since been published in a pamphlet. The fact is, Miss Willard is no better or worse than the great bulk of white Americans on the Negro questions. They are all afraid to speak out, and it is only British public opinion which will move them, as I am thankful to see it has already begun to move Miss Willard. I am, etc.,

May 21.   IDA B. WELLS.

Unable to deny the truth of these assertions, the charge has been made that I have attacked Miss Willard and misrepresented the W. C. T. U. If to state facts is misrepresentation, then I plead guilty to the charge.

I said then and repeat now, that in all the ten terrible years of shooting, hanging and burning of men, women and children in America, the Women's Christian Temperance Union never suggested one plan or made one move to prevent those awful crimes. If this statement is untrue the records of that organization would disprove it before the ink is dry. It is clearly an issue of fact and in all fairness this charge of misrepresentation should either be substantiated or withdrawn.

It is not necessary, however, to make any representation concerning the W. C. T. U. and the lynching question. The record of that organization speaks for itself. During all the years prior to the agitation begun against Lynch Law, in which years men, women and children were scourged, hanged, shot and burned, the W. C. T. U. had no word, either of pity or protest; its great heart, which concerns itself about humanity the world over, was, toward our cause, pulseless as a stone. Let those who deny this speak by the record. Not until after the first British campaign, in 1893, was even a resolution passed by the body which is the self constituted guardian for "God, home and native land."

Nor need we go back to other years. The annual session of that organization held in Cleveland in November, 1894, made a record which confirms and emphasizes the silence charged against it. At that session, earnest efforts were made to secure the adoption of a resolution of protest against lynching. At that very time two men were being tried for the murder of six colored men who were arrested on charge of barn burning, chained together, and on pretense of being taken to jail, were driven into the woods where they were ambushed and all six shot to death. The six widows of the butchered men had just finished the most pathetic recital ever heard in any court room, and the mute appeal of twenty-seven orphans for justice touched the stoutest hearts. Only two weeks prior to the session, Gov. Jones of Alabama, in his last message to the retiring state legislature, cited the fact that in the two years just past, nine colored men had been taken from the legal authorities by lynching mobs and butchered in cold blood—and not one of these victims was even charged with an assault upon womanhood.

It was thought that this great organization, in face of these facts, would not hesitate to place itself on record in a resolution of protest against this awful brutality towards colored people. Miss Willard gave assurance that such a resolution would be adopted, and that assurance was relied on. The record of the session shows in what good faith that assurance was kept. After recommending an expression against Lynch Law, the President attacked the anti-lynching movement, deliberately misrepresenting my position, and in her annual address, charging me with a statement I never made.

Further than that, when the committee on resolutions reported their work, not a word was said against lynching. In the interest of the cause I smothered the resentment. I felt because of the unwarranted and unjust attack of the President, and labored with members to secure an expression of some kind, tending to abate the awful slaughter of my race. A resolution against lynching was introduced by Mrs. Fessenden and read, and then that great Christian body, which in its resolutions had expressed itself in opposition to the social amusement of card playing, athletic sports and promiscuous dancing; had protested against the licensing of saloons, inveighed against tobacco, pledged its allegiance to the Prohibition party, and thanked the Populist party in Kansas, the Republican party in California and the Democratic party in the South, wholly ignored the seven millions of colored people of this country whose plea was for a word of sympathy and support for the movement in their behalf. The resolution was not adopted, and the convention adjourned.

In the Union Signal Dec. 6, 1894, among the resolutions is found this one:

Resolved, That the National W. C. T. U., which has for years counted among its departments that of peace and arbitration, is utterly opposed to all lawless acts in any and all parts of our common lands and it urges these principles upon the public, praying that the time may speedily come when no human being shall be condemned without due process of law; and when the unspeakable outrages which have so often provoked such lawlessness shall be banished from the world, and childhood, maidenhood and womanhood shall no more be the victims of atrocities worse than death.

This is not the resolution offered by Mrs. Fessenden. She offered the one passed last year by the W. C. T. U. which was a strong unequivocal denunciation of lynching. But she was told by the chairman of the committee on resolutions, Mrs. Rounds, that there was already a lynching resolution in the hands of the committee. Mrs. Fessenden yielded the floor on that assurance, and no resolution of any kind against lynching was submitted and none was voted upon, not even the one above, taken from the columns of the Union Signal, the organ of the national W. C. T. U.!

Even the wording of this resolution which was printed by the W. C. T. U., reiterates the false and unjust charge which has been so often made as an excuse for lynchers. Statistics show that less than one-third of the lynching victims are hanged, shot and burned alive for "unspeakable outrages against womanhood, maidenhood and childhood;" and that nearly a thousand, including women and children, have been lynched upon any pretext whatsoever; and that all have met death upon the unsupported word of white men and women. Despite these facts this resolution which was printed, cloaks an apology for lawlessness, in the same paragraph which affects to condemn it, where it speaks of "the unspeakable outrages which have so often provoked such lawlessness."

Miss Willard told me the day before the resolutions were offered that the Southern women present had held a caucus that day. This was after I, as fraternal delegate from the Woman's Mite Missionary Society of the A. M. E. Church at Cleveland, O., had been introduced to tender its greetings. In so doing I expressed the hope of the colored women that the W. C. T. U. would place itself on record as opposed to lynching which robbed them of husbands, fathers, brothers and sons and in many cases of women as well. No note was made either in the daily papers or the Union Signal of that introduction and greeting, although every other incident of that morning was published. The failure to submit a lynching resolution and the wording of the one above appears to have been the result of that Southern caucus.

On the same day I had a private talk with Miss Willard and told her she had been unjust to me and the cause in her annual address, and asked that she correct the statement that I had misrepresented the W. C. T. U., or that I had "put an imputation on one-half the white race in this country." She said that somebody in England told her it was a pity that I attacked the white women of America. "Oh," said I, "then you went out of your way to prejudice me and my cause in your annual address, not upon what you had heard me say, but what somebody had told you I said?" Her reply was that I must not blame her for her rhetorical expressions—that I had my way of expressing things and she had hers. I told her I most assuredly did blame her when those expressions were calculated to do such harm. I waited for an honest unequivocal retraction of her statements based on "hearsay." Not a word of retraction or explanation was said in the convention and I remained misrepresented before that body through her connivance and consent.

The editorial notes in the Union Signal, Dec. 6, 1894, however, contains the following:

"In her repudiation of the charges brought by Miss Ida Wells against white women as having taken the initiative in nameless crimes between the races, Miss Willard said in her annual address that this statement 'put an unjust imputation upon half the white race.' But as this expression has been misunderstood she desires to declare that she did not intend a literal interpretation to be given to the language used, but employed it to express a tendency that might ensue in public thought as a result of utterances so sweeping as some that have been made by Miss Wells."

Because this explanation is as unjust as the original offense, I am forced in self-defense to submit this account of differences. I desire no quarrel with the W. C. T. U., but my love for the truth is greater than my regard for an alleged friend who, through ignorance or design misrepresents in the most harmful way the cause of a long suffering race, and then unable to maintain the truth of her attack excuses herself as it were by the wave of the hand, declaring that "she did not intend a literal interpretation to be given to the language used." When the lives of men, women and children are at stake, when the inhuman butchers of innocents attempt to justify their barbarism by fastening upon a whole race the obloque[11] of the most infamous of crimes. It is little less than criminal to apologize for the butchers today and tomorrow to repudiate the apology by declaring it a figure of speech.

[11] Obloquy.

CHAPTER IX. LYNCHING RECORD FOR 1894

The following tables are based on statistics taken from the columns of the Chicago Tribune, Jan. 1, 1895. They are a valuable appendix to the foregoing pages. They show, among other things, that in Louisiana, April 23–28, eight Negroes were lynched because one white man was killed by the Negro, the latter acting in self defense. Only seven of them are given in the list.

Near Memphis, Tenn., six Negroes were lynched—this time charged with burning barns. A trial of the indicted resulted in an acquittal, although it was shown on trial that the lynching was prearranged for them. Six widows and twenty-seven orphans are indebted to this mob for their condition, and this lynching swells the number to eleven Negroes lynched in and about Memphis since March 9, 1892.

In Brooks county, Ga., Dec. 23rd, while this Christian country was preparing for Christmas celebration, seven Negroes were lynched in twenty-four hours because they refused, or were unable to tell the whereabouts of a colored man named Pike, who killed a white man. The wives and daughters of these lynched men were horribly and brutally outraged by the murderers of their husbands and fathers. But the mob has not been punished and again women and children are robbed of their protectors whose blood cries unavenged to Heaven and humanity. Georgia heads the list of lynching states.

MURDER

Jan. 9, Samuel Smith, Greenville, Ala.; Jan. 11, Sherman Wagoner, Mitchell, Ind.; Jan. 12, Roscoe Parker, West Union, Ohio; Feb. 7, Henry Bruce, Gulch Co., Ark.; March 5, Sylvester Rhodes, Collins, Ga.; March 15, Richard Puryea, Stroudsburg, Pa.; March 29, Oliver Jackson, Montgomery, Ala.; March 30, ———— Saybrick, Fisher's Ferry, Miss.; April 14, William Lewis, Lanison, Ala.; April 23, Jefferson Luggle, Cherokee, Kan.; April 23, Samuel Slaugate, Tallulah, La.; April 23, Thomas Claxton, Tallulah, La.; April 23, David Hawkins, Tallulah, La.; April 27, Thel Claxton, Tallulah, La.; April 27, Comp Claxton, Tallulah, La.; April 27, Scot Harvey, Tallulah, La.; April 27, Jerry McCly, Tallulah, La.; May 17, Henry Scott, Jefferson, Tex.; May 15, Coat Williams, Pine Grove, Fla.; June 2, Jefferson Crawford, Bethesda, S.C.; June 4, Thondo Underwood, Monroe, La.; June 8, Isaac Kemp, Cape Charles, Va.; June 13, Lon Hall, Sweethouse, Tex.; June 13, Bascom Cook, Sweethouse, Tex.; June 15, Luke Thomas, Biloxi, Miss.; June 29, John Williams, Sulphur, Tex.; June 29, Ulysses

Hayden, Monett, Mo.; July 6, ——— Hood, Amite, Miss.; July 7, James Bell, Charlotte, Tenn.; Sept. 2, Henderson Hollander, Elkhorn, W.Va.; Sept. 14, Robert Williams, Concordia Parish, La.; Sept. 22, Luke Washington, Meghee, Ark.; Sept. 22, Richard Washington, Meghee, Ark.; Sept. 22, Henry Crobyson, Meghee, Ark.; Nov. 10, Lawrence Younger, Lloyd, Va.; Dec. 17, unknown Negro, Williamston, S.C.; Dec. 23, Samuel Taylor, Brooks County, Ga.; Dec. 23, Charles Frazier, Brooks County, Ga.; Dec. 23, Samuel Pike, Brooks County, Ga.; Dec. 23, Harry Sherard, Brooks County, Ga.; Dec. 23, unknown Negro, Brooks County, Ga.; Dec. 23, unknown Negro, Brooks County, Ga.; Dec. 23, unknown Negro, Brooks County, Ga.; Dec. 26, Daniel McDonald, Winston County, Miss.; Dec. 26, William Carter, Winston County, Miss.

RAPE

Jan. 17, John Buckner, Valley Park, Mo.; Jan. 21, M. G. Cambell, Jellico Mines, Ky.; Jan. 27, unknown, Verona, Mo.; Feb. 11, Henry McCreeg, near Pioneer, Tenn.; April 6, Daniel Ahren, Greensboro, Ga.; April 15, Seymour Newland, Rushsylvania, Ohio; April 26, Robert Evarts, Jamaica, Ga.; April 27, James Robinson, Manassas, Va.; April 27, Benjamin White, Manassas, Va.; May 15, Nim Young, Ocala, Fla.; May 22, unknown, Miller County, Ga.; June 13, unknown, Blackshear, Ga.; June 18, Owen Opliltree, Forsyth, Ga.; June 22, Henry Capus, Magnolia, Ark.; June 26, Caleb Godly, Bowling Green, Ky.; June 28, Fayette Franklin, Mitchell, Ga.; July 2, Joseph Johnson, Hiller's Creek, Mo.; July 6, Lewis Bankhead, Cooper, Ala.; July 16, Marion Howard, Scottsville, Ky.; July 20, William Griffith, Woodville, Tex.; Aug. 12, William Nershbread, Rossville, Tenn.; Aug. 14, Marshall Boston, Frankfort, Ky.; Sept. 19, David Gooseby, Atlanta, Ga.; Oct. 15, Willis Griffey, Princeton, Ky.; Nov. 8, Lee Lawrence, Jasper County, Ga.; Nov. 10, Needham Smith, Tipton County, Tenn.; Nov. 14, Robert Mosely, Dolinite, Ala.; Dec. 4, William Jackson, Ocala, Fla.; Dec. 18, unknown, Marion County, Fla.

UNKNOWN OFFENSES

March 6, Lamsen Gregory, Bell's Depot, Tenn.; March 6, unknown woman, near Marche, Ark.; April 14, Alfred Brenn, Calhoun, Ga.; June 8, Harry Gill, West Lancaster, S.C.; Nov. 23, unknown, Landrum, S.C.; Dec. 5, Mrs. Teddy Arthur, Lincoln County, W.Va.

DESPERADO

Jan. 14, Charles Willis, Ocala, Fla.

SUSPECTED INCENDIARISM

Jan. 18, unknown, Bayou Sarah, La.

SUSPECTED ARSON

June 14, J. H. Dave, Monroe, La.

ENTICING SERVANT AWAY

Feb. 10, ———— Collins, Athens, Ga.

TRAIN WRECKING

Feb. 10, Jesse Dillingham, Smokeyville, Tex.

HIGHWAY ROBBERY

June 3, unknown, Dublin, Ga.

INCENDIARISM

Nov. 8, Gabe Nails, Blackford, Ky.; Nov. 8, Ulysses Nails, Blackford, Ky.

ARSON

Dec. 20, James Allen, Brownsville, Tex.

ASSAULT

Dec. 23, George King, New Orleans, La.

NO OFFENSE

Dec. 28, Scott Sherman, Morehouse Parish, La.

BURGLARY

May 29, Henry Smith, Clinton, Miss.; May 29, William James, Clinton, Miss.

ALLEGED RAPE

June 4, Ready Murdock, Yazoo, Miss.

ATTEMPTED RAPE

July 14, unknown Negro, Biloxi, Miss.; July 26, Vance McClure, New Iberia, La.; July 26, William Tyler, Carlisle, Ky.; Sept. 14, James Smith, Stark, Fla.; Oct. 8, Henry Gibson, Fairfield, Tex.; Oct. 20, ———— Williams, Upper Marlboro, Md.; June 9, Lewis Williams, Hewett Springs, Miss.; June 28, George Linton, Brookhaven, Miss.; June 28, Edward White,

Hudson, Ala.; July 6, George Pond, Fulton, Miss.; July 7, Augustus Pond, Tupelo, Miss.

RACE PREJUDICE

June 10, Mark Jacobs, Bienville, La.; July 24, unknown woman, Sampson County, Miss.

INTRODUCING SMALLPOX

June 10, James Perry, Knoxville, Ark.

KIDNAPPING

March 2, Lentige, Harland County, Ky.

CONSPIRACY

May 29, J. T. Burgis, Palatka, Fla.

HORSE STEALING

June 20, Archie Haynes, Mason County, Ky.; June 20, Burt Haynes, Mason County, Ky.; June 20, William Haynes, Mason County, Ky.

WRITING LETTER TO WHITE WOMAN

May 9, unknown Negro, West Texas.

GIVING INFORMATION

July 12, James Nelson, Abbeyville, S.C.

STEALING

Jan. 5, Alfred Davis, Live Oak County, Ark.

LARCENY

April 18, Henry Montgomery, Lewisburg, Tenn.

POLITICAL CAUSES

July 19, John Brownlee, Oxford, Ala.

CONJURING

July 20, Allen Myers, Rankin County, Miss.

ATTEMPTED MURDER

June 1, Frank Ballard, Jackson, Tenn.

ALLEGED MURDER

April 5, Negro, near Selma, Ala.; April 5, Negro, near Selma, Ala.

WITHOUT CAUSE

May 17, Samuel Wood, Gates City, Va.

BARN BURNING

April 22, Thomas Black, Tuscumbia, Ala.; April 22, John Williams, Tuscumbia, Ala.; April 22, Toney Johnson, Tuscumbia, Ala.; July 14, William Bell, Dixon, Tenn.; Sept. 1, Daniel Hawkins, Millington, Tenn.; Sept. 1, Robert Haynes, Millington, Tenn.; Sept. 1, Warner Williams, Millington, Tenn.; Sept. 1, Edward Hall, Millington, Tenn.; Sept. 1, John Haynes, Millington, Tenn.; Sept. 1, Graham White, Millington, Tenn.

ASKING WHITE WOMAN TO MARRY HIM

May 23, William Brooks, Galesline, Ark.

OFFENSES CHARGED FOR LYNCHING

Suspected arson, 2; stealing, 1; political causes, 1; murder, 45; rape, 29; desperado, 1; suspected incendiarism, 1; train wrecking, 1; enticing servant away, 1; kidnapping, 1; unknown offense, 6; larceny, 1; barn burning, 10; writing letters to a white woman, 1; without cause, 1; burglary, 1; asking white woman to marry, 1; conspiracy, 1; attempted murder, 1; horse stealing, 3; highway robbery, 1; alleged rape, 1; attempted rape, 11; race prejudice, 2; introducing smallpox, 1; giving information, 1; conjuring, 1; incendiarism, 2; arson, 1; assault, 1; no offense, 1; alleged murder, 2; total (colored), 134.

LYNCHING STATES

Mississippi, 15; Arkansas, 8; Virginia, 5; Tennessee, 15; Alabama, 12; Kentucky, 12; Texas, 9; Georgia, 19; South Carolina, 5; Florida, 7; Louisiana, 15; Missouri, 4; Ohio, 2; Maryland, 1; West Virginia, 2; Indiana, 1; Kansas, 1; Pennsylvania, 1.

LYNCHING BY THE MONTH

January, 11; February, 17; March, 8; April, 36; May, 16; June, 31; July, 21; August, 4; September, 17; October, 7; November, 9; December, 20; total colored and white, 197.

WOMEN LYNCHED

July 24, unknown woman, race prejudice, Sampson County, Miss.; March 6, unknown woman, unknown offense, Marche, Ark.; Dec. 5, Mrs. Teddy Arthur, unknown cause, Lincoln County, W.Va.

CHAPTER X. THE REMEDY

It is a well established principle of law that every wrong has a remedy. Herein rests our respect for law. The Negro does not claim that all of the one thousand black men, women and children, who have been hanged, shot and burned alive during the past ten years, were innocent of the charges made against them. We have associated too long with the white man not to have copied his vices as well as his virtues. But we do insist that the punishment is not the same for both classes of criminals. In lynching, opportunity is not given the Negro to defend himself against the unsupported accusations of white men and women. The word of the accuser is held to be true and the excited bloodthirsty mob demands that the rule of law be reversed and instead of proving the accused to be guilty, the victim of their hate and revenge must prove himself innocent. No evidence he can offer will satisfy the mob; he is bound hand and foot and swung into eternity. Then to excuse its infamy, the mob almost invariably reports the monstrous falsehood that its victim made a full confession before he was hanged.

With all military, legal and political power in their hands, only two of the lynching States have attempted a check by exercising the power which is theirs. Mayor Trout, of Roanoke, Virginia, called out the militia in 1893, to protect a Negro prisoner, and in so doing nine men were killed and a number wounded. Then the mayor and militia withdrew, left the Negro to his fate and he was promptly lynched. The business men realized the blow to the town's were given light sentences, the highest being one of twelve financial interests, called the mayor home, the grand jury indicted and prosecuted the ringleaders of the mob. They months in State prison. The day he arrived at the penitentiary, he was pardoned by the governor of the State.[12]

---

[12] For sense, the passage should read: "The business men realized the blow to the town's financial interests, [and] called the mayor home. The grand jury indicted and prosecuted the ringleaders of the mob. They were given light sentences, the highest being one of twelve months in State prison. The day he arrived at the penitentiary, he was pardoned by the governor of the State."

The only other real attempt made by the authorities to protect a prisoner of the law, and which was more successful, was that of Gov. McKinley,[13] of Ohio, who sent the militia to Washington Courthouse, O., in October, 1894, and five men were killed and twenty wounded in maintaining the principle that the law must be upheld.

In South Carolina, in April, 1893, Gov. Tillman aided the mob by yielding up to be killed, a prisoner of the law, who had voluntarily placed himself under the Governor's protection. Public sentiment by its representatives has encouraged Lynch Law, and upon the revolution of this sentiment we must depend for its abolition.

Therefore, we demand a fair trial by law for those accused of crime, and punishment by law after honest conviction. No maudlin sympathy for criminals is solicited, but we do ask that the law shall punish all alike. We earnestly desire those that control the forces which make public sentiment to join with us in the demand. Surely the humanitarian spirit of this country which reaches out to denounce the treatment of the Russian Jews, the Armenian Christians, the laboring poor of Europe, the Siberian exiles and the native women of India—will not longer refuse to lift its voice on this subject. If it were known that the cannibals or the savage Indians had burned three human beings alive in the past two years, the whole of Christendom would be roused, to devise ways and means to put a stop to it. Can you remain silent and inactive when such things are done in our own community and country? Is your duty to humanity in the United States less binding?

What can you do, reader, to prevent lynching, to thwart anarchy and promote law and order throughout our land?

1st. You can help disseminate the facts contained in this book by bringing them to the knowledge of every one with whom you come in contact, to the end that public sentiment may be revolutionized. Let the facts speak for themselves, with you as a medium.

2d. You can be instrumental in having churches, missionary societies, Y. M. C. A.'s, W. C. T. U.'s and all Christian and moral forces in connection with your religious and social life, pass resolutions of condemnation and protest every time a lynching takes place; and see that they are sent to the place where these outrages occur.

3d. Bring to the intelligent consideration of Southern people the refusal of capital to invest where lawlessness and mob violence hold sway. Many labor organizations have declared by resolution that they

---

[13] William McKinley (Republican) served two terms as governor of Ohio and in 1896 was elected president of the United States. He died in office in 1901.

would avoid lynch infested localities as they would the pestilence when seeking new homes. If the South wishes to build up its waste places quickly, there is no better way than to uphold the majesty of the law by enforcing obedience to the same, and meting out the same punishment to all classes of criminals, white as well as black. "Equality before the law," must become a fact as well as a theory before America is truly the "land of the free and the home of the brave."

4th. Think and act on independent lines in this behalf, remembering that after all, it is the white man's civilization and the white man's government which are on trial. This crusade will determine whether that civilization can maintain itself by itself, or whether anarchy shall prevail; whether this Nation shall write itself down a success at self government, or in deepest humiliation admit its failure complete; whether the precepts and theories of Christianity are professed and practiced by American white people as Golden Rules of thought and action, or adopted as a system of morals to be preached to heathen until they attain to the intelligence which needs the system of Lynch Law.

5th. Congressman Blair[14] offered a resolution in the House of Representatives, August, 1894. The organized life of the country can speedily make this a law by sending resolutions to Congress indorsing Mr. Blair's bill and asking Congress to create the commission. In no better way can the question be settled, and the Negro does not fear the issue. The following is the resolution:

"Resolved, By the House of Representatives and Senate in congress assembled, That the committee on labor be instructed to investigate and report the number, location and date of all alleged assaults by males upon females throughout the country during the ten years last preceding the passing of this joint resolution, for or on account of which organized but unlawful violence has been inflicted or attempted to be inflicted. Also to ascertain and report all facts of organized but unlawful violence to the person, with the attendant facts and circumstances, which have been inflicted upon accused persons alleged to have been guilty of crimes punishable by due process of law which have taken place in any part of the country within the ten years last preceding the passage of this resolution. Such investigation shall be made by the usual methods and agencies of the Department of Labor, and report made to Congress as soon as the work can be satisfactorily done, and the sum of $25,000, or so much thereof as may be necessary, is hereby

---

[14] Senator Henry W. Blair, Republican from New Hampshire.

appropriated to pay the expenses out of any money in the treasury not otherwise appropriated."

The belief has been constantly expressed in England that in the United States, which has produced Wm. Lloyd Garrison, Henry Ward Beecher, James Russell Lowell, John G. Whittier[15] and Abraham Lincoln there must be those of their descendants who would take hold of the work of inaugurating an era of law and order. The colored people of this country who have been loyal to the flag believe the same, and strong in that belief have begun this crusade. To those who still feel they have no obligation in the matter, we commend the following lines of Lowell on "Freedom."

> Men! whose boast it is that ye
> Come of fathers brave and free,
> If there breathe on earth a slave
> Are ye truly free and brave?
> If ye do not feel the chain,
> When it works a brother's pain,
> Are ye not base slaves indeed,
> Slaves unworthy to be freed?
>
> Women! who shall one day bear
> Sons to breathe New England air,
> If ye hear without a blush,
> Deeds to make the roused blood rush
> Like red lava through your veins,
> For your sisters now in chains, —
> Answer! are ye fit to be
> Mothers of the brave and free?
>
> Is true freedom but to break
> Fetters for our own dear sake,
> And, with leathern hearts, forget
> That we owe mankind a debt?

---

[15] William Lloyd Garrison, publisher of the antislavery newspaper *The Liberator*, was a supporter of several African Americans, including Maria Stewart, the first known African American female political speaker; Charlotte Forten, educator, poet, and club-woman; and Frederick Douglass. A Congregational minister and distinguished orator, Henry Ward Beecher was an outspoken abolitionist before the Civil War and a supporter of moderate Reconstruction policies afterward. James Russell Lowell, an influential nineteenth-century poet and literary critic from Massachusetts, served also as minister to Spain and ambassador to Great Britain. John Greenleaf Whittier was a highly respected poet, journalist, and abolitionist from Massachusetts.

No! true freedom is to share
All the chains our brothers wear,
And, with heart and hand, to be
Earnest to make others free!

There are slaves who fear to speak
For the fallen and the weak;
They are slaves who will not choose
Hatred, scoffing, and abuse,
Rather than in silence shrink
From the truth they needs must think;
They are slaves who dare not be
In the right with two or three.

A Field for Practical Work

The very frequent inquiry made after my lectures by interested friends is, "What can I do to help the cause?" The answer always is, "Tell the world the facts." When the Christian world knows the alarming growth and extent of outlawry in our land, some means will be found to stop it.

The object of this publication is to tell the facts, and friends of the cause can lend a helping hand by aiding in the distribution of these books. When I present our cause to a minister, editor, lecturer, or representative of any moral agency, the first demand is for facts and figures. Plainly, I can not then hand out a book with a twenty-five cent tariff on the information contained. This would be only a new method in the book agents' art. In all such cases it is a pleasure to submit this book for investigation, with the certain assurance of gaining a friend to the cause.

There are many agencies which may be enlisted in our cause by the general circulation of the facts herein contained. The preachers, teachers, editors and humanitarians of the white race, at home and abroad, must have facts laid before them, and it is our duty to supply these facts. The Central Anti-Lynching League, Room 9, 128 Clark St., Chicago, has established a Free Distribution Fund, the work of which can be promoted by all who are interested in this work.

Anti-lynching leagues, societies and individuals can order books from this fund at agents' rates. The books will be sent to their order, or, if desired, will be distributed by the League among those whose co-operative aid we so greatly need. The writer hereof assures prompt distribution of books according to order, and public acknowledgment of all orders through the public press.

Excerpt from

CRUSADE FOR JUSTICE

The Autobiography of Ida B. Wells

———————

Edited by Alfreda M. Duster

CHAPTER 10. THE HOMESICK EXILE

Every week from that first remarkable issue I had my regular two columns in the *New York Age*.[1] Before leaving the South I had often wondered at the silence of the North. I had concluded it was because they did not know the facts, and had accepted the southern white man's reason for lynching and burning human beings in this nineteenth century of civilization. Although the *Age* was on the exchange list of many of the white periodicals of the North, none so far as I remember commented on the revelations I had made through its columns.

Eventually these facts did get into the white press of the country, but through an agency that was little expected. About two months after my appearance in the columns in the *New York Age*, two colored women remarked on my revelations during a visit with each other and said they thought that the women of New York and Brooklyn should do something to show appreciation of my work and to protest the treatment which I had received. They thought they could get other friends together to talk over the idea. These two women were Mrs. Victoria Earle Matthews of New York and Miss Maritcha Lyons, a Brooklyn schoolteacher.

The meeting was held and the idea adopted with enthusiasm. This led to further meetings, which grew in interest and numbers until no house was large enough to hold those who came. They met in the lecture rooms of the churches, and the slogan adopted was to raise enough to enable Miss Wells to publish her paper again. A committee of two hundred and fifty women was appointed, and they stirred up sentiment throughout the two cities which culminated in a testimonial at Lyric Hall on 5 October 1892.

This testimonial was conceded by the oldest inhabitants to be the greatest demonstration ever attempted by race women for one of their number. New York, then as now, had the name of being cold-blooded and selfish in its refusal to be interested in anybody or anything who was not to the manner born, whose parents were not known, or who

---

[1] Citizens of Memphis were apprised of the activities of Ida B. Wells. "Since leaving Memphis she has gone to New York, where she had connected herself with a paper called *The Age* in which she has continued to publish matter not a whit less scandalous than that which aroused the ire of the whites just prior to her departure. This matter has appeared in *The Age* from week-to-week, and since the same has been running, *The Age* has been put in circulation in this city." The *Memphis Appeal-Avalanche*, 30 June 1892, p. 5.

did not belong to their circle. New York looked down on Brooklyn, her sister city across the bridge. Yet the best womanhood of those two cities, led by the two women named above, responded wonderfully to their appeal. It resulted in the most brilliantly interesting affair of its kind ever attempted in these United States.

The hall was crowded with them and their friends. The leading colored women of Boston and Philadelphia had been invited to join in this demonstration, and they came, a brilliant array. Mrs. Gertrude Mossell of Philadelphia, Mrs. Josephine St. Pierre Ruffin of Boston, Mrs. Sarah Garnett, widow of one of our great men, a teacher in the public schools of New York City, Dr. Susan McKinney of Brooklyn, the leading woman physician of our race, were all there on the platform, a solid array behind a lonely, homesick girl who was an exile because she had tried to defend the manhood of her race.

The arrangements for that meeting were perfect. An electric light spelled "Iola," my pen name, at the back of the platform. The programs were miniature copies of the *Free Speech*. Mrs. Victoria E. Matthews presided, and after a beautiful program of speeches, resolutions, and music, I was introduced to tell my story.

When the committee told me I had to speak I was frightened. I had been a writer, both as correspondent and editor, for several years. I had some little reputation as an essayist from schoolgirl days, and had recited many times in public recitations which I had committed to memory. In canvassing for my paper I had made talks asking for subscriptions. But this was the first time I had ever been called on to deliver an honest-to-goodness address.

Although every detail of that horrible lynching affair was imprinted on my memory, I had to commit it all to paper, and so got up to read my story on that memorable occasion. As I described the cause of the trouble at home and my mind went back to the scenes of the struggle, to the thought of the friends who were scattered throughout the country, a feeling of loneliness and homesickness for the days and the friends that were gone came over me and I felt the tears coming.

A panic seized me. I was afraid that I was going to make a scene and spoil all those dear good women had done for me. I kept saying to myself that whatever happened I must not break down, and so I kept on reading. I had left my handkerchief on the seat behind me and therefore could not wipe away the tears which were coursing down my cheeks. The women were all back of me on the platform and could not see my plight. Nothing in my voice, it seemed, gave them an inkling of the true state of affairs. Only those in the audience could see the tears dropping. At last I put my hand behind me and beckoned even as I kept reading. Mrs. Matthews, the chairman, came forward and I asked her for my handkerchief. She brought it and I wiped my nose and streaming face, but I kept on reading the story which they had come to hear.

I was mortified that I had not been able to prevent such an exhibition of weakness. It came on me unawares. It was the only time in all those trying months that I had so yielded to personal feelings. That it should come at a time when I wanted to be at my best in order to show my appreciation of the splendid things those women had done! They were giving me tangible evidence that although my environment had changed I was still surrounded by kind hearts. After all these years I still have a feeling of chagrin over that exhibition of weakness. Whatever my feelings, I am not given to public demonstrations. And only once before in all my life had I given way to woman's weakness in public.

But the women didn't feel that I had spoiled things by my breakdown. They seemed to think that it had made an impression on the audience favorable to the cause and to me. Mr. C. S. Morris, who had married Frederick Douglass's granddaughter, was among those present, and he said that it did more to convince cynical and selfish New York of the seriousness of the lynching situation than anything else could have done. He said that if I had deliberately sought a way to arrest their attention I could not have done anything more effective. I had no knowledge of stage business, but I was relieved and happy to know that they did not consider that I had spoiled things on my first appearance before a New York audience.

The women gave me five hundred dollars and a gold brooch made in the shape of a pen, an emblem of my chosen profession. The money was placed in the bank against the time when I would be able to start my own paper. The brooch I wore for the next twenty years on all occasions. So many things came out of that wonderful testimonial.

First, it was the real beginning of the club movement among the colored women in this country. The women of New York and Brooklyn decided to continue that organization, which they called the Women's Loyal Union. These were the first strictly women's clubs organized in those two cities. Mrs. Ruffin of Boston, who came over to that testimonial, invited me to be her guest in Boston later on. She called a meeting of the women at her home to meet me, and they organized themselves into the Woman's Era Club of that city. Mrs. Ruffin had been a member of the foremost clubs among white women in Boston for years, but this was her first effort to form one among colored women.[2] She also made dates for me in other nearby cities, where she called the women together and organized them into clubs of their own. This was done in New Bedford, Providence, and Newport, Rhode Island, and several other towns. Several years later, on a return visit to New England, I helped the women of New Haven, Connecticut, to organize their first club.

It was during this visit to Boston that I had my first opportunity to address a white audience. Joseph Cook, who was a famous preacher at that time, invited me to speak at his Monday morning lecture. Dr. Zacshufski, a pioneer woman physician and suffragist, had me to address her group. Mr. William Lloyd Garrison, son and namesake of the famous abolitionist, used his influence as a businessman to turn down a loan solicited by Memphis, Tennessee. He gave as his reason for that refusal the conditions I pictured as existing there. The *Boston Transcript* and *Advertiser* gave the first notices and report of my story of any white northern papers.

Second, that testimonial was the beginning of public speaking for me. I have already said that I had not before made speeches, but invitations came from Philadelphia, Wilmington, Delaware, Chester, Pennsylvania, and Washington, D.C., besides the ones I have already mentioned. In these meetings I read my paper, the same one that I had read at the first meeting in New York. The Washington meeting was held in the Metropolitan A.M.E. Church and was very poorly attended. Frederick Douglass was there with his wife, his sons, and their wives. Mr. Douglass spoke and apologized for Washington's seeming indifference to the important message I brought and invited me to come again, when he would undertake to have a larger meeting for me.

In Philadelphia I was the guest of William Still, who wrote *The Underground Railroad.* My meeting was attended by many old "war horses." Miss Catherine Impey of Street, Somerset, England, was visiting Quaker relatives of hers in the city and at the same time trying to learn what she could about the color question in this country. She was the editor of *Anti-Caste,* a magazine published in England in behalf of the natives of India, and she was therefore interested in the treatment of darker races everywhere.

---

[2] For an account of Mrs. Ruffin's activities and difficulties, see Rayford W. Logan, *The Negro in American Life and Thought: The Nadir 1877–1901* (New York: Dial Press, 1954), pp. 236–38.

She was present at my meeting at the Quaker City and called on me at Mr. Still's home. She was shocked over the lynching stories I had told, also the indifference to conditions which she found among the white people in this country. She was especially hurt that this should be the fact among those of her own sect and kin. We deplored the situation and agreed that there seemed nothing to do but keep plugging away at the evils both of us were fighting.

This interview was held in November of 1892 and began what brought about the third great result of that wonderful testimonial in New York the previous month. Although we did not know it at the time, that interview between Miss Impey and myself resulted in an invitation to England and the beginning of a worldwide campaign against lynching. I am very glad at this late day to make acknowledgment of the wonderful results of that initial effort of the women of New York and Brooklyn to give me their loyal endorsement and support.

CHAPTER 11. LIGHT FROM THE HUMAN TORCH

On the third day of February 1893, I was back in Washington, D.C., to fill the return date Mr. Douglass had requested. True to his promise, he had called together the leading women of Washington, and they filled Metropolitan Church with one of the biggest audiences I had ever seen. Mr. Douglass himself presided and had Mrs. Mary Church Terrell introduce me. Mrs. Terrell was president of Bethel Literary and was just beginning her public career. She was the daughter of the Mr. Church who had shown himself a friend while I was a teacher in Memphis. Like myself, she seemed to be making a maiden speech. Mrs. Anna J. Cooper, principal of the high school, Miss Lucy Moten, head of the normal school and most of the brilliant women of Washington aided our "grand old man." That meeting ended in a blaze of glory and a donation of nearly two hundred dollars to aid the cause.

The next morning the newspapers carried the news that while our meeting was being held there had been staged in Paris, Texas, one of the most awful lynchings and burnings this country has ever witnessed. A Negro had been charged with ravishing and murdering a five-year-old girl. He had been arrested and imprisoned while preparations were made to burn him alive. The local papers issued bulletins detailing the preparations, the schoolchildren had been given a holiday to see a man burned alive, and the railroads ran excursions and brought people of the surrounding country to witness the event, which was in broad daylight with the authorities aiding and abetting this horror. The dispatches told in detail how he had been tortured with red-hot irons searing his flesh for hours before finally the flames were lit which put an end to his agony. They also told how the mob fought over the hot ashes for bones, buttons, and teeth for souvenirs.

I had said in newspaper articles and public speeches that we should be in a position to investigate every lynching and get the facts for ourselves. If there was no chance for a fair trial in these cases, we should have the facts to use in an appeal to public opinion. Accordingly, I felt that the first thing we should do in this case was to get the facts.

We had no organization and no funds for that purpose, but the women of Washington had just given me $150 the night before. I used that to have Pinkerton's send an honest, unprejudiced man from the Chicago office to bring unbiased facts. Instead, a man was sent from the Kansas City office, who sent back clippings from the local press, rather than personal investigation, and the photograph sent was that of an innocent child of tender years.

The man died protesting his innocence. He had no trial, no chance to defend himself, and to this day the world has only the word of his accusers that he committed that terrible crime against innocent childhood. For that reason there will always be doubts as to his guilt. There is no doubt whatever as to the guilt of those who murdered and tortured and burned alive this victim of their blood lust. They openly admitted and gloried in their shame. Miss Laura Dainty-Pelham was traveling through Texas a year later and she often told how the wife of the hotel keeper kept talking about it as if it were something to be proud of. While she talked, her eight-year-old daughter, who was playing about the room, came up to her mother and shaking her by the arm said, "I saw them burn the nigger, didn't I Mamma?" "Yes, darling, you saw them burn the nigger," said the complacent mother, as matter-of-factly as if she had said she saw them burn a pile of trash.

The fire lighted by this human torch flamed round the world. It was the subject of conversation at a breakfast table in Aberdeen, Scotland, the next day. Mrs. Isabelle Fyvie Mayo, a Scottish authoress, had invited Miss Catherine Impey to visit her. She had read *Anti-Caste* and wanted to know the woman who, like herself, was fighting caste in India as practiced by Great Britain.

Mrs. Mayo's interest had taken practical form. Her house had been a sanctuary for a long while for East Indians who wanted education and help. Mrs. Mayo wanted to know of Miss Impey if she had learned, when in America the year before, why the United States of America was burning human beings alive in the nineteenth century as the red Indians were said to have done three hundred years before. Miss Impey's reply was evidently not satisfactory. Mrs. Mayo asked if she knew anyone in the states who could come over and tell them about it. She thought that if this could be done, they might arouse public sentiment against such horrible practices. Miss Impey told her about the women's meeting in New York and my story. Mrs. Mayo said, "Write and ask her to come over. If she will do so, we will find the money for her expenses and provide opportunity for airing this intolerable condition."

Thus it was that I received the invitation to go to England. I was a guest in Mr. Douglass's home when the letter came, forwarded from New York. It said that they knew Mr. Douglass was too old to come, and that if for that reason I could not come, to ask him to name someone else. I gave him the letter to read and when he finished he said, "You go, my child; you are the one to go, for you have the story to tell."

It seemed like an open door in a stone wall. For nearly a year I had been in the North, hoping to spread the truth and get moral support for my demand that those accused of crimes be given a fair trial and punished by law instead of by mob. Only in one city—Boston—had I been given even a meager hearing, and the press was dumb. I refer, of course, to the white press, since it was the medium through which I hoped to reach the white people of the country, who alone could mold public sentiment.

CHAPTER 12. THROUGH ENGLAND AND SCOTLAND

In one of the little books furnished passengers on the steamships, I find in the brief spaces of blank pages left for daily record of the passage the following entries:

DIARY

First Day, Wednesday, April 5, 1893

Sailed for England today. First voyage across the ocean. Day is fine and trip so far enjoyable. Have four traveling companions bound for Africa.

Second Day

No seasickness. Hope to get thru alright. At any rate Miss Patton is with me. She is a doctor and will take care of me, but I don't think I am going to need her.

Third Day

Seasick. So is Dr. Georgia E. L. Patton. We have a stateroom to ourselves and lie in the two lower berths looking at each other. Ugh.

Fourth Day

Seasick still. Am afraid to lift my head. How I hate the sight of food.

Fifth Day

Seasicker.

Sixth Day

Seasickest. Ugh. How I wish I was on land. Got better this evening after
swallowing half the ship doctor's medicine chest contents.

Seventh Day

Have eaten a little something but have no appetite yet. Indigestion holds
me for its own. I do not advise anybody to start on a sea voyage with a
disordered system. Wrote a number of letters today.

Eighth Day

We got to Queenstown this morning and our letters back to the states
were mailed. I also received unexpectedly a letter and telegram from Miss
Impey telling me to come directly to her home in Somerset. I had cabled
her when I sailed. We reached Liverpool too late tonight to land.

Ninth Day

Woke up this morning to find out ship standing in the middle of the
Mersey River opposite Liverpool. Landed about 9:30 a.m. Went thru the
customs office assisted by the baggage master of Bywater Taugery & Co.,
who directed us to Shaftsbury Hotel where I shall stay with Miss Patton
until she sails Saturday, then go to Miss Impey.

Miss Patton was a graduate of Meharry Medical College, one of its first
woman graduates, if not the first. She was early imbued with the desire
to go to Africa as a medical missionary. The three young lads with her
were protégés of the Methodist Episcopal church who were returning
to their home in Monrovia, Liberia, for which point Miss Patton was
bound. The names they wrote in this little book of mine were Harold M.

Wood, Monrovia, Liberia, Africa, and Gilbert B. Haven. I have never heard of them since and do not know if they are still living.

Georgia Patton stayed in Liberia a number of years practicing medicine, until her health broke down and she returned to the United States. She settled in Memphis, my old home, and built up a practice there. She afterward married David Washington, one of the most highly respected letter carriers there and one of the few substantial citizens who did not leave Memphis when the rest of us did. Georgia Patton Washington had one child, which died, and later she herself passed away before she had reached the noonday of life.

Miss Impey, her mother, and her sister Kate welcomed me to their home in Street, Somersetshire, where I remained a few days to recuperate from my trip. She told me of her new friend, Mrs. Mayo, who was so interested in the work and who was going to be a co-worker in the cause; she said that the first effort was to start from her home in Aberdeen in the north of Scotland. Accordingly, we journeyed there in a few days and received a most hearty welcome from Mrs. Isabella Fyvie Mayo, who was well known in Scotland and England under the pen name of Edward Garrett.

Mrs. Mayo's home was an asylum for East Indians, who enjoyed her practical friendship. Dr. George Ferdinands, a native of Ceylon, had finished his collegiate and medical course at the University of Aberdeen and was practicing his profession of dentistry. Another young man, a relative of his, was attending school. The third member of the household was a German music teacher, who had plenty of music pupils in the town.

These three protégés of Mrs. Mayo threw themselves wholeheartedly into the work of helping to make preparations for our campaign: writing letters, arranging meetings, seeing the press, helping to mail out ten thousand copies of *Anti-Caste*, which went out to inform the British people of the organization of the Society for the Brotherhood of Man, with Mrs. Mayo and Miss Impey as leaders and co-editors of the little magazine. A happy two weeks were thus spent in busily working out plans.

The beginning of my share of the work was a drawing-room meeting of the local celebrities in Mrs. Mayo's home, where, after explanations, the audience formed itself into a membership of our new society. When introduced to speak, I told the same heart-stirring episodes which first gained for me the sympathy and good will of my New York friends. The facts I related were enough of themselves to arrest and hold the attention. They needed no embellishment, no oratory from me. *Society*, one of the periodicals of London, in its issue of 6 May 1893, had the following from one of its staff:

A very interesting young lady is about to visit London in the hope of arousing sympathy for the Blacks, whose treatment in the United States is not seldom fiendishly cruel. Miss Ida Wells is an American Negro lady, who is fortunate enough to have secured as an ally Mrs. Isabella Fyvie Mayo, one of our cleverest writers of sound and useful literature. Miss Wells has opened her campaign in Aberdeen with a drawing-room meeting at Mrs. Mayo's home.

Besides the meetings arranged for me in Aberdeen, Mrs. Mayo took me to a crowded men's Pleasant Saturday Evening meeting. There were an estimated fifteen hundred men there, and we had seats on the platform. It is possible that Mrs. Mayo had arranged to have me introduced at this meeting, but besides this, the chairman came to us during the singing and stated that the speaker scheduled could not be present, and asked me to use the fifteen minutes allotted to that speaker. This I was glad to do, and I began by telling of conditions in the South since the Civil War, jim crow laws, ballot-box intimidation, and laws against intermarriage. I told how in spite of such laws to prevent the mixing of the races, the white race had so bleached the Afro-Americans that a race of mulattoes, quadroons, and octoroons had grown up within the race, and that such laws put a premium on immorality. I also told of the cruel physical atrocities vented upon my race, and of the failure of the whites to allow a fair trial to any accused.

When I finished I found that I had been talking twenty-five minutes instead of the allotted fifteen, and no one had interrupted or called time on me. Mrs. Mayo was elated, said that it was the best I had done, and urged me to continue along those lines. After this successful start in Aberdeen, Mrs. Mayo and I went on to Huntly, Glasgow, and Edinburgh, while Miss Impey went on to arrange other meetings for us in the United Kingdom, working largely through the Society of Friends, of which she and her family were members.

The *Peterhead Sentinel and Buchan Journal* of 2 May 1893 said:

During the past week meetings have been held in several of the large towns of Scotland, at which addresses have been delivered by Miss Ada B. Wells [sic], an American Negro lady, who has been accompanied by Mrs. Fyvie Mayo, Aberdeen, and Miss Catherine Impey, who resides in Somerset. The object of these meetings is set forth in a little pamphlet which lies before me. It is a special number of *Anti-Caste*, a journal which advocates "the brotherhood of mankind irrespective of colour or descent." This number is made up of "some facts respecting lynch law occuring within the past few months in the United States; a selection only, drawn from reliable sources by Catherine Impey, Editor of

Anti-Caste, Somerset, England, and Isabelle Fyvie Mayo (Edward Garrett) Aberdeen, Scotland.

The facts that are set forth go to show very clearly that although slavery in the southern states of America is believed to have been abolished when the American war closed[,] the lot of the coloured people in these parts is little better than when slavery was in full force. These people are uniformly treated as people of an inferior caste, they are subjected to every possible indignity, they are denied all the rights of citizens, and when they give any manner of offence to the white man, they are tried according to the summary methods of Judge Lynch. Some horrible stories are told in this pamphlet, which one cannot read without burning indignation. Were it not that the facts are spoken to by ladies, whose reputation for truth and carefulness is beyond suspicion, one would fain believe that such things could not be in these days of civilization and freedom. But a case has been made out by these ladies that cannot be ignored by those who care for the good name of the United States; and it is no wonder that so much sympathy has gone out to the ladies who have come to tell the people of this country how freedom is mocked in the country that boasts herself the freest in the world.

And this from the *Edinburgh Evening Gazette* of 1 May 1893:

Apropos of the recent visit to Aberdeen of Miss Ida B. Wells, the American Negro lady who addressed a meeting last Monday evening in the Ball Room, Music Hall Building, a correspondent writes me as follows:

Miss Wells has been in Edinburgh since Thursday night. On Friday afternoon she addressed an influential meeting in the Bible Society Rooms, St. Andrew Square. Today, Saturday, she spoke to a drawing-room meeting convened in the Free Church Manse, Kirkliston (Rev. Mr. Lendrum) and afterwards to a crowded assembly in the hall of the Carubbers' Close Mission. She has everywhere been heard with deep attention and interest, and has evoked unanimous expressions of sympathy. On Monday she spoke in the rooms of the Y.M.C.A., South St. Andrew Street, as per enclosed. On Tuesday she goes to Glasgow, where she is to find an audience in the Friends' Meeting House. The Society for the Furtherance of the Brotherhood of Man, the proposed basis for protests against violence and prejudice, and for expression of sympathy with sufferers therefrom, has already enrolled many names, and every post is bringing more.

In Edinburgh we were the guests of Eliza Wigham, an old friend of Frederick Douglass's Anti-Slavery campaign. She was head of the new society there and everybody was jubilant over the great interest already aroused and the excellent press notices and ready response of those asked to join.

CHAPTER 13. BREAKING THE SILENT INDIFFERENCE

Miss Impey and I then went on to Newcastle, Birmingham, and Manchester. The meetings were all largely attended and secured good notices from the press. The *Newcastle Leader* of 10 May 1893 gave the following account:

> Yesterday she addressed public meetings held afternoon and evening in the Society of Friends Meeting House, Pilgrim Street, Newcastle. At night the audience was so large that two meetings were held, one presided over by Mr. David Richardson, and the other by Mr. Thomas Hunter, postmaster. Miss Wells, who is a young lady with a strong American accent, and who speaks with an educated and forceful style, gave some harrowing instances of the injustice to the members of her race, of their being socially ostracised and frequently lynched in the most barbarous fashion by mobs on mere suspicion, and without any trial whatever. These lynchings are on the increase, and have risen from 52 in 1882 to 169 in 1891, and 159 in 1892. Up to April, 1893, 93 black men and women had been lynched, and since April 5th three black men have been so treated. Her object in coming to England, she said, was to arouse public sentiment on this subject. England has often shown America her duty in the past, and she has no doubt that England will do so again.

The Birmingham papers gave columns of reports of our meetings, and splendid editorials. The *Birmingham Daily Gazette* of 18 May 1893 had a wonderful, full two-column editorial, and another full-column news report of the Birmingham meetings. The *Birmingham Daily Post* of the same date also carried a column report of the meetings under the caption LYNCH LAW IN AMERICA.

> A meeting was held yesterday at the Young Men's Christian Association assembly room, Needles Alley, to hear addresses upon the treatment of Negroes in the southern states of the American Union. Among those present were several ministers, members of the Society of Friends and ladies and gentlemen interested in local philanthropic work. Mr. R. L. Impey presided briefly, introduced Miss Ida B. Wells, an American Negro lady, and expressed sympathy with her object in coming to England.

Miss Wells in a quiet but effective address said it had been asked why she should have come four thousand miles to tell the people of Birmingham about something that could be dealt with very properly by the local authorities in America. She thought her story would answer that question. . . . Since 1875 the southern states had been in possession each of its own state government, and the privilege had been used to make laws in every way restrictive and proscriptive of the Negro race. One of the first of these laws was that which made it a state prison offense for black and white to inter-marry. That law was on the statute books of every southern state.

Another of these restrictive laws had only been adopted within the last half dozen years. It was one that made it a crime by fine and imprisonment for black and white people to ride in the same carriage. ("Shame.") Some of these laws were only passed last year, so that recollections of the Civil War could not be pleaded as an excuse.

A Negro woman carrying a white child would be received in a railway car, but an educated self-respecting woman with Negro blood in her veins, could she get past the sentinel at the door and enter as a passenger in her own right, she would be dragged out of the car. Her presence would be regarded as contamination. That of the nurse would be acceptable. It was the same at hotels and in the churches. A colored man might be employed as a janitor or to ring the bells, but would not dare walk into the same church simply to hear the preacher. ("Shame.") A Christian minister would not even administer the sacrament to a Negro side-by-side with a white communicant. ("Shame.")

Having given some particulars showing flimsy evidence on which people who had afterwards been proved innocent were lynched, Miss Wells said that when the woman was black and the man who assaulted her was white the offender was not even punished by the law. The white men of the South had forgotten entirely that in the war when their fathers and brothers were away the white women of the South had been in charge of the black men, against whose freedom their masters were fighting and not one black man was accused of betraying his trust ("applause"). . . .

One of the prominent citizens had vowed to shoot Miss Wells if she returned to her home at any time within twenty years and a well-known Christian woman, though she had disproved [*sic*] of the lynching of the three men, had expressed her approval of the course that had been taken in regard to Miss Wells. ("Shame.")

Having given details of other cases of lynching including three in which the victims had been burned to death, and showing that the authorities could not or would not interfere, Miss Wells argued from the result of the antislavery agitation that British public opinion if properly aroused would have good effect upon the people of the United

States, and strengthen the hand of those in America who were desirous of putting an end to these cruel proceedings.

In conclusion Miss Wells read the resolution which had been sent to her unsolicited and which was passed on Sunday night simply in consequence of what had appeared in the papers ("applause"). . . .

In reply to a question Miss Wells said that an attempt had been made but without success by representatives of Negroes to approach the Senate and Congress of the United States on the subject of lynching. Also, at a convention of seven governors held a short time ago to consider the best means of promoting immigration and the influx of capital into their states, a deputation of Negroes attended but were refused admission and told to state their business to the doorkeeper. ("Shame.") The Southerners appeared totally unable to realize the common humanity of the Negroes with themselves, and that was why it was desirable that they should learn the views of Englishmen whom they regarded as their equals and whose good opinion they valued. ("Hear, hear.")

It is very probable that the appearance of the following correspondence in the *Birmingham Daily Post* of the week before undoubtedly helped to give us the splendid audience we had in Birmingham:

A Wearied Councillor's Protest

To the Editor of the *Daily Post*
Sir:

If Solomon were living now he would say "Overmuch philanthropy is a weariness of the flesh." This morning I got a packet of literature relating to the prevalence of lynch law in the United States of America, and announcing meetings to be held in Birmingham next week on the subject.

They appear to be called on the initiative of an American Negro lady herself a victim of a Tennessee mob, and an English lady who edits a newspaper. A list is appended of Birmingham men who "have expressed their cordial sympathy with the objects of the meetings," and I am invited to attend.

My time is valuable, my powers are limited and I feel justified in asking what possible practical object can be attained by such meetings? I have no wish to disparage the zeal or to question the motives of a lady who, having been I presume, ill treated by a Tennessee mob, has come four thousand miles to raise a question which could be dealt with effectually only on the spot.

But I fail to see what ground there is for Birmingham people to dictate on questions of detail in the local police arrangements of certain towns in the United States. As a public man, I cannot find time to do all that I should wish for our own city; and I protest against being expected to give my attention to matters of municipal detail in a civilized country at a great distance, any interference with which by English people would be an impertinence.

A City Councillor

Birmingham, May 12th

On 16 May, a day before our meetings, the following answer appeared in the same paper:

LYNCH LAW IN THE UNITED STATES

To the Editor of the *Daily Post*
Sir:

A City Councillor asks in Saturday's *Post* what possible practical object can be attained by such meetings. He refers to the meeting to be held Wednesday in which an exposition of Lynch Law in the Southern states of America will be given by the writer.

I beg space to answer that question. Resentment because of the freedom and citizenship of the Negro race has been constantly shown by southern whites. In the ten years succeeding the Civil War thousands of Negroes were murdered for the crime (?) of casting a ballot. As a consequence their vote is entirely nullified throughout the entire South. The laws of the Southern states make it a crime for whites and Negroes to intermarry or even ride in the same railway carriage. Both crimes (?) are punishable by fine and imprisonment. The doors of churches, hotels, concert halls and reading rooms are alike closed against the Negro as a man, but every place is open to him as a servant.

The latest culmination of this war against Negro progress is the substitution of mob rule for courts of justice throughout the South. Judges, juries, sheriffs, and jailors in these states are all white men, and thus makes it impossible for a Negro to escape the penalty for any crime he commits. Then whenever a black man is charged with any crime against a white person these mobs without disguise take him from the jail in broad daylight, hang, shoot or burn him as their fancy dictates. A coroner's jury renders a verdict that "The deceased came to his death at the hands of parties unknown to the jury."

In the past ten years over a thousand black men and women and children have met this violent death at the hands of a white mob. And the rest of America has remained silent. Not even when three men were burned alive in the past twelve months, has she opened her mouth to protest against this barbarism. One religious body which met in Philadelphia last June refused to pass a resolution condemning lynching because it feared to offend the southern delegates present.

The pulpit and press of our own country remains silent on these continued outrages and the voice of my race thus tortured and outraged is stifled or ignored wherever it is lifted in America in a demand for justice. It is to the religious and moral sentiment of Great Britain we now turn. These can arouse the public sentiment of America so necessary for the enforcement of law. The moral agencies at work in Great Britain did much for the final overthrow of chattel slavery. They can in like manner pray, write, preach, talk and act against civil and industrial slavery; against the hanging, shooting and burning alive of a powerless race.

America cannot and will not ignore the voice of a nation that is her superior in civilization, which makes this demand in the name of justice and humanity. If the moral reforms of the age have been brought about by Christianity here is one which calls loudly for Christian and moral effort. I am in Great Britain today because I believe that the silent indifference with which she has received the charge that human beings are burned alive in Christian (?) Anglo-Saxon communities is born of ignorance of the true situation; and that if she really knew she would make the protest loud and long.

The horror and amazement with which my story has been received in Scotland and England; the prompt and vigorous resolutions of protest and condemnation of lynch law, have convinced me of the truth of my supposition. And I believe the people of Birmingham when they hear the story, will be not one whit less willing nor too busy to lend their moral influence to check what is fast becoming a national evil.

Ida B. Wells

of Memphis, Tennessee   66 Gough Road
United States, America   Birmingham,
                                         May 14

From here we went on to Manchester and had almost the same result in our wonderfully interesting meetings there. Mr. Axon, whose guests we were, was also editor of the *Guardian*, the leading daily paper of Manchester. The reports of the meetings were practically the same as those in the Birmingham papers because my subject matter was the same in every case. The *Guardian* had this notice:

Miss Ida B. Wells who is to visit Ashton and to address a gathering in Temperance Hall is a Negro lady of great natural ability.

She was being educated at the Rust University when the death of her parents called her back to her native place, Holly Springs, Mississippi, to keep a home for five younger brothers and sisters. Her earliest work was that of a school teacher, but having strong literary sympathies she became well known as a valued contributor to the press. "Iola" is the press name adopted by Miss Wells. She has an unbounded popularity with both men and women of the Negro race.

Her brave and outspoken contention for justice and common fairness in the treatment of the Negro race made Miss Wells obnoxious to her white neighbors, and she was driven from the State of Tennessee by a mob. She will be accompanied on Sunday by Miss Catherine Impey, a member of the Society of Friends who is well known for her philanthropic and temperance work, and by Mr. W. E. A. Axon, President of the Manchester and Salford Temperance Union, whose guests the ladies are.

It was in the home of Mr. and Mrs. Axon that the vegetarian propaganda was most forcefully brought to my attention. The few days I had spent in Miss Impey's home in Somersetshire had made known to me that her family were vegetarians. Although this was true they always had plenty of meat on the table for any visitors or friends who might not be members of the cult. Having been somewhat of a meat eater all my life, I ate roast beef or whatever other meat they had on the table. But in Mr. Axon's home in Manchester there was never any meat of any kind served and it all seemed new and strange to me.

All our meetings had aroused considerable interest and a good deal of newspaper comment. But on account of Mrs. Mayo's activity this ended the meetings which had been arranged by Miss Impey before the separation. From there we went to her home in Somersetshire.

CHAPTER 14.   AN INDISCREET LETTER

Mrs. Mayo received a letter one morning while we were in Edinburgh planning for the future, which in almost the twinkling of an eye changed the entire outlook. She sent at once for Miss Impey to join us there, and when she came she put in her hands the letter which caused all the trouble.

It was from Miss Impey herself, written to Dr. George Ferdinands after we had left Aberdeen. In it she declared that she returned the affection she felt sure he had for her; that she was taking this advance step because she knew he hesitated to do so because he was of a darker race; that she had written to her family acquainting them with the state of affairs, and telling them to prepare to receive him as her husband and that she rejoiced to give this proof to the world of the theories she had approved—the equality of the brotherhood of man.

The letter was a surprise to Dr. Ferdinands, who had revered Miss Impey for her work in behalf of India, but who had never dreamed of her in any such connections as her letter indicated. Fearing for the success of the work for which they were all making sacrifices, he sent the letter to

Mrs. Mayo. When Miss Impey came, Mrs. Mayo confronted her with this letter and demanded that she withdraw from the work. This she refused to do; then Mrs. Mayo declared she would not go on with her and insisted on the destruction of the entire issue of *Anti-Caste* which had their names jointly as editors and a recalling of dates, and demanded that I quit Miss Impey and go with her in an effort to carry on the work, which Miss Impey would disgrace if she continued with us.

But I could not see why because she had fallen in love with Dr. Ferdinands, and had been indiscreet enough to tell him so, that that incident which need not be known by anyone but ourselves would harm our work. Then Mrs. Mayo insisted that Miss Impey was the type of maiden lady who used such work as an opportunity to meet and make advances to men; that if we went on, she was likely to write such letters to others who might strike her fancy and throw suspicion and ridicule on our cause.

This conclusion I could not accept. I was young and inexperienced, it was true. I had never heard the word nymphomaniac before Mrs. Mayo used it in that connection with Miss Impey, and did not know its meaning until she told me. I had never heard one woman talk to another as she did, nor the scorn and withering sarcasm with which she characterized her. Poor Miss Impey was no match for her even if she had not been in the wrong. I really think it the most painful scene in which I ever took part. I had spent such a happy two weeks in the society of two of the best representatives of the white race in an atmosphere of equality, culture, refinement, and devotion to the cause of the oppressed darker races. To see my two ideals of noble womanhood divided in this way was heartrending. When it was demanded that I choose between them it was indeed a staggering blow.

I spent a sleepless night praying for guidance and in the morning told Mrs. Mayo that I could not do as she wished; that I was willing to concede that Miss Impey had made a mistake in yielding to her feelings and writing such a letter, but I could not see that she had committed a crime by falling in love and confessing it—but that I did not believe she would do it again anywhere, and I could not believe her to be the type of woman she had accused her of being. I reminded her that Miss Impey was my friend and had proved herself a friend of the race years before, that she had sacrificed time and money fighting for us, and that I could not be such an ingrate as to desert her or accent Mrs. Mayo's belief, after all these years of faithful, honorable service before the public in our behalf. I also reminded her that it was through Miss Impey that I came to know her, and that my people at home would never understand if through any act of mine they were made to seem ungrateful to her.

Mrs. Mayo, stern upright Calvinistic Scotchwoman that she was, could not see anything but that I was hurting the cause, and parted from me in what to her was righteous anger. She cast me into outer darkness with Miss Impey and I never saw her again. I wrote her pleading for a more charitable treatment of Miss Impey. I told her I did not know one woman could be so cruel to another and begged her to have a kinder feeling, but she could not see my point. Dr. Ferdinands himself wrote and strongly condemned me for staying with Miss Impey. But although I did not answer his letter I often wonder if he ever realized his mistake in passing on the offending letter instead of destroying it.

CHAPTER 15.　FINAL DAYS IN LONDON

The time came for going to London to appear at the May meetings. There had already appeared in the *Ladies Pictorial* an announcement of my coming. This magazine was one of the leading women's journals of the country, and it had this following very pleasing article in my behalf:

> Miss Ida Bell Wells, a negro lady who has come to England on the invitation of Miss Catherine Impey, has been lecturing with great success on a subject somewhat new to British audiences, namely, "Lynch Law in the United States," especially as it affects the colored people of the South. It is hoped that by this means the moral sentiment of this country may be aroused in favor of the just and equal treatment of the Negro race throughout the world. Miss Wells comes from Holly Springs, Mississippi, and was first engaged in teaching and then in journalistic work. She has attractive manners and a pleasant voice, and is exceedingly pleased with the reception accorded her in this country. The statements she made in a recent interview will probably startle some of our readers, who think that the prejudice against the colored race has passed away. When asked if the spread of education and growth of property among the Negro race was increasing, she replied that "the color line" was as distinctly drawn as ever. For instance, no "Afro-American"—whatever his moral, financial, or educational standing—can enter a white church, Y.M.C.A., school or railway car. In the theatres they may only go into the gallery, a part of which is railed off to separate them even there. One sign that the feeling is not on the decrease is that several Southern states have within the last six years passed laws to prevent the admission of Afro-Americans to the same railway car as the whites. When asked if she preferred the term "Afro-American" as a name for her people, she said it accurately described the position and had become

a popular designation. "Negro leaves out the element of nationality, and we are all Americans, nor has the Republic more faithful and loyal citizens than those of our race. Some of the 'colored' people are not distinguishable from whites, so far has their Negro blood been diluted, but they are all Afro-Americans—that is, Americans of African descent."

"Could not an Afro-American obtain damages for breach of contract if a railway refused to give him the accommodation for which he had paid and his ticket refused?" said the interviewer. And Miss Wells replied that she was herself dragged out of a railway car in Tennessee and on refusing to go into the "Jim Crow car," was left behind in the station, to the great delight of the passengers who stood up on their seats and applauded the action of the conductor, baggagemaster, and station-master in expelling her. Any one who has traveled through America knows the horrors of the "colored car," and will sympathise with Miss Wells. The dislike of the South is not to the Negroes as laborers or servants, but to the recognition of them as citizens. As a servant a Negro may enter places from which, whatever her wealth, intellect, education, or refinement, she is still ruthlessly excluded as a citizen. Miss Wells seems to think that as the Negro advances in education and in the qualities of good citizenship, the disinclination to allow him civil rights becomes deeper. Her revelations with regard to the lynchings were horrible. "The mob," she said, "are no longer content with shooting and hanging, but burn Negroes alive," and she justly appeals for a fair trial and legal punishment when the offense is proven. She maintains that British opinion and protest will have great force, and for this reason has determined to hold meetings in the principal cities here. She is delighted with the reception hereto accorded her, and feels greatly encouraged."

Every national organization in Great Britain goes up to London for its annual meeting in May. Parliament is in session, the society season is at its best, and everybody is in town. Mrs. Mayo had protested against every public appearance of Miss Impey since our separation; she declared that she must not appear in London but insisted that she send someone with me at her own expense.

Miss Impey acquiesced in this ultimatum and a German maiden lady was sent with me. She was a fine companion and chaperon but was not well enough known to secure entrance for me at these important meetings. Guided by the newspapers we went to most of the places where different meetings were announced. I was successful only in having a few minutes granted me at the British Women's Temperance meeting. This meeting was presided over by Lady Henry Somerset, and Miss Frances E. Willard, head of the Women's Christian Temperance Union of the United States, was present as her guest. I was given a few minutes by this body at which time Lady Somerset herself offered a resolution which she had drawn up.

With this I had to be contented, accepting a few small meetings. As the summer was coming on and very few meetings were held indoors, I sailed home from Southampton. The invitation which was the cause of my going to England said that the committee would guarantee all my expenses but could pay me nothing for my services. They loyally kept faith with me, since every item of expense had been met by them. My duty was to tell the story wherever an opening had been made, so when the time came for no more meetings it was the appropriate hour for me to return.

Miss Impey accompanied me to Southampton and stayed with me until the sailing of the boat. She blamed herself bitterly for the sudden ending of what had promised so well. I too regretted the separation, but I never ceased to believe that I had taken the right step, and never for a moment did I ever believe that Miss Impey had been actuated by any but the purest motives and the highest idealism.

I never intended to say anything about this story, but when I reached New York I found that Mrs. Mayo had written to Mr. Fortune, editor of the *New York Age*, to Frederick Douglass, and to Judge Albion W. Tourgee, who was the "Bystander" of the *Chicago Inter-Ocean*. She wrote also to several others of note in the country. She was most vindictive against Miss Impey in these letters and let them know she blamed me for going along with her. To these correspondents I gave a true version of the matter from my standpoint, and was very glad that every one of these experienced men of public affairs agreed with me that I had done the right thing. They also said that the best appreciation of Miss Impey's work for humanity was to keep the story to ourselves.

It is now thirty years since all this happened, and even now I hesitate long, before setting the facts down here, over whether I should tell the story after all these years. So far as I know the principals, except Mrs. Mayo, are still alive. But the matter has been much garbled and I have come to feel that it is only just to Miss Impey as well as to myself to set down here the unvarnished truth. Especially do I feel this way when I remember that in a subsequent visit to England I found that many of Miss Impey's relatives and friends seemed to feel that I was in some way to blame for the odium cast upon her. They felt this way very naturally because they had never heard the whole story.

They knew that something happened to put a stop to the work while I was with Miss Impey, and that shortly afterward I had left the country and the movement quieted down. Not having heard the real facts I suppose that it was the most natural deduction for them to conclude that I was in some way to blame. I am quite sure that Mrs. Mayo was sincere in her belief that she was doing the best thing for the work to which they were both committed, but I am also still convinced that she judged Miss Impey too harshly.

While we waited in Southampton for the boat which brought me home, Miss Impey took me to call upon Canon Wilberforce, who was dean of the cathedral of that town. As he was the grandson of the great antislavery agitator, I was especially glad to meet him and enjoyed our half-hour's visit very much. He regretted that there was not time to have a meeting in Southampton. After giving me a splendid autographed photograph of himself, he bade us farewell, wishing me a safe journey across the water.

The only other occurrence of special importance which happened during this trip had to do with the questions that were asked me after each lecture. Almost invariably, when I said that the Christian and moral sentiment of my own country remained silent in the face of these mob outrages, someone would ask, What about Rev. D. L. Moody and Miss Frances Willard? Both of these persons were well known and highly esteemed by the British people. Rev. Moody had visited and preached throughout Great Britain on several occasions. Miss Willard had been and was still the guest of Lady Henry Somerset and as such had traveled all over the United Kingdom visiting local temperance organizations.

My answer to these queries was that neither of those great exponents of Christianity in our country had ever spoken out in condemnation of lynching, but seemed on the contrary disposed to overlook that fashionable pastime of the South. I remembered very clearly that when Rev. Moody had come to the South with his revival sermons the notices printed said that the Negroes who wished to attend his meetings would have to go into the gallery or that a special service would be set aside for colored people only. I had noticed mention of this in colored newspapers printed in the towns where Rev. Moody had spoken.

Not in one instance was there ever any word to show that Rev. Moody objected to this segregation. In every case he appeared and spoke to the segregated gathering. Perhaps he thought it better to put over the gospel in this left-handed way than not to preach to poor benighted Negroes at all. Or he might have thought that he would destroy his influence with the good southern white Christians if he attempted to rebuke their unchristian attitude. Whatever the cause, no Negroes had ever heard of Rev. Moody's refusal to accept these jim crow arrangements, or knew of any protest of his against lynchings.

As to Miss Willard, I had very keen recollection of her first trip throughout the South in her capacity as president of the National Women's Christian Temperance Union. She had been figuratively wined and dined by the best white people of the South. She had made an opening for and received recognition of her organization such as had never occurred before. She was charmed by the culture and hospitality of those by whom she was entertained.

When she went back North there appeared an interview in the *New York Voice*, the organ of the temperance forces, in which she practically condoned lynchings. Every Negro newspaper in the South quoted and criticized that interview. Marked copies of their journals were sent to her, my own among the number. But so far as anyone knew, Miss Willard had never retracted or explained that interview.

Having this in mind I could not truthfully say that Miss Willard had ever said anything to condemn lynching; on the contrary she had seemed to condone it in her famous interview after returning from her first visit in the South. Of course, my statements were challenged by temperance followers. Not having a copy of the interview with me, I could not verify my statement. It looked as if I was making an attack on the two most noted Americans abroad. But I never mentioned the names of these two individuals in my lectures. I spoke only in a general way as to conditions among our Christian and moral forces. But when someone in the audience would ask the pointed question naming these two persons, there seemed nothing else for me to do but to tell the truth as I knew it.

My return voyage was most delightful. First, there were few if any white Americans on board. Second, there were fifteen young Englishmen in one party on their way to visit the World's Fair. I had not met any of them previously, but one [or] two of them were members of the Society of Friends and they had read about my trip. They were as courteous and attentive to me as if my skin had been of the fairest. It was indeed a delightful experience. We traveled together practically all the way to Chicago and they seemed to take great pleasure in shocking the onlookers by their courteous and respectful attention to me. All of this I enjoyed hugely, because it was the first time I had met any of the members of the white race who saw no reason why they should not extend to me the courtesy they would have offered to any lady of their own race.

A Wells Chronology
(1862–1931)

1862   Ida Bell Wells is born in Holly Springs, Mississippi, on July 16 to James Wells (a carpenter) and Elizabeth Warrenton Wells (a cook). Wells would be the eldest of eight children, four females and four males, two of whom died in early childhood.

Mary Jane Patterson becomes the first African American woman to receive a bachelor of arts degree from an established American college, Oberlin College in Ohio.

1863   President Abraham Lincoln signs the Proclamation of Amnesty and Reconstruction and the Emancipation Proclamation.

The Port Royal Commission establishes the first "official" school for freed slaves in the South on St. Helena Island off the coast of South Carolina.

1864   Rebecca Lee graduates from the New England Female Medical College and becomes the first female African American physician in the United States.

1865   The Civil War ends.

President Lincoln is assassinated, and Andrew Johnson becomes the seventeenth U.S. president.

Congress establishes the Bureau of Refugees, Freedmen, and Abandoned Lands.

Congress ratifies the Thirteenth Amendment.

The southern states begin adopting Black Codes.

Vassar College, among the oldest women's colleges in the United States, is founded.

1866   The Ku Klux Klan is organized in Pulaski, Tennessee.

Fisk University (Tennessee), Atlanta University (Georgia), and Rust College (Mississippi) are founded.

The Equal Rights Association, an organization dedicated to advancing the civil rights of African Americans and women, is established, with Elizabeth Cady Stanton as president, Frederick Douglass as vice president, and Susan B. Anthony as secretary.

1867 Congress passes the Reconstruction Acts, and military oversight in the southern states begins.

1868 Congress ratifies the Fourteenth Amendment.

1870 Congress ratifies the Fifteenth Amendment.

The first African Americans elected to the Senate (Hiram R. Revels from Mississippi) and the House of Representatives (Joseph H. Rainey from South Carolina) begin their terms.

All southern states have been readmitted to the Union.

Southern states begin establishing state-supported public education.

1872 Charlotte E. Ray, an African American, is awarded a law degree from Howard University and becomes one of the first women of any race to be admitted to the bar in Washington, DC.

1874 The Woman's Christian Temperance Union (WCTU) is founded.

1877 Control of legislatures by Democrats is reestablished in all southern states.

President Rutherford B. Hayes removes the last military troops from the South.

Radical Reconstruction ends.

1878 The yellow fever epidemic of 1878 began in New Orleans and spread inland quickly along the rivers and railways of the Mississippi Valley with an estimated 150,000 cases and 20,000 deaths. In Holly Springs, there were 1,239 cases recorded with 309 deaths. Among the dead were James and Elizabeth Wells and their youngest child. In Memphis, the numbers were even larger with over 5,000 dead, among them the spouse of Ida's Aunt Belle (her mother's sister), who would encourage Ida B. Wells to move to Memphis. Wells becomes the family provider. She leaves Rust College and begins a teaching career.

1880 Wells is invited by her aunt to move to Memphis, Tennessee, where she secures a better teaching position. She participates in social and political activities.

1881 The Atlanta Baptist Female Seminary (later Spelman College), the oldest college for women of African descent, is founded.

1884 Wells sues the Chesapeake, Ohio, and Southwestern Railroad and wins, but the suit is overturned by the Tennessee Supreme Court.

Wells writes her first article for the *Living Way* about her railroad lawsuit.

1889   Wells becomes co-owner, with Rev. Taylor Nightingale and J. L. Fleming, of the *Free Speech and Headlight.*

1890   The National American Woman Suffrage Association unifies the National Woman Suffrage Association and the American Woman Suffrage Association.

1891   Wells writes an editorial against the all-white Memphis Board of Education, loses her teaching job, and becomes a full-time journalist.

1892   Thomas Moss, Calvin McDowell, and Wil Stewart are lynched on March 9. Wells publishes her "Eight Men Lynched" editorial in the *Free Speech* on May 21. Forced into exile from the South by terrorist threats, Wells accepts a position as a reporter for the *New York Age.*

This year marks the first peak of mob violence against African Americans.

At the invitation of clubwomen from New York and Brooklyn, Wells begins a career as a public speaker. She addresses 250 African American women from three states on October 5 at Lyric Hall in New York City at a testimonial dinner given in her honor.

Wells publishes *Southern Horrors: Lynch Law in All Its Phases* as a pamphlet with five hundred dollars raised for her at the testimonial dinner.

Anna Julia Cooper, educator and community activist, appeals for the rights, interests, and recognition of African American women in the essay collection *A Voice from the South.*

1893   Wells makes her first speaking tour of England, Scotland, and Wales.

With Frederick Douglass, Ferdinand L. Barnett, and I. Garland Penn, Wells publishes an eighty-one-page pamphlet, *The Reason Why the Colored American Is Not in the World's Columbian Exposition.*

1894   Wells makes her second speaking tour of England, Scotland, and Wales, sending home articles that are published in the Chicago *Inter Ocean* as "Ida B. Wells Abroad."

John W. Jacks, president of the Missouri Press Association, sends an incendiary letter regarding African American women to Florence Balgarnie, secretary of the Anti-Lynching Society of England. Florida Ruffin Ridley, corresponding secretary of the Woman's Era Club in Boston, writes to Laura Ormiston Chant, a British social reformer and writer, in defense of the "colored women of America."

1895   Wells publishes *A Red Record,* her second pamphlet.

Wells marries Ferdinand L. Barnett and begins raising a family.

Frederick Douglass dies on February 20.

1896   The National Association of Colored Women (NACW) is founded; Mary Church Terrell is named its first president.

1900   Wells publishes *Mob Rule in New Orleans,* her third pamphlet.

1902   Gertrude Bustill Mossell, journalist and activist, publishes the essay collection *Afro-American Women and Work.*

1909   The National Association for the Advancement of Colored People (NAACP) is founded as an interracial organization dedicated to social and legal reform.

1919   This year is the second peak of mob violence against African Americans.

1920   An interracial network of moderate southern leaders organizes the Commission on Interracial Cooperation, which grows in the mid-1920s to become the major interracial reform organization in the South.

1922   At the request of the NAACP, Mary Burnett Talbert, NACW president from 1916 to 1920, organizes the Anti-Lynching Crusaders, a group that draws from a broadly based network of female African American community activists.

1930   This year is the third peak of mob violence against African Americans.

Jessie Daniels Ames organizes the Association of Southern Women for the Prevention of Lynching, the first organization of white women against lynching.

1931   Wells dies on March 25. Lynchings of African Americans continue to be reported each year after her death until 1953, when there are none reported for the first time since 1882. After 1953, lynchings continue to be reported.

Between 1882 and 1931, according to figures collected by the NAACP, 3,318 African American men, women, and children were lynched "at the hands of parties unknown."

Questions for Consideration

1. As a "public woman," Ida B. Wells can be viewed as unusual among nineteenth-century women. What makes her so?

2. The title of Wells's autobiography is *Crusade for Justice*. How would you characterize Wells as a "crusader"?

3. What impression of Wells as an activist do you glean from her account of herself in *Crusade for Justice*? What does your perception of her self-identity and the personality that she presents in her autobiography suggest to you about her achievements or the achievements of women generally in the nineteenth century?

4. Wells made a point of using data from white newspapers to support her claims about mob violence. What was the advantage of this strategy?

5. Consider Wells's British campaign. Why was it important to position lynching as an international concern? What did Wells expect to gain?

6. As historical documents, what do the pamphlets in this collection suggest about the conditions and challenges that confronted African Americans? Women? African American women? Identify and discuss issues related to race, gender, and class.

7. Given the excerpt from *Crusade for Justice*, how would you describe Wells's British campaign? What sort of experience was it for Wells? How does the British campaign compare to her domestic campaign? What evidence can you find of the success of the British campaign?

8. Discuss the following themes in Wells's pamphlets: women's place, justice, equality, political and economic power, law and order.

9. What evidence can you find of cooperation and division between African American women and white women during this era?

10. What do you consider to be the most distinctive features of the pamphlets? What stands out most when you study these pamphlets as "public" documents designed to enlighten and persuade?

11. Why did the accusation of rape make an effective excuse for mob violence? On what grounds did Wells claim these acts of violence to be unlawful?

12. What solutions did Wells offer to the problem of mob violence? Can these solutions be seen as having led to the decline of mob violence in the twentieth century? If so, how?

Selected Bibliography

BY AND ABOUT IDA B. WELLS

Bay, Mia, ed. *Ida B. Wells: The Light of Truth; Writings of an Anti-Lynching Crusader*. New York: Penguin Books, 2014.

Bressey, Caroline. *Empire, Race, and the Politics of Anti-Caste*. New York: Bloomsbury Academic, 2013.

DeCosta-Willis, Miriam. *Ida B. Wells: The Memphis Diaries*. Boston: Beacon Press, 1994.

Duster, Alfreda M. *Crusade for Justice: The Autobiography of Ida B. Wells*. Chicago: University of Chicago Press, 1970.

Duster, Michelle, ed. *Ida from Abroad: The Timeless Writings of Ida B. Wells from England in 1894*. Chicago: Benjamin Williams, 2010.

Giddings, Paula J. *Ida, a Sword among Lions: Ida B. Wells and the Campaign against Lynching*. New York: Amistad, 2008.

Greaves, William, producer. *Ida B. Wells: A Passion for Justice*. Installment of the PBS series *The American Experience*. New York: Video Dub, 1990.

Humrich, Shauna Lea. "Ida B. Wells-Barnett: The Making of a Reputation." Master's thesis, University of Colorado, 1989.

Hutton, Mary M. B. "The Rhetoric of Ida B. Wells: The Genesis of the Anti-Lynch Movement." PhD diss., University of Indiana, 1975.

McMurry, Linda O. *To Keep the Waters Troubled: The Life of Ida B. Wells*. New York: Oxford University Press, 1998.

Royster, Jacqueline Jones. "'To Call a Thing by Its True Name': The Rhetoric of Ida B. Wells." In *Reclaiming Rhetorica*, edited by Andrea Lunsford, 167–84. Pittsburgh: University of Pittsburgh Press, 1995.

———. "Wells-Barnett, Ida B." In *America in the World, 1776 to the Present: A Supplement to the Dictionary of American History*, edited by Edward J. Blum. 2 vols. Farmington Hills, Mich.: Charles Scribner's Sons, 2016.

Schechter, Patricia A. *Ida B. Wells-Barnett and American Reform, 1880–1930*. Chapel Hill: University of North Carolina Press, 2001.

Silkey, Sarah L. *Black Woman Reformer: Ida B. Wells, Lynching, and Transatlantic Activism*. Athens: University of Georgia Press, 2015.

Thompson, Mildred I. *Ida B. Wells-Barnett: An Exploratory Study of an American Black Woman, 1893–1930*. Vol. 15 of *Black Women in United States History*. Brooklyn, N.Y.: Carlson, 1990.

Wells, Ida B. *Mob Rule in New Orleans.* 1900. Bel Air, Calif.: Qontro Classic Books, 2010.

LYNCHING

Bederman, Gail. "'Civilization,' the Decline of Middle-Class Manliness, and Ida B. Wells's Antilynching Campaign (1892–94)." *Radical History Review* 52 (1992): 5–30.

Berg, Manfred. *Popular Justice: A History of Lynching in America.* American Ways Series. Lanham, Md.: Rowman and Littlefield, 2015.

Brundage, W. Fitzhugh. *Lynching in the New South: Georgia and Virginia, 1880–1930.* Urbana: University of Illinois Press, 1993.

Cameron, James. *A Time of Terror: A Survivor's Story.* Baltimore: Black Classic Press, 1994.

Carby, Hazel V. "'On the Threshold of Woman's Era': Lynching, Empire, and Sexuality in Black Feminist Theory." *Critical Inquiry* 12 (Autumn 1985): 262–77.

Dray, Phillip. *At the Hands of Persons Unknown: The Lynching of Black America.* New York: Modern Library, 2002.

Feimster, Crystal N. *Southern Horrors: Women and the Politics of Rape and Lynching.* Cambridge: Harvard University Press, 2011.

Ginzburg, Ralph. *100 Years of Lynching.* Baltimore: Black Classic Press, 1988.

Grant, Donald L. *The Anti-Lynching Movement: 1883–1932.* San Francisco: R & E Research Associates, 1975.

Hall, Jacqueline Dowd. *Revolt against Chivalry.* New York: Columbia University Press, 1993.

Harris, Trudier. *Exorcising Blackness: Historical and Literary Lynching and Burning Rituals.* Bloomington: Indiana University Press, 1984.

Jones, Nancy Baker. "Association of Southern Women for the Prevention of Lynching." *Handbook of Texas Online.* Texas State Historical Association. June 9, 2010. www.tshaonline.org/handbook/onlinearticles/via01.

Karcher, Carolyn L. "Ida B. Wells and Her Allies against Lynching." *Comparative American Studies* 3(2): 131–51.

"Lynching." *Oxford English Dictionary.* Compact edition. 1971.

"Lynch Law." *Oxford English Dictionary.* Compact edition. 1971.

Page, Amy Louise Wood. *Lynching and Spectacle: Witnessing Racial Violence in America, 1890–1940.* New Directions in Southern Studies. Chapel Hill: University of North Carolina Press, 2011.

Raper, Arthur F. *The Tragedy of Lynching.* Chapel Hill: University of North Carolina Press, 1933.

Zangrando, Robert L. *The NAACP Crusade against Lynching, 1909–1950.* Philadelphia: Temple University Press, 1980.

POST–CIVIL WAR HISTORY

Anderson, James D. *The Education of Blacks in the South, 1860–1935*. Chapel Hill: University of North Carolina Press, 1988.

Bloom, Khaled J. *The Mississippi Valley's Great Yellow Fever Epidemic of 1878*. Baton Rouge: Louisiana State University Press, 1993.

Brown, Thomas. *American Eras: Civil War and Reconstruction, 1850–1877*. Farmington Hills, Mich.: Gale, 1997.

Bullock, Penelope. *The Afro-American Periodical Press, 1838–1909*. Baton Rouge: Louisiana State University Press, 1981.

Byrd, W. Michael, and Linda A. Clayton. *An American Health Dilemma: A Medical History of African Americans and the Problem of Race*. New York: Routledge, 2000.

Cimbala, Paul A., and Randall M. Miller, eds. *The Freedmen's Bureau and Reconstruction*. New York: Fordham University Press, 1999.

Cox, LaWanda, and John H. Cox, eds. *Reconstruction, the Negro, and the New South*. Columbia: University of South Carolina Press, 1973.

Crumpler, Rebecca. *A Book of Medical Discourses*. 1883. U.S. National Library of Medicine Digital Collections. http://resource.nlm.nih.gov/67521160R.

Downs, Jim. *Sick from Freedom: African-American Illness and Suffering during the Civil War and Reconstruction*. New York: Oxford University Press, 2012.

Du Bois, William E. B. *Black Reconstruction*. New York: Harcourt, Brace & Co., 1935.

Foner, Eric. *A Short History of Reconstruction, 1863–1877*. New York: HarperCollins e-books, 2010.

Franklin, John Hope. *Reconstruction: After the Civil War*. 2nd ed. Chicago: University of Chicago Press, 1994.

———— and Alfred A. Moss Jr. *From Slavery to Freedom: A History of Negro Americans*. 6th ed. New York: McGraw-Hill, 1988.

Gordon, Lynn D. *Gender and Higher Education in the Progressive Era*. New Haven, Conn.: Yale University Press, 1990.

Humphreys, Margaret. *Yellow Fever and the South*. Baltimore: Johns Hopkins University Press, 1992.

Jones, Jacqueline. *Soldiers of Light, Soldiers of Love: Northern Teachers and Georgia Blacks, 1865–1873*. Chapel Hill: University of North Carolina Press, 1980.

Long, Gretchen. *Doctoring Freedom: The Politics of African American Medical Care in Slavery and Emancipation*. Chapel Hill: University of North Carolina Press, 2012.

May, Ernest R. *American Imperialism: A Speculative Essay*. New York: Atheneum, 1968.

McPherson, James M. *The Abolitionist Legacy*. Princeton, N.J.: Princeton University Press, 1975.

McWhiney, Grady, ed. *Reconstruction and the Freedmen.* Chicago: Rand McNally, 1963.

Myrdal, Gunnar. *An American Dilemma.* New York: Harper & Brothers, 1944.

Nuwer, Deanne Stephens. *Plague among the Magnolias: The 1878 Yellow Fever Epidemic in Mississippi.* Tuscaloosa: University of Alabama Press, 2015.

Perlo, Victor. *American Imperialism.* New York: International Publishers, 1951.

Rozwenc, Edwin C., and Thomas Lyons. *Reconstruction and the Race Problem.* Boston: D. C. Heath, 1968.

Said, Edward. *Culture and Imperialism.* New York: Alfred A. Knopf, 1993.

Savitt, Todd L., and James Harvey Young, eds. *Disease and Distinctiveness in the American South.* Knoxville: University of Tennessee Press, 1988.

Smith, Page. *The Rise of Industrial America: A People's History of the Post-Reconstruction Era.* New York: Penguin Books, 1990.

Stampp, Kenneth M. *The Era of Reconstruction, 1865–1877.* New York: Vintage, 1967.

Summers, Mark Wahlgren. *The Ordeal of the Reunion: A New History of Reconstruction.* Chapel Hill: University of North Carolina Press, 2014.

Woodward, C. Vann. *Origins of the New South, 1877–1913.* Rev. ed. Baton Rouge: Louisiana State University Press, 1981.

_____. *The Strange Career of Jim Crow.* Commemorative ed. New York: Oxford University Press, 2001.

WOMEN'S HISTORY

Aptheker, Bettina. *Woman's Legacy: Essays on Race, Sex, and Class in American History.* Amherst: University of Massachusetts Press, 1982.

Bay, Mia, Farah J. Griffin, Martha S. Jones, and Barbara Dianne Savage, eds. *Toward an Intellectual History of Black Women.* The John Hope Franklin Series in African American History and Culture. Chapel Hill: University of North Carolina Press, 2015.

Berkeley, Kathleen C. "'Colored Ladies Also Contributed': Black Women's Activities from Benevolence to Social Welfare, 1866–1896." In *Black Women in American History: From Colonial Times through the Nineteenth Century*, edited by Darlene Clark Hine, 61–83. Vol. 1 of *Black Women in United States History.* Brooklyn, N.Y.: Carlson, 1990.

"Black Girls Matter." African American Policy Forum. www.aapf.org.

Carby, Hazel V. *Reconstructing Womanhood: The Emergence of the Afro-American Woman Novelist.* New York: Oxford University Press, 1987.

Cooper, Anna Julia. *A Voice from the South.* Schomburg Library of Nineteenth-Century Black Women Writers. New York: Oxford University Press, 1988.

Dickson, Lynda F. "Toward a Broader Angle of Vision in Uncovering Women's History: Black Women's Clubs Revisited." In *Black Women's History:*

Theory and Practice, edited by Darlene Clark Hine, 103–19. Vol. 9 of *Black Women in United States History*. Brooklyn, N.Y.: Carlson, 1990.

Dubois, Ellen Carol, and Lynn Dumenil. *Through Women's Eyes, Combined Volume: An American History with Documents*. 3rd ed. Boston: Bedford/ St. Martin's, 2012.

Gates, Henry Louis, Jr., ed. *The Schomburg Library of Nineteenth-Century Black Women Writers*. New York: Oxford University Press, 1988.

Guy-Sheftall, Beverly, ed. *Words of Fire: An Anthology of African-American Feminist Thought*. New York: New Press, 1995.

Harley, Sharon. *Sister Circle: Black Women and Work*. Piscataway, N.J.: Rutgers University Press, 2002.

Helly, Dorothy O., and Susan M. Reverby, eds. *Gendered Domains: Rethinking Public and Private in Women's History*. Ithaca, N.Y.: Cornell University Press, 1992.

Hine, Darlene Clark, ed. *Black Women in America*. 2nd ed. 3 vols. New York: Oxford University Press, 2005.

Hull, Akasha (Gloria T.), Patricia Bell-Scott, and Barbara Smith, eds. *All the Women Are White, All the Blacks Are Men: But Some of Us Are Brave*. New York: Feminist Press of City University of New York, 2015.

Jones, Beverly Washington. *Quest for Equality: The Life and Writings of Mary Eliza Church Terrell, 1863–1954*. Vol. 13 of *Black Women in United States History*. Brooklyn, N.Y.: Carlson, 1990.

Kerber, Linda K., Jane Sherron DeHart, and Cornelia H. Dayton. *Women's America: Refocusing the Past*. 7th ed. New York: Oxford University Press, 2010.

Lengermann, Patricia Madoo, and Ruth A. Wallace. *Gender in America: Social Control and Social Change*. Englewood Cliffs, N.J.: Prentice-Hall, 1985.

Lerner, Gerda. *The Creation of Feminist Consciousness: From the Middle Ages to 1870*. New York: Oxford University Press, 1993.

Lubiano, Wahneema. "Black Ladies, Welfare Queens, and State Minstrels: Ideological War by Narrative Means." In *Race-ing Justice, En-gendering Power*, edited by Toni Morrison, 323–63. New York: Pantheon Books, 1992.

Matthews, Glenna. *The Rise of Public Woman*. New York: Oxford University Press, 1992.

Morrison, Toni, ed. *Race-ing Justice, En-gendering Power*. New York: Pantheon Books, 1992.

Moss, Alfred A., Jr. *The American Negro Academy: Voice of the Talented Tenth*. Baton Rouge: Louisiana State University Press, 1981.

Mossell, N. F. *The Work of the African American Woman*. Schomburg Library of Nineteenth-Century Black Women Writers. New York: Oxford University Press, 1988.

Neverdon-Morton, Cynthia. *Afro-American Women of the South and the Advancement of the Race, 1895–1925*. Knoxville: University of Tennessee Press, 1989.

Noble, Jeanne L. *The Negro Woman's College Education*. New York: Columbia University Press, 1956.

Pearson, Carol S., Donna L. Shavlik, and Judith G. Touchton, eds. *Educating the Majority: Women Challenge Tradition in Higher Education*. New York: American Council on Education, 1989.

Porter, Dorothy. "The Organized Educational Activities of Negro Literary Societies, 1828–1846." *Journal of Negro Education* 5 (October 1936): 555–74.

Royster, Jacqueline Jones. *Traces of a Stream: Literacy and Social Change among African American Women*. Pittsburgh: University of Pittsburgh Press, 2000.

——— and Gesa E. Kirsch. *Feminist Rhetorical Practices: New Horizons for Rhetoric, Composition, and Literacy Studies*. Carbondale: Southern Illinois University Press, 2012.

Sage: A Scholarly Journal on Black Women 1, no. 1 (Spring 1984). Black Women's Education.

Salem, Dorothy. *To Better Our World: Black Women in Organized Reform, 1890–1920*. Vol. 14 of *Black Women in United States History*. Brooklyn, N.Y.: Carlson, 1990.

Terrell, Mary Church. "The Duty of the NACW to the Race." In *Quest for Equality*, edited by Beverly Washington Jones, 139–50. Vol. 13 of *Black Women in United States History*. Brooklyn, N.Y.: Carlson, 1990.

Vance, Carole S. *Pleasure and Danger: Exploring Female Sexuality*. Boston: Routledge & Kegan Paul, 1984.

Wesley, Charles Harris. *The History of the National Association of Colored Women's Clubs: A Legacy of Service*. Washington, D.C.: National Association of Colored Women's Clubs, 1984.

White, Deborah Gray. *Too Heavy a Load: Black Women in Defense of Themselves, 1894–1994*. New York: W. W. Norton, 1999.

SELECTED WEB SITES

African American Policy Forum. www.aapf.org.

Arlington National Cemetery. www.arlingtoncemetery.mil.

The Freedmen's Bureau. African American Records. www.archives.gov.

The Online Reference Guide to African American History. www.blackpast.org.

United Nations. www.un.org.

U.S. National Library of Medicine. www.nlm.nih.gov.

Index

abolitionist movement, 16, 21–22, 32
Advertiser, on Wells's public speaking, 156
Afric-American Female Intelligence Society, 22
African American community. *See also* economic life of African Americans; Jim Crow laws; political activity of African Americans
anti-lynching organizations, establishing, 8
Black Codes and, 6–7
Columbian Exposition, exclusion from, 33–34
mass meetings and political conventions, organizing, 7–8, 66
post-Reconstruction era and, 7
response to mob violence and lynching, 3, 6–8, 31, 62, 65
responsibilities of, 39
self-government abilities of, 63
social life and, 3, 6–7, 25
Southern Horrors call for self-help in, 65–68
violence against. *See* lynchings; mob violence; violence
Wells's early years in, 8–9
yellow fever and, 10–12, 176
African American men
interracial relationships and, 50–56, 74, 114–17
lynchings, number of, 5, 57, 70
race and gender stereotypes in lynching and, 26–27
rape charges against. *See* rape charges against African American men
African American women
anti-lynching movement and, 22–23, 34, 39
clubs and, 20–23, 34, 39, 155–56
education opportunities for, 18
movement for social equality and legal reform, 19
post-Reconstruction era and, 21–22, 27
professional organizations for, 19
race and gender stereotypes in lynching and, 26–27
rape charges against white men by, 27, 55–56, 123–25
Wells's prominence among, 19–20

African Methodist Episcopal (AME) Church, 13, 15, 21, 63, 156
Afro-American Council, 37
Afro-American League, 8
Afro-American Women and Work (Mossell), 180
Alexander, Sadie T. M., 18
Ames, Jessie Daniels, 44*n*36, 180
Anthony, Susan B., 176–77
Anti-Lynching Bureau, 37
Anti-Lynching Committee, 33–34, 36
Anti-Lynching Crusaders, 23, 180
anti-lynching movement
African American organizations for, 8, 22–23, 34, 39, 155–56
British influence on, 32, 125, 130–32, 137, 150
Free Speech editorial by Wells and, 1, 3, 15, 27, 29
mass meetings and political conventions organized against, 7–8
modern, 39–40
Wells's arguments in, 25–30
Wells's contributions to, 2, 15, 23, 37–41, 125–32. *See also* Wells, Ida B., publications
Woman's Era magazine and, 21, 22
women's movement for social equality and legal reform and, 19
Anti-Lynching Society of England, 35, 179
Appeal-Avalanche on lynchings, 111
Arkansas Race Riot, The (Wells), 38
Association of Southern Women for the Prevention of Lynching (ASWPL), 23, 29, 39, 44*n*36, 180
Atlanta Baptist Female Seminary, 18, 178

Balgarnie, Florence, 35, 131, 137, 179
Barnett, Ferdinand L., 34, 37, 179, 180
Beckwith, Byron De La, 40
Beecher, Henry Ward, 150
Birmingham Daily Gazette, on Wells's public speaking, 164–68
Biscoe, Hamp, 83–86
Black Codes, 6–7, 177
Blair, Henry W., 149, 149*n*14
Blair Bill, 37, 39, 149–50
Bloom, Khalid J., 10

189